A MARMAC GUIDE TO

PHILADELPHIA

Edited by
Judith Minkoff Pransky

Assistant Editor
Robert Joseph Pransky

PELICAN PUBLISHING COMPANY
Gretna 2001

ISBN: 1-56554-759-4
ISSN: 0736-8127

The Marmac Guidebook series was created by Marge McDonald of Atlanta, Georgia. As owner of a convention and sightseeing service in Atlanta for fourteen years, she learned from visitors and those relocating to Atlanta what information was important to them. She also served as President and CEO of the Georgia Hospitality and Travel Association for four years and in 1978 was named Woman of the Year in Travel by the Travel Industry Association of America.

Information in this guidebook is based on authoritative data available at the time of printing. Prices and hours of operation of businesses listed are subject to change without notice. Readers are asked to take this into account when consulting this guide.

Printed in Canada
Published by Pelican Publishing Company, Inc.
1000 Burmaster Street, Gretna, Louisiana 70053

CONTENTS

MAPS

KEY TO LETTER CODE			
E	Expensive	CH	Entrance Charge
M	Moderately Expensive	NCH	No Charge
I	Inexpensive		

FOREWORD

The Marmac guidebooks are designed for the resident and traveler who seek comprehensive information in an easy-to-use format and who have a zest for the best in each city and area mentioned in this national series.

We have chosen to include only what we can recommend to you on the basis of our own research, experience, and judgment. Our inclusions are our reputation.

We first escort you into the city or area, introducing you to a new or perhaps former acquaintance, and we relate the history and folklore that is indigenous to this particular locale. Secondly, we assist you in *learning the ropes*—the essentials of the community, necessary matters of fact, transportation systems, lodging and restaurants, nightlife, attractions, and the visual and performing arts. Thirdly, we point you toward available activities—sightseeing, museums and galleries, shopping, sports, and excursions into the heart of the city and to its environs. And lastly, we salute the special needs of special people—the new resident, the international traveler, students, children, senior citizens, and persons with disabilities.

A key area map is placed at the opening of each book, always at your fingertips for quick reference. The margin index, keyed 1-6 and A-F, provides the location code to each listing in the book. Subsidiary maps include a downtown street map keyed 7-12 and G-L, and in-town and out-of-town touring maps. A comprehensive index at the back of the book makes the Marmac guidebook a breeze to use. Please write to us with your comments and suggestions at Pelican Publishing Company, P.O. Box 3110, Gretna, LA 70054-3110. We will always be glad to hear from you.

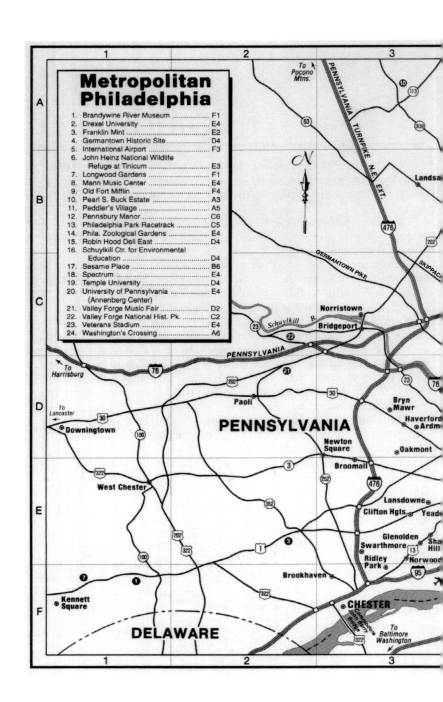

Metropolitan Philadelphia

To Pocono Mtns.

PENNSYLVANIA TURNPIKE N.E. EXT.

Landsa

GERMANTOWN PIKE

SKIPPAC

Norristown

Schuylkill R.

Bridgeport

PENNSYLVANIA

To Harrisburg

Paoli

PENNSYLVANIA

Bryn Mawr

Haverford
Ardm

To Lancaster

Downingtown

Newton Square

Oakmont

West Chester

Broomall

Lansdowne

Clifton Hgts.

Yeade

Glenolden

Swarthmore

Sha Hill

Ridley Park

Norwood

Brookhaven

CHESTER

Kennett Square

To Baltimore Washington

DELAWARE

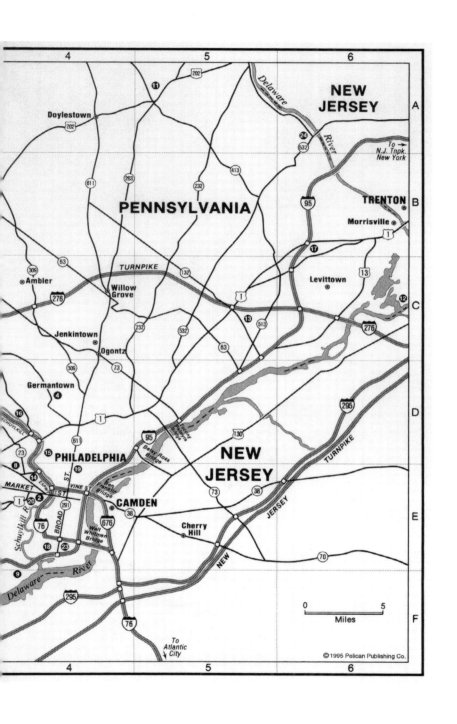

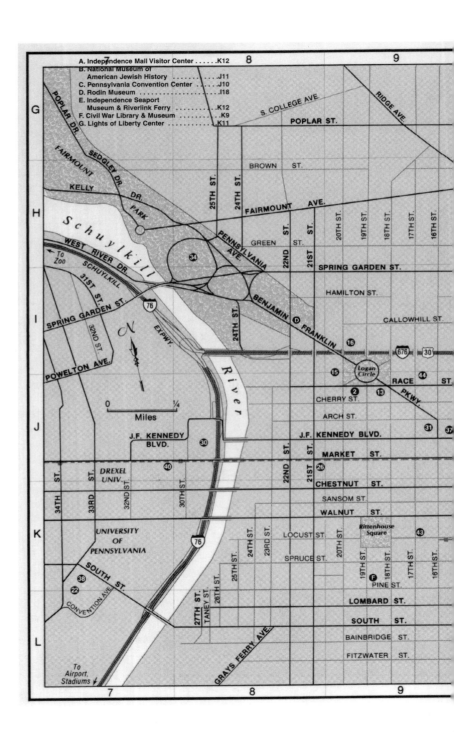

A. Independence Mall Visitor Center K12
B. National Museum of
   American Jewish History J11
C. Pennsylvania Convention Center J10
D. Rodin Museum I18
E. Independence Seaport
   Museum & Riverlink Ferry K12
F. Civil War Library & Museum K9
G. Lights of Liberty Center K11

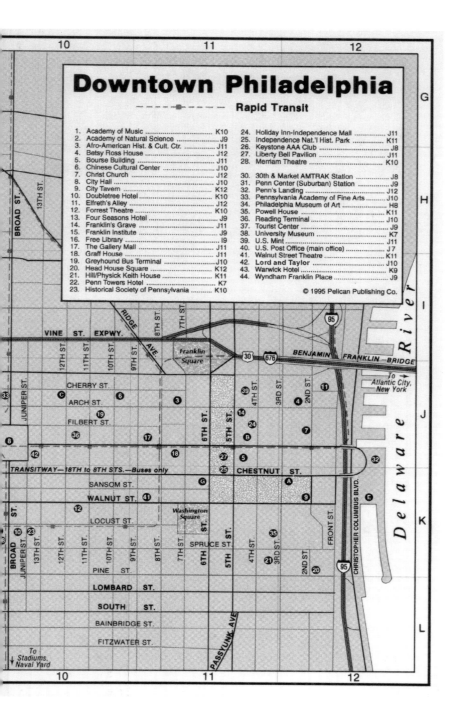

Downtown Philadelphia

- - - - - ◼ - - - - - **Rapid Transit**

© 1995 Pelican Publishing Co.

Liberty Bell on Independence Mall

*Greater Philadelphia Tourism
Marketing Corporation*

A MARMAC GUIDE TO
PHILADELPHIA

PHILADELPHIA PAST

Indian Origins

Four hundred years ago, The City of Brotherly Love was inhabited by a tribe of Native-American Indians known as the Lenni Lenape (The Original People), a trusting, sharing tribe that saw no threat in the arrival of the first British and Dutch seamen in the early 1600s. With the area's lush and game-filled forests, its rivers and streams teeming with fish, the Lenni Lenape believed that there was plenty for everyone. By 1640, they had helped Swedish settlers establish a tiny colony along the Delaware River.

Eventually the newcomers from Europe began fighting for control of the area. The Lenni Lenape, the first Americans, were also the first casualties. Today, this Native-American Indian heritage remains in the Philadelphia area in the nomenclature of such towns and creeks as Tacony—"the empty place," Passyunk—"the level place," Wissinoming—"the place of fear," and Wissahickon—"the catfish stream."

William Penn

Before they disappeared forever, the Lenni Lenape made a lasting friendship with a man they called "the white truth-teller." He insisted upon buying land from them instead of taking it. In admiration and respect, the tribe gave this man a belt of wampum, its beads depicting a clasp of hands, one red, the other white.

The man's name was William Penn. Raised in the British aristocracy, Penn became, at an early age, a believer in religious freedom. In 1667 he shunned the Church of England to join the highly persecuted Society of Friends, the Quakers. He was imprisoned three times for his writing and preaching.

Fortunately, the Crown owed Penn's late father a debt of some $80,000. In 1681 Penn persuaded King Charles II to repay the debt

13

with land in the New World, and the following year he sailed across the Atlantic to breathe reality into his dream that men could co-exist in freedom and peace regardless of their religious beliefs.

A "Holy Experiment" is what Penn called his plan. It was to unfold in a city called Philadelphia, Greek for "brotherly love," and in a colony known as Pennsylvania or "Penn's woods," in memory of his father. Many of the principles that Penn wrote into his Frame of Government after his arrival in October of 1682 were the same principles that the colonists would go to war for less than a century later.

Because his beliefs had been widely publicized in Europe, Penn was followed to his "greene Countrie Towne" by thousands of people suffering from religious persecution. As a result, Philadelphia quickly became known not only as a city of religious freedom, but also as one of economic opportunity. Its location on the Delaware River made the city a hub of shipping and trade in the colonies.

The Revolutionary War

Among the many people that Philadelphia attracted was a 17-year-old printer from Boston named Benjamin Franklin. Though he arrived with little more than the shirt on his back, Franklin was soon running the colonies' most successful newspaper, and in 1731 he published his first issue of Poor Richard's Almanac. As a burgeoning inventor, author, and philosopher, he also became Philadelphia's top civic leader, as well as one of the colonies' most influential statesmen.

Freedom of thought and expression was so important in Philadelphia that after the British imposed unpopular trade policies and taxes in the mid-1700s, the city became the logical choice as a convention site to formalize the rights of the colonies. In July of 1774 the First Continental Congress convened in Carpenter's Hall; less than a year later, following the initial salvos of the Revolutionary War, the Second Continental Congress met in the Pennsylvania State House, now Independence Hall. It was there that the Declaration of Independence was adopted on July 4, 1776.

On that same day, more than 30,000 British troops arrived in New York Harbor and immediately began marching south. As they burned and looted their way through New Jersey in the ensuing months, George Washington, the general of the Continental Army, wrote, "I tremble for Philadelphia."

A year later on September 26, 1777, the British finally captured Philadelphia, paving their way with their victory at the Battle of Brandywine. A week after that, Washington tried to regain the city in a surprise attack on Germantown. After being turned back, he took his army to Valley Forge and settled in for the winter.

On February 5, 1778, France officially joined the colonists' war effort and, though the winter months had been hard ones, Washington's army emerged from Valley Forge in the spring as a unified fighting force. In June, the British pulled out of Philadelphia to avoid being trapped by the French fleet.

In July, Congress again met in Philadelphia and continued to do so until 1783. Four years later, the Constitution of the United States was signed in Independence Hall, and from 1790 to 1800 Philadelphia served as the capital of the new nation.

The Pennsylvania Dutch

In 1793, Philadelphia was struck by a severe epidemic of yellow fever that claimed 5,000 lives and drove thousands farther inland. Among those forced to move were waves of Moravian Germans who settled in the rich farmland of Lancaster, Berks, York, and other interior counties. Though none were actually from the Netherlands, these people became known as the Pennsylvania Dutch because the word "Deutsch," which means "German," had been misinterpreted. Their genius for farming turned the region into a veritable garden spot, and today they still honor centuries-old habits of work and dress. Among these settlers were the Amish and the Mennonites, many of whom still refuse to use such necessities of modern life as cars and tractors.

The City Flourishes

Freed of British trade restrictions as a result of the successful war for independence, Philadelphia continued to grow and prosper. Coal mines flourished to the west, railroads were built, and new canals were dug. Individual fortunes were amassed in iron, shipping, machinery, and textiles.

By the late 1700s, Philadelphia had become the site of the first life insurance company, the first commercially-chartered bank, the first bank partly-owned by the government, the first stock exchange, the first mint, and the first building and loan society. Through the efforts of financier Robert Morris, who, assisted by broker Haym Salomon had raised huge sums of money to finance the Continental Army during the war, Philadelphia became known as "the cradle of finance."

Waves of Immigration and the Civil War—

In the early 1800s, thousands of Irish Catholics arrived in Philadelphia, followed in mid-century by Germans and Italians.

Although the first blacks were slaves, many more came later as freemen as a result of the Quakers' anti-slavery movement.

During the Civil War, Philadelphia, already one of the busiest manufacturing centers in the country, continued to flourish. The wealthy built mansions in Rittenhouse Square and along what became known as "the Main Line." In an inspired bit of foresight 20 years earlier, the city had bought many of the estates along the Schuylkill River and produced Fairmount Park, the largest city park in the world. It was there in 1876 on the one hundredth anniversary of the birth of the nation that the first World's Fair in the Western Hemisphere was staged.

At the turn of the century, still more Europeans flocked to Philadelphia; from 1880 to 1920, the city's population swelled from 850,000 to 1,800,000.

Turn of the Century

Not everyone in Philadelphia was making fortunes, however, for by the turn of the century slums had begun to appear in the city's core. Those who could afford to move left the city to build homes, mansions, and estates in outlying areas. A substantial part of the city's tax base left with these people, and the only major municipal project to be approved around the turn of the century was construction of the Benjamin Franklin Parkway. Over the next 40 years, many of the city's homes, buildings, streets, and historical sites lapsed into decay.

By the end of World War II, Philadelphians were appalled at the status of their once-proud city. More than 400,000 attended the Better Philadelphia Exposition in 1947, and the vast majority of those polled said that they would pay higher taxes to see the designs of the exposition reach fruition. The federal government shared their desires, declaring the Independence Hall area a national park and providing partial funds for restoration.

Urban Revitalization

A new city charter was quick to follow in 1951, along with the rise to power of Democratic party reformers Joseph S. Clark and Richardson Dilworth in City Hall. A year later, the Chinese Wall, a mass of elevated railroad tracks on Market Street that had prevented Center City redevelopment, was torn down. Replacing it was the commercial complex known as Penn Center.

Elsewhere, the old Dock Street produce markets were razed, clearing the way for the revitalization of Old Philadelphia and the construction of Society Hill Towers. Rittenhouse Square was given a facelift and a host of new shops and restaurants arose around it. With city government and private enterprises working hand-in-hand, Philadelphia embarked upon an era of restoration and new construction that lasted into the mid-1960s.

The city then began gearing up for the Bicentennial. The year 1976, however, proved to be a disappointment. The federal government provided only half the money Philadelphia had expected. The Tall Ships, a primary attraction, headed instead for New York. The summer also brought the tragedy of Legionnaires' disease. By the end of the year, 7 million tourists had visited Philadelphia when 20 million had been expected.

Century IV to the Present

Six years later, the city celebrated its 300th birthday with a year-long party called Century IV, an event which proved that more than a few lessons had been learned from the Bicentennial experience. For a fraction of the money that had been spent in 1976, Philadelphia offered, along with a host of special events, attractions that truly accented the past, present, and future of the city. Among these was the internationally-famous Flower Show featuring 300 years of gardening, an outdoor Restaurant Festival on Benjamin Franklin Parkway, and a Neighborhoods Festival in which some 50 of the city's "small towns" opened their arms to welcome thousands of visitors.

This time, not only did the Tall Ships come in splendor, but the world's mightiest ocean liner, the Queen Elizabeth II, also breezed in, having sailed the identical course that William Penn followed when he crossed the Atlantic Ocean 300 years before.

Century IV's impact on Philadelphia was by all accounts a glorious success. Urban celebration and national publicity caught onto the soaring Philadelphia spirit.

A truly restored "City of Brotherly Love," Philadelphia was the site of the nation's celebration of the U.S. Constitutional Convention's 200th anniversary during the summer of 1987. The successful celebration drew millions of visitors for parades, special exhibits, lectures, and appearances by a variety of dignitaries. "A Promise of Permanency," an interactive computer exhibit on the Constitution, was installed at the Independence National Historical Park Visitor's Center. "Born Out of Time," a multi-media sound-and-light show that illustrates Ben Franklin's many contributions to the modern world, became a permanent exhibit at the Franklin Institute Science Museum.

Philadelphia spent 1994 celebrating William Penn's 350th birthday and using the occasion to further re-establish itself as a premiere place to visit or call home. The building of the $522 million Convention Center in Center City was a catalyst to establish an Avenue of the Arts, refurbish existing museums, improve transportation, build hotels, restore neighborhoods, and open businesses. Philadelphia truly deserved its award as one of 1994's Top 10 All-American Cities.

The city continued revitalizing and renewing itself as it entered the twenty-first century. Millennium Philadelphia comprised 18 months of festivities that began with the flash of the Photo of the Century—a group photograph at Independence Hall of 100 Americans born on the Fourth of July, one each year, from 1900 to 1999. The Independence Hall historic district itself was energized with the new "Lights of Liberty" extravaganza—a one-hour, 3-D, multimedia theatrical experience that transports visitors back in time to Revolutionary America. The Franklin Institute Science Museum celebrated its 175th anniversary with the new "Franklin—He's Electric" exhibit. The Philadelphia Zoo, America's oldest, celebrated its 125th birthday with the opening of the new Primate Reserve. The Avenue of the Arts, and the Convention Center and waterfront areas increased their hotel, restaurant and tourist sites. And the list goes on.

The city is moving ahead at a breathtaking pace, with bulldozers and jackhammers forging new vistas while a commitment to the past preserves and renews historic sights. It is a place to discover and enjoy. But most of all, it is a city to visit, revisit, or call home.

PHILADELPHIA TODAY

The "greene Countrie Towne" that William Penn envisioned more than 300 years ago is today a vibrant, exciting city whose heritage remains remarkably apparent as eighteenth-century homes play neighbor to gleaming twentieth-century skyscrapers. The home of America's independence, this burgeoning metropolis and fifth largest city in the United States is composed of many individual neighborhoods and small towns, each with its own ethnic character, flavor, and traditions. The result is a city so uniquely diverse that even Philadelphia's natives have difficulty defining it.

Founded on a stretch of land between the Delaware and Schuylkill Rivers, as Philadelphia grew, so did its boundaries. As a result, many old memories of the past were spared from the wrecking crew. It is this permanence that lends such a strong feeling of nostalgia and history to Philadelphia. Society Hill, a model of urban restoration with Federal-style townhouses, cobblestone streets, Franklin lamps, and a wealth of museums, boutiques, and restaurants, is just one of the city's fascinating landmarks. The historic splendor of Independence Mall and Old City, the waterfront area of Penn's Landing, the beauty of Fairmount Park, the heritage of Germantown, and the flag-draped vistas of "America's Champs-Elysees," Benjamin Franklin Parkway, all contribute to make Philadelphia a city unlike any other.

Beyond the historic, Philadelphia offers even more through its people, their accomplishments, and their offerings. The huge Victorian train stations that workers labored to erect a century ago still stand. Freighters move silently along the Delaware, a reminder of the city's ever-busy port. Philadelphia offers the best in elegant and unusual shopping. The city is also a grab bag of ethnic culinary wonders, right down to Philly's own soft pretzels and cheese steaks. The sleek office buildings and hotels of Center City are evidence of Philadelphia's status as an international city. Beneath the grit of raucous sports crowds lie proud hearts that truly care about their hometown teams. Mario Lanza, Eddie Fisher, Frankie Avalon, Bobby Rydell, David Brenner, Eugene Ormandy, the late Princess Grace of Monaco, Wilt

Chamberlain, Sylvester Stallone, and Bill Cosby have all called Philadelphia home. In addition to its world-famous Philadelphia Orchestra, Philadelphia's quiet excellence in education, medicine, art, and culture will astound you.

Separated from both New York and Washington, D.C., by short train rides, Philadelphia is also within easy reach of exciting Atlantic City to the east and the magnificent Pocono Mountains to the north. Visitors have always enjoyed this historic city; since the Bicentennial, the 200th birthday of the Constitution, and the Millennium Philadelphia celebration, however, tourists and residents alike have continued in growing numbers to discover Philadelphia. There can be no greater joy in doing this than by exploring the city on foot and intermingling with its people. What one finds is a large city with a small-town friendliness, in the words of painter and native Philadelphian William Wharton, "a blend of tradition and change, immutability and progress."

Cultural and Educational Center ——————

Without question, Philadelphia is one of the most prolific cultural and educational cities in the world. It is the site of the Walnut Street Theater, which, having presented its first play in 1809, is the oldest active theater in the nation. The magnificent Academy of Music, circa 1857, is the oldest opera house in the United States and home to the famed Philadelphia Orchestra since it was founded in 1900 and until its 2001 relocation to the new Regional Performing Arts Center. The Academy, will become a part of the arts center and remain home to the Pennsylvania Ballet, the Opera Company of Philadelphia, and numerous theatrical productions. The Benjamin Franklin Parkway has more museums than any other boulevard in the world, including the Philadelphia Museum of Art, the Rodin Museum, the Academy of Natural Sciences (founded in 1812, the oldest natural science museum in the country), and the Franklin Institute (founded in 1824, the nation's first museum of science and technology).

The Pennsylvania Academy of Fine Arts operates the nation's oldest art museum, circa 1805, while the Historical Society of Pennsylvania offers a host of paintings about the history of the state and the nation. Established by Benjamin Franklin in 1731, the Library Company of Philadelphia was the first U.S. lending library and still contains volumes that once belonged to William Penn, George Washington, and Thomas Jefferson. The Free Library has its main location on the parkway and 48 branches throughout the five-county area.

With 20 colleges and universities within its boundaries, including the University of Pennsylvania, Temple, LaSalle, Drexel, and St.

Joseph's, and another 30 colleges and universities nearby, Philadelphia and its counties provide an atmosphere of intellectual stimulation. Among Philadelphia's educational "firsts" are the Pennsylvania Academy of Fine Arts, the oldest art school in the country, and the Moore College of Art which opened in 1844, the oldest art school for women in the nation.

Boom Town?

Philadelphia may well be *the* American city of the new millennium. It has been transformed from a center of heavy manufacturing into a center for service industries, including finance, insurance, real estate, communications, management, investment, and electronics. Philadelphia has always been one of the nation's foremost centers of medical training, research, and treatment, with numerous medical colleges, teaching hospitals, pharmaceutical companies, and bio-technical facilities. The city has six medical schools and more than 100 general and specialized hospitals within or near its boundaries.

Revitalization of Center City

Philadelphia "offers a complete range of settings, scenery, facilities, transport, prices, sports, and savvy . . . Philadelphia is the biggest rebirth of a metropolis since Toronto." At the heart of this rebirth is Center City in downtown Philadelphia, a sleek and exciting collection of shopping malls, terrific restaurants, hotels, condominiums, and office buildings. Motivated by federal aid and attractive real-estate opportunities, private developers have invested millions of dollars in this area. And now, with the launching of the $522 million Pennsylvania Convention Center, the second largest in the Northeast, they are investing even more. New roadways have been laid, more hotels have been built, businesses are opening, museums are expanding, and neighborhoods are being restored.

Philadelphia has been the scene of a "restaurant renaissance," too, with new eateries constantly opening. Center City is just one of the sections in Philadelphia that has gained from this culinary explosion. Add to this the wealth of diversified shopping opportunities, as well as the number of businesses located here, and you will find that Center City is an exciting, sophisticated, and beautiful area surrounded and enhanced by the parks, ethnic neighborhoods, and historic sites of Philadelphia.

Center City Skyline

Bob Krist for the Greater Philadelphia Tourism Marketing Corporation

The city's revival is the product of its maturing urban renewal programs and its emergence as a regional service center. The outlook for further growth and expansion continues because land for development in the area is available at prices generally more reasonable than elsewhere in the country.

One of the most tangible signs that Philadelphia has moved into a new era is the construction of Liberty Place in Center City. After much debate, this elegant skyscraper was allowed to be built higher than the statue of William Penn atop City Hall, traditionally the "ceiling" on Philadelphia's skyscrapers. The new skyline has a very modern look.

And as the city is building "up," so is it building out, revitalizing its waterfront along the Delaware River in a manner similar to the waterfront development in Boston in the 1970s. The waterfront already bustles with marinas, innovative restaurants, new luxury apartments, tennis piers, museums, and many more projects are in the works, such as the Family Entertainment Center at Penn's Landing slated to open in 2002. Farther west, on Broad Street, the city has created the Avenue of the Arts, a "cultural corridor" several miles long, with already established theaters and concert halls showcasing Philadelphia's performing arts, and anchored by the soon-to-be-completed, state-of-the-art, Regional Performing Arts Center.

International Network

With its history of international diplomacy, world trade, and cultural and educational exchange, Philadelphia ranks among the nation's leading cities in its response to both corporate and public participation in the international scene. Local corporate and community leaders strive to make Philadelphia a truly "international city" that serves as a home for internationally oriented industries and organizations, with the social, cultural, and educational atmosphere to sustain such business.

Philadelphia's efforts in this endeavor are advanced by several major nonprofit organizations. Among them is The International Visitors Council of Philadelphia (215-683-0999) which introduces leading foreign visitors, tour groups, and international conference participants to the economic, cultural, and academic atmosphere of Philadelphia, as well as to its historic contributions to the nation as a whole. A second organization is International House of Philadelphia (215-387-5125), a residence and cultural center, which promotes international and intercultural understanding. A third is the World Affairs Council of Philadelphia (215-731-1100) which provides lectures, seminars, debates, and conferences on international events and issues, and assists business leaders in developing an awareness of international issues among their employees.

A Port of Prominence

When the Queen Elizabeth II sailed up the Delaware River to dock in Philadelphia during the 1982 Century IV celebration, it appeared that every boat in Pennsylvania, Delaware, and southern New Jersey had turned out to greet her, and with good reason. Since William Penn decided to place his city "where most ships may best ride," Philadelphia has become one of the largest ports for waterborne commerce in the nation.

Only 90 miles up the Delaware River from the sea, the Port of Philadelphia trades with almost 300 ports in more than 100 countries and handles 66 million tons of international cargo annually worth more than $12 billion. Most of this tonnage is comprised of fruit, vegetables, meat, paper products, plywood, chemicals, iron, and steel. Philadelphia is also the largest oil-refining center on the East Coast. In all, the port has 50 piers, with dockworkers loading and unloading 2,600 ships per year. It is this kind of activity, combined with the network of rail, air, and highway routes through the city, that makes Philadelphia the same major hub of transportation that it was during colonial times.

Philadelphia and Its Counties

Embracing Philadelphia County, which is the city's limits, are four more counties—Bucks, Montgomery, Delaware, and Chester—that enhance the entire Philadelphia area. Large areas of the four counties have developed into surging business centers in recent years; still, historical roots run deep, rolling hills and stands of trees grace the countryside, and the region is packed with numerous outposts of charm and interest.

A number of buildings and former homes have been restored and transformed into restaurants, as have some of the old taverns along former Conestoga wagon and stagecoach trails. Some of these taverns have been in continuous operation for 200 years. Inside is still to be found good food, drink, and when the weather is the least bit nippy outside, a crackling fireplace. Also to be found in the surrounding counties are old covered bridges (Pennsylvania leads the nation with 390 of them) and "the great stone barns" of brown, white, and green in Bucks and Chester counties.

Each county has special attractions that draw thousands of Philadelphia-area inhabitants and tourists every year. Bucks County has New Hope, a cluster of antique and craft shops where William Lathrup founded the nation's first art colony in 1900. History buffs will head for Pennsbury, the faithful reconstruction of William Penn's manor on the Delaware. Montgomery County has the Peter Wentz Farmstead, a restored colonial farmhouse used by Washington before and after the Battle of Germantown. Delaware County is the site of the Brandywine Battlefields, the Franklin Mint museum, and the nation's first fox hunt club, the Rose Tree Club. Chester County, the largest and least populated of the counties, is currently the fastest-growing county in the state; within its borders are Swiss Pines, Longwood Gardens, and Valley Forge. Chester County is also the mushroom capital of America, producing 125 million pounds of mushrooms per year. It's fox-hunting country, too, with numerous events that include the prestigious Pennsylvania Hunt Cup Race in November.

Climate and Dress

With the Atlantic Ocean to its east and the Appalachian Mountains to its west, Philadelphia benefits from a moderate climate. Conditions change rapidly, and periods of extreme temperature or high humidity rarely last for more than a few days. Philadelphians enjoy four distinct and dramatic seasons, highlighted by dazzling autumns and sparkling springs. Two or three substantial snowfalls can be expected each winter. Rainfall is fairly evenly distributed, with the heaviest precipitation in rapidly-moving thunderstorms in late July and August. Because of fast-changing conditions, it is recommended that you dress in layers of clothing that may be adjusted according to the weather, particularly during fall and winter.

Philadelphia is as fashionable as many of its sites are old-fashioned. In the downtown business district you will find formality in dress during both working hours and in the evening. A more casual approach is in evidence in the suburban areas, particularly at night.

The City's People

Philadelphia displays its heritage not only though its historical landmarks, but also through its people. In a country as young as the United States, a city as old as Philadelphia holds a special place in the hearts of its residents, symbolizing as it does so much of the richness of background and tradition that has made this country what it is today.

This sense of the past allows a unique melding of the old with the new. Surrounded by modern business and shopping complexes, natives of this city still cling to their "hometown" ethnic neighborhoods. From these people come the wealth of food, events, and sites that bestow on Philadelphia the honor of being "one of the best kept secrets in the world."

Some Philadelphians may be happy to keep their marvelous city a secret, but that is no longer possible, especially since it was named one of the Top 10 American Cities. Philadelphia is claiming its rights as an area as rich in the arts and academe as New York or Washington, D.C. With an enthusiasm that would have made William Penn proud, this city's natives are opening their arms to people the world over who wish to share in the special attractions that Philadelphia has to offer.

MATTERS OF FACT

AAA—Keystone Motor Club; 215-569-4321. For emergencies: 800-HELP. Website: www.AAA.com.

African-American and Latino Cultural Organizations, Coalition of—215-765-5055.

Ambulance—Allied Medical Ambulance Inc.; 215-477-1700; 610-664-4601.

AMTRAK—800-USA-RAIL.

Area Codes—215 and 610. Dial "1" before the area code and number.

Babysitter—Check with your hotel's front desk.

Calendar of Events—Friday supplements to *The Philadelphia Inquirer* ("Weekend" section) and *The Philadelphia Daily News* ("Friday" section); Sunday editions of *The Philadelphia Inquirer*, and *Philadelphia Magazine*.

Chamber of Commerce—Suite 700, 200 S. Broad St., Phila., PA 19102; 215-545-1234.

Civil Defense—610-565-8700.

Climate—Annual averages:
Rainfall: 41.18 inches.
Snowfall: 20.3 inches (30 inches in northwest suburbs).
Sunny days: Average 91.
Partly sunny days: Average 100.
Days above 90 degrees: Average 19.
Days below 32 degrees: Average 19.
Driest month: October.
Rainiest month: August.
Coldest month: January.
Warmest month: July.
Wind: West-southwest prevailing.

Convention and Visitors Bureau—1515 Market St., Suite 2020, Phila., PA 19102; 215-636-1666; 800-537-7676; TDD: 215-636-3403; Website: www.libertynet.org/phila-visitor.

Currency Exchange—Thomas Cook Currency Services; 1800 John F. Kennedy Blvd; 800-287-7362. First Union Bank; Sixteenth and Market Sts.; 215-973-4402.

Customs, U.S.—215-596-1972.

Dentist—American Dental Association; 215-925-6050 from 9 am-5 pm weekdays.

Disabilities, Mayor's Commission on People with—215-686-2798.

Doctor—Philadelphia County Medical Society; 215-563-5343 from 9 am-5 pm weekdays; evenings and weekends, contact hotel doctor or visit nearest hospital (see below).

Emergency Counseling—215-686-4420.

Emergency Room—215-955-6840 (Thomas Jefferson University Hospital).

Fairmount Park Commission—215-685-0000.

Federal Information Operator—800-688-9889.

Fire—911 (emergency).

Health, PA Dept. of—800-692-7254.

Help, First Call For (information and referral service of the United Way)—215-568-3750.

Hotel Association, Greater Philadelphia—215-557-1900.

Foreign Language Translation—Inlingua; 215-735-7646; 800-361-6444.

Hospitals—

Bryn Mawr Hospital, 130 S. Bryn Mawr Ave., Bryn Mawr; 610-526-3000; TDD: 610-645-3493.

Children's Hospital of Philadelphia, Thirty-fourth Street and Civic Center Blvd.; 215-590-1000.

Einstein Medical Center, York and Tabor Rds.; 215-456-7890

Graduate Hospital, 1800 Lombard St.; 215-893-2000.

Hahnemann University Hospital, 230 N. Broad St.; 215-762-7000.

Hospital of the University of Pennsylvania, 3400 Spruce St.; 215-662-4000.

Lankenau Hospital, Lancaster and City Line Aves., Wynnewood; 610-645-2000; TDD: 610-645-3493.

St. Christopher's Hospital for Children, Erie Ave. at Front St.; 215-427-5000.

Temple University Hospital, Broad and Ontario Sts.; 215-707-2000.

Thomas Jefferson University Hospital, Eleventh and Walnut Sts.; 215-955-6000.

Wills Eye Hospital, 900 Walnut St.; 215-928-3000.

Lawyer—Lawyer Referral and Information Service of the Philadelphia Bar Association; 215-238-6333.

Legal Aid—Community Legal Services; 215-683-5127; American Civil Liberties Union; 215-592-1513.

Library, Public—Central branch, Free Library of Philadelphia, Logan Sq.; 215-686-5322.

Liquor Laws—Legal drinking age, 21. All alcoholic beverages in Pennsylvania, except beer, sold in state-owned liquor stores; special beverage stores sell beer. Bars close at 2 am; no liquor sales until 1 pm on Sunday.

Newspapers—*The Philadelphia Inquirer,* *The Philadelphia Daily News, Philadelphia Weekly, City Paper,* and numerous local and suburban newspapers.

Passport Information—Philadelphia Passport Agency; 215-597-7480. (Message in English and Spanish.)

Pets—Humane Society of Pennsylvania; 215-426-6300; The Women's Humane Society of Pennsylvania; 215-750-3100.

Poison Control—215-386-2100; 800-722-7112.

Police—911 (emergency).

Police, State—215-560-6200.

Population—1.6 million.

Port of Philadelphia—The Delaware River Port System is the No. 1 port of foreign waterborne commerce in the United States. It trades with 300 ports in 100 countries and handles 66 million tons of international cargo annually, producing more than $328 million in U.S. Customs' receipts. Philadelphia Regional Port Authority; 215-928-9100.

Post Office—Main Office, Thirtieth and Market Sts.; 215-895-8000.

Radio Stations—

AM—

WFIL (560) Christian talk.

WIP (610) Sports, talk.

WPHE (690) Spanish/religious.

WVCH (740) Religious.

WWDB (860) Religious.

WEMG (900) Spanish/English dance/contemporary.

WPEN (950) Oldies.

WZZD (990) Religious.

KYW (1060) "All news all the time."

WPHT (1210) "Talk Radio 1210." (Don Imus, Dr. Laura, Rush Limbaugh, etc.)

WSSJ (1310) Spanish oldies.

WHAT (1340) African-American oriented talk.

WCOJ (1420) News, talk, adult contemporary.

WNPV (1440) News, talk. (Ask the Doctor, Legally Speaking, etc.)

WDAS (1480) Religious/gospel.

WNWR (1540) Ethnic/multi-lingual.

FM—

WXPN (88.5) Progressive music. (University of Pennsylvania)

WRTI (90.1) Jazz and some classical. (Temple University)

WHYY (90.9) National Public Radio; talk, public affairs, news.

WXTU (92.5) Country.

WMMR (93.3) Rock music.

WYSP (94.1) Classic Rock and Roll.

WEJM (95.7) Urban oldies. (Hy Lit)

WWDB (96.5) Talk.

WOGL (98.1) Oldies.

WUSL (98.9) Urban contemporary.

WPLY (100.3) Alternative rock/ contemporary music.

WBEB (101.1) Adult contemporary.

WIOQ (102.1) Contemporary music.

WMGK (102.9) Classic hits.

WPHI (103.9) Urban contemporary.

WLCE (104.5) Rock hits.

WDAS (105.3) Urban contemporary.

WJJZ (106.1) Smooth jazz.

Recreation, Department of, City of Philadelphia—215-683-3600.

Red Cross, American—Emergency Services; 215-299-4000.

Sales Tax—6% minimum. No sales tax on food or clothing.

Senior Citizens—Mayor's Commission on Services to the Aging; 215-686-3587.

Social Services—United Way of Southeastern Pennsylvania; 215-568-3750.

Television Stations—

Channel 3 (CBS) KYW.

Channel 6 (ABC) WPVI.

Channel 10 (NBC) WCAU.

Channel 12 (PBS) WHYY.

Channel 17 (WB) WPHL.

Channel 28. Spanish language.

Channel 29 (FOX) WTXF.

Channel 35 WYBE. Educational/ international/multilingual.

Channel 48 WGTW. Brunson Broadcasting.

Channel 57 (UPN) WGBS. Grant Broadcasting.

Channel 61 WPPX. Family programming.

Tickets—Upstages, 215-735-0631; TicketMaster, 215-336-2000; Online, www.ticketmaster.com.

Time—215-846-1212 (TI6-1212).

Time Zone—Eastern Standard Time. Daylight Savings, April to October.

Transportation—Southeastern Pennsylvania Transportation Authority (SEPTA Bus and Rail)— 6 am to midnight daily, altered service on weekends and holidays; 215-580-7800.

Tourist Information—Philadelphia Visitors Center, 1525 JFK Blvd.; 215-636-1666; 800-537-7676; TDD: 215-636-3403; Website: www.libertynet.org/phila-visitor.

Independence National Historical Park Visitors Center— 215-597-8787.

Traffic Laws, State—Right turn allowed on red light, except where posted otherwise.

Traveler's Aid—215-546-0571; 215-523-7580.

Weather—215-936-1212 (WE6-1212).

TRANSPORTATION

Philadelphia is in the heart of the busy "northeast corridor" of the United States, with Boston to the northeast, Baltimore and Washington to the south, and New York City only 90 miles away. The following information will help you travel to Philadelphia via air, rail, car, or bus, and enable you to move about the metropolitan area as well.

TO PHILADELPHIA

Air

Philadelphia International Airport

The airport underwent a billion-dollar facelift and is the site of more than 1400 departures and arrivals daily. The Overseas Terminal is host to flights from Europe, Canada, Mexico, and the Caribbean, and is also a departure and receiving point for connecting flights to the Orient. The airport is served by a number of commuter airlines that take passengers to and from New York, Washington, Atlantic City, and the Pocono Mountains.

Located on Route 291, Philadelphia International Airport is eight miles southwest of Center City (or 20 minutes by cab), and is accessible from all directions by major highways.

Philadelphia International Airport—215-937-6800; 800-PHL-GATE; Website: www.phl.org. Airport information can be heard on 1610 AM within five miles of the airport.

Airlines serving Philadelphia International, including their reservations and information telephone numbers, are:

Domestic
Airtrain Airlines 800-825-8538
American Airlines 800-433-7300
America West 800-235-9292
Continental Airlines 800-525-0280
Delta Air Lines 800-221-1212

30

Midway Airlines 800-446-4392
Northwest Airlines 800-225-2525
ProAir 800-939-9551
Trans World Airlines 800-221-2000
United Airlines 800-241-6522
US Airways 800-428-4322

Commuter
American Eagle 800-433-7300
Continental Express 800-525-0280
Delta Connection 800-221-1212
Midwest Express 800-452-2022
Northwest Airlink 800-225-2525
Trans World Express 800-221-2000
United Express 800-241-6522
US Airways Express 800-428-4322

International
Air Canada 800-776-3000
Air Jamaica 800-523-5585
British Airways 800-AIRWAYS
Northwest Airlines 800-225-2525
Swissair 800-221-4750
Trans World Airlines Charters 800-221-2000
US Airways 800-622-1015

Ground Service to and from the Airport

SEPTA (Southeastern Pennsylvania Transportation Authority) Airport Express Service; 215-580-7800. SEPTA runs a train between Center City and the airport, running every half hour from 4 am to midnight. Center City stops include Market East, Suburban Station, and Thirtieth Street Station. Travel time is approximately 26 minutes. Price $5 (one way).

Taxi service has improved markedly in recent years, in both the number of cabs available and companies from which to choose. Cabs should be waiting outside your arrival terminal; the approximate fare to Center City is $20 on the meter. (See taxi listing below. Also see limousine listing under Auto Rental.)

Animals—Ground Services to and from the Airport

The transportation of animals is handled by the individual airlines.

Aircraft Rental and Charter

Aero Taxi, at Wilmington (Delaware) Airport; 800-551-8555.
Atlantic Aviation, at Philadelphia International Airport; 215-492-2970.
Koro Aviation at Hazelton (PA) Airport; 800-833-5676.
Wings Charter Services, at Blue Bell; 215-646-1800.

Automobile

The Philadelphia area is embraced by a network of major highways. Principal access routes from the north and south are the New Jersey Turnpike and I-95, and from east and west, the Pennsylvania Turnpike, via the Schuylkill Expressway.

Bus

Greyhound has a major terminal in Center City. **Greyhound,** Tenth and Filbert Sts.; 215-931-4035; 800-231-2222.

Rail

AMTRAK service is so comprehensive that some Philadelphians commute to and from jobs in New York City and various stops in-between. Many of the trains operating between Boston and Washington are Metroliners traveling in excess of 100 miles per hour, and virtually all of them stop at Thirtieth Street Station. Tickets are available at Thirtieth Street Station, at a few suburban stations in the area, and through a travel agent. Call AMTRAK; USA-RAIL; Website: www.amtrak.com.

Package Tours

Package tours are growing in popularity nationwide, but have always been a hot item in the Philadelphia area. They include weekends or several days at special prices, and can include hotel room, attraction tickets, meals, and chauffeured limousines. Many major hotels, especially those in Atlantic City, offer attractive packages. For further information, call **Rosenbluth Travel Service**; 215-563-1070, or **International Travel Exchange**; 800-752-6050 or 215-332-2444.

AROUND PHILADELPHIA

Auto Rental ————————————————

Rental cars are available by the day, week, or longer. Rental locations include the airport and various locations throughout the city, including major hotels. Major credit cards expedite the procedure, and be sure to have your driver's license. Prices vary greatly, so it is wise to check with various companies for rates and specials that suit your particular needs.

Alamo Rent-A-Car 800-327-9633
Avis Rent-A-Car 800-831-2847
Budget Rent-A-Car 215-492-9447;
                                               800-527-0700;
                                               TDD: 800-826-5100
Dollar Rent-A-Car . . . . .215-365-2700 or
                                               800-800-4000
Enterprise Rent-A-Car 800-RENT-A-CAR
                                               (800-736-8222);
                                               Out of town: 800-325-8007
Express Car and Truck Rental 800-826-7368
Hertz Rent-A-Car 800-654-3131
National Rent-A-Car . . . . .800-CAR RENT
                                               (800-227-7368)

Chauffeured Limousine Service
Dav El 215-334-7900; 800-727-1957
Dave's Best Limousine Service 215-288-1000
USA Limousine Service 215-546-4044;
                                               800-327-5466
Worldwide Limousine 215-639-1599;
                                               800-833-7633

Private Car————————————————

Thanks to the grid plan designed by William Penn in 1682, Philadelphia streets run north-south and east-west between the Delaware and Schuylkill rivers. Going west from Front Street on the Delaware River, north-south streets are numbered (Second, Third, Fourth, etc.) except for Broad Street, which would have been

Fourteenth. Elsewhere, streets, roads, and state routes can meander and be much less predictable, so consult maps.

Major access arteries are I-95, which runs parallel to the Delaware River from northeast to southwest, and the Schuylkill Expressway, I-76, which links Center City with King of Prussia, Valley Forge, and the northwestern suburbs. During the morning and evening rush hours, however, it is wise to avoid these two routes—especially the Schuylkill, which, in some sections, offers only two lanes in each direction.

To the immediate west of the city lies I-476 (known to locals as "The Blue Route"). This major artery runs from I-95 near Chester, going through Springfield, Villanova, and King of Prussia, until it ends at Plymouth Meeting. There, it connects with I-276, the Pennsylvania Turnpike, and becomes its northeast extension.

Once within the city, numerous garages and lots provide ample parking. Rates are $1 per hour on parking meters.

In case of emergency or when in need of assistance, call:
Philadelphia Police .... .911.
Pennsylvania State Police .... .215-560-6200.

Public Transportation ──────────────

SEPTA, Southeastern Pennsylvania Transportation Authority, is Philadelphia's public transportation system. It operates 2,500 public buses, trolleys, subways, elevated trains, and commuter trains in the region.

A $325-million Center City Commuter Terminal, running from Penn Center to a portal north of Spring Garden Street between Eighth and Ninth Streets, joins the six former Reading commuter rail lines with the six former Penn Central lines.

SEPTA's transit stops are indicated at mid-block or on street-corner locations. For schedules and maps of SEPTA routes, visit the Customer Service office in the underground concourse at Fifteenth and Market Streets, or call 215-580-7800; Website: www.septa.com. SEPTA charges $1.60 per ride on buses and subways; exact change is required. A transfer is 40¢ extra. SEPTA's tourist-friendly Day Pass costs $5. Trans passes for SEPTA buses are $16 weekly and $58 monthly. A package of 10 tokens costs $10.50. Senior citizens pay reduced fares and sometimes travel for free. Train schedules vary greatly, so be sure to consult SEPTA for times and schedules.

SEPTA Services for the Handicapped. Extensive facilities are available for the handicapped resident and visitor. To register for Paratransit service call 215-580-7145. Many Philadelphia routes have lift-equipped buses. For a listing and schedule call 215-580-7800. For reduced fare information and registration, call 215-580-7365. In the suburbs, lift-equipped buses can be arranged with a one-day advance reservation by contacting "Suburban On Call" at 215-580-3455. Hearing impaired persons can call the TTD number; 215-580-7853.

Patco High Speed Line, Port Authority Transit Corp.; 215-922-4600 or 856-772-6900. A high-speed commuter rail line that whisks you between Philadelphia and New Jersey. It begins at Sixteenth and Locust Streets, and stops at Thirteenth, Tenth, Ninth and Locust, and Eighth and Market. As it crosses the Benjamin Franklin Bridge, you will enjoy a magnificent view of the Delaware River. Website: www.drpa.org/patco.

At the Broadway Station in New Jersey, the line connects with the New Jersey Transit Aqualink shuttle bus to the NJ State Aquarium and Children's Garden in Camden, and the new E-Centre—the Blockbuster-Sony Music Entertainment Centre.

Phlash Downtown Tourist Loop. 215-4-PHLASH. The purple buses of this friendly, local service stop at the major tourist attractions. A one-way ticket is $1.50, but you can ride all day and night for only $3. Call for routes and times.

Taxis

More and better cab service is available in Philadelphia than ever before. Rates are $1.80 for the first mile and $1.80 per mile thereafter. Some suggested cab companies:

Liberty 215-389-8000
Olde City Taxi 215-338-0838
Quaker City 215-728-8000
Yellow 215-922-8400

Tours

Several companies offer daytime and candlelight sightseeing bus tours of the city and attractions in nearby areas. The following is only a partial list. Call for times and tours or check at your hotel.

Academy Bus Tours; . . . . .800-430-1339.
African American Historical Tours; . . . . .215-895-4054.

All About Philadelphia Tours; . . . . .215-389-2510.
American Jewish Committee Historic Tours; . . .215-665-2300.
Centipede, Inc.; . . . . .215-735-3123.
Culture Tours; . . . . .215-947-8991.
Martz/Gray Line Tours; . . . . .215-569-3666.

Unique Ways to See Philadelphia

See it from the air with Sterling Helicopter, taking off from Penn's Landing; 215-271-2510.

Or see it on the ground with **Philadelphia Trolley Works.** Philadelphia's most popular Bicentennial feature, the Fairmount Park Trolley was custom-made to capture the flavor of the old trolley that once operated in the park. The present-day trolleys travel a scenic 90-minute loop through Center City, making stops at cultural, historic, and recreational treasures along the way. Board and reboard as often as you like with an All-Day Pass.

Other tours are offered through Fairmount Park, America's largest urban park: The West Fairmount Park tour, passing historic mansions, the Horticultural Center, the Japanese House and Gardens, and the Zoo; and the East Park tour, passing six other historic mansions, and the fascinating Smith Memorial Playground. For schedules, fares, boarding locations, and further information, call 215-925-TOUR (925-8687). You can also call American Trolley Tours; 215-333-2119.

SEPTA's trolleys offer a rather refreshing experience, too. There are five trolley lines that cover the city, and two that reach into the suburbs. For schedules and information, call 215-580-7800.

Carriage Rides are a delightful way to ride through historic areas of Philadelphia. Three companies are at your service. Standard pickup points are Independence Hall and Head House Square.

Ben Franklin Carriages; 215-923-8516.
Philadelphia Carriage Company; 215-922-6840.
'76 Carriage Company; 215-925-TOUR (925-8516).

Boats and Ferries. To see Philadelphia the way William Penn first saw it, we recommend a cruise up the Delaware River. This is available on pleasure boats that serve lunch, dinner, late-night meals, or Sunday brunch while they sail the waters. See the listings in the Dining section under "Waterfront," or consult the Visitors Center—215-636-1666.

For a relaxed ride to Camden, take the **RiverLink** from Penn's

Horse and Buggy in Society Hill

*Bob Krist for the Greater Philadelphia
Tourism Marketing Corporation*

Landing in Philadelphia to the Camden waterfront adjacent to the NJ State Aquarium. The 400-passenger ferry runs every 30 minutes. Fare: $2 each way. For information call 215-925-5465.

And for a unique land and river tour of the waterfront, try the Philly Splash, the new amphibious craft scheduled to begin coasting along the shoreline in the late summer of 2000. For information call the Penn's Landing Corporation; 215-922-2FUN. Website: www.pennslanding-corp.com.

Another type of experience is the **Driving Tour of Philadelphia Movie Sites,** available from the Greater Philadelphia Film Office. The tour takes you past locations shot in *Blow Out, Witness, Birdy, Trading Places, Mannequin,* etc. Approximate driving time is two hours. Call for a copy, 215-686-2668; Hotline: 215-686-3663.

Walking

The walker who enjoys a few hours seeing the city will be delighted with the compact nature of Center City Philadelphia. We recommend the daylight hours for walking and taxi service during the evening. An excellent spot to start is the **Philadelphia Convention and Visitors Center,** 1525 John F. Kennedy Blvd., where maps, brochures, and expert advice are available. Hours are 9 am-5 pm every day except Thanksgiving and Christmas; 215-636-1666. (See DOWNTOWN WALKING TOUR of Center City, Philadelphia).

The following is only a selection of available guided walking tours:

Chef's Tour of the Italian Market; 215-772-0739.
Chinatown Tour; 215-772-0739.
Foundation for Architecture Tours; 215-569-3187.
Ghost Tours of Philadelphia; 215-413-1997.
Lights of Liberty interactive, 3-D, multimedia tour of Independence Mall; 877-GO-2-1776. (See SIGHTS.)
Tippler's Tour—a guided eighteenth-century pub-crawl. For this and other Historic Philadelphia, Inc. programs, call 800-76-HISTORY.

LODGING

Philadelphia has been increasing its number of hotel rooms in its goal to compete as a major convention city in the United States. With the opening of the Convention Center in Center City, the building of more hotels, and the elegant renovation of many others, accommodations in and near Center City have been greatly increased and enhanced. Indeed, the success of these efforts is evidenced by the fact that the Republican National Convention was held in Philadelphia in the summer of 2000.

The 1,200-room Philadelphia Marriot is actually connected to the Convention Center, while other new venues are close by. Elsewhere, in the northeast, in the Valley Forge area that boasts its own convention facilities, in West Philadelphia, and near the airport, lodging is equal to the demand, with hotels and motels to suit every mood, taste, and budget. In an effort to generate more tourism, Philadelphia approved a 13% tax on hotel room bills with the funds earmarked for promotion of the city's many attractions and historical sites. This tax also applies in Delaware and Montgomery counties.

Below we have listed hotels, motels, inns, resorts, and campgrounds that are anxious to make your visit to Philadelphia a most pleasant and enjoyable one.

The following key is used at the end of each listing.

D	Discounts offered.
FP	Family plans offered.
MAP	Modified American plan.
PA	Pets allowed.
PAC	Packages available.

We will abbreviate the following recipients:

AP	Airline personnel.
C	Clergy.
CR	Commercial rates for corporate business.
F	Faculty.
GI	Government/Military.
SC	Senior citizens.
ST	Students.
TA	Travel agents.

Remember that although all lodgings have rates that will be categorized as expensive, moderate, or inexpensive, they may offer discounts or weekend specials that may reduce these rates. Some rates may fluctuate according to the season of the year. Call for information.

E   Expensive, $100 and up for a double room;
M   Moderate, $75-$100 for a double room;
I   Inexpensive, less than $75 for a double room.

LODGING BY AREA

BUCKS COUNTY
Best Western—New Hope, M.
Black Bass Hotel, M.
Colonial Woods Family Campground, I.
Logan Inn, M.
Sheraton Bucks County Hotel, M-E.
Tohickon Family Campground, I.
The Warrington Motor Lodge, I.

CENTER CITY
Clarion Suites—Convention
    Center, M.
Comfort Inn at Penn's Landing, M.
Crowne Plaza Philadelphia
    Center City, E.
Doubletree Hotel, E.
Hawthorn Suites Philadelphia at
    the Convention Center, E.
Holiday Inn—City Centre, E.
Holiday Inn—Express Midtown, E.
Park Hyatt Philadelphia at the
    Bellevue, E.
Latham Hotel, M.
Warwick, E.
Wyndham Franklin Plaza, E.

CENTER CITY—PARKWAY
Best Western Center City Hotel, M.
Embassy Suites Hotel, E.
Four Seasons Hotel, E.
The Hotel Windsor, E.
Korman Suites Hotel and
    Conference Center, E.

Loews Philadelphia Hotel, E.
The Rittenhouse Hotel, E.
The Ritz-Carlton, Philadelphia, E.
Sheraton Rittenhouse Square Hotel, E.
Walnut Street Inn, E.

CHESTER COUNTY
Coventry Forge Inn, I.
Holiday Inn—Express, M.
Holiday Inn West Chester, M.
Philadelphia/West Chester KOA, I.
Wyndham Suites Valley Forge, M.

CITY AVENUE
Adams Mark Hotel, E.
Holiday Inn—City Line, E.

DELAWARE COUNTY
Christopher's Alpine Inn
    Motor Lodge, I.
Executive Motor Inn, I.
Radnor Hotel, E.
Ramada Inn Chadds Ford, M.
Summit Motor Inn, I.
The Wayne Hotel, E.

LANCASTER COUNTY
All Seasons Resort, I-E.
Holiday Inn—Lancaster Visitors
    Center, M-E.
Mill Bridge Village Campground, I.
Shady Grove Campground, I.
Willow Valley Inn, M.

MONTGOMERY COUNTY
Best Western—The Inn at King of
    Prussia, M.
Best Western Inn, M.
Desmond Hotel and Conference
    Center, E.
Eagle Lodge Conference Center and
    Country Club, E.
Holiday Inn—Fort Washington, M.
Holiday Inn—Valley Forge, M.
Inn at Plymouth Meeting, I.
Park Ridge atValley Forge, E.
Philadelphia Marriot West, E.
Sheraton Valley Forge Hotel and
    Convention Center, E.
Valley Forge Hilton, M.
The Greater Valley Forge Picnic
    and Sports Complex, I-E.
Wyndham Suites Valley Forge, M.

NORTHEAST PHILADELPHIA
Best Western Hotel Philadelphia
    NE, M.
Club Hotel by Doubletree, M.
Days Inn, I.
Holiday Inn—Northeast, M.
Howard Johnson Hotel, M.
Radisson Philadelphia Northeast
    Hotel, M.

NORTHWEST PHILADELPHIA
Chestnut Hill Hotel, M-E.
Sugarloaf Conference Center, E.

OLD CITY-SOCIETY HILL
Best Western Independence Park
    Inn, E.

Holiday Inn—Independence
    Mall, E.
Omni Hotel at Independence
    Park, E.
Penn's View Hotel, E.
Sheraton Society Hill, E.
Society Hill Hotel, M-E.
Thomas Bond House, M-E.

SOUTH PHILADELPHIA
Airport Tower Hotel, M.
Days Inn Hotel/Philadelphia
    International Airport, M.
Econolodge/Philadelphia
    International Airport, I.
Embassy Suites Hotel, E.
Hampton Inn Philadelphia
    International Airport, E.
Hilton Philadelphia Airport, E.
Holiday Inn Airport, M.
Holiday Inn, Philadelphia
    Stadium, E.
Howard Johnson's Airport
    South, M.
Philadelphia Airport Marriot, E.
Radisson Hotel Philadelphia
    Airport, M-E.
Ramada Inn Airport, M.
Sheraton Philadelphia International
    Airport Hotel, E.
Westin Suites, Airport, M.

UNIVERSITY CITY
Penn Towers, M-E.
Sheraton University City
    Hotel, M-E.

HOTELS AND MOTELS

ADAM'S MARK HOTEL, City Ave. and Monument Rd., Philadelphia, 19131; 215-581-5000, 800-231-5858. E. This sleek hotel has 515 deluxe rooms and 66 suites in the heart of the City Line business and media center. Located only 10 minutes from Center City and

20 minutes from Philadelphia International Airport, the Adam's Mark has a wide range of facilities for meetings, banquets, and exhibits. For the female business traveler, it offers a special floor with upgraded rooms and special amenities. *The Marker*, one of Philly's hottest restaurants, features excellent contemporary American cuisine, dazzling desserts, and an extensive wine list. Another dining room, *Appleby's*, is priced for the entire family. Fine shopping is within walking distance. For relaxation, the hotel features two racquetball courts, indoor and outdoor swimming pools, and a health club with Nautilus exercise equipment, a whirlpool, a sauna, and steam rooms. Free parking. Scheduled limousine to and from the airport. PAC.

AIRPORT TOWER HOTEL, 2015 Penrose St., Philadelphia, 19145; 215-336-4600. M. Five blocks from the sports complex, two-and-a-half miles from the airport, and close to ethnic South Philadelphia, this hotel offers 204 rooms, as well as a heated outdoor pool, meeting and banquet facilities, and free airport limousine. *Waldo Pepper's Bar and Grill* is ready to serve you. D (AP,CR,G,SC,ST), FP, PA, PAC.

BEST WESTERN HOTELS
Best Western, Center City Hotel, Twenty-second St. and Benjamin Franklin Parkway, Philadelphia, 19130; 215-568-8300. M. This budget motor lodge offers 181 rooms and convenient access to some of the city's most famous historical sites. There's free parking, the *Rodin Restaurant*, an outdoor café, and an outdoor pool. D, FP, SC, PAC.

Best Western Independence Park Inn, 235 Chestnut St., Philadelphia, 19106; 215-922-4443; 800-624-2988. E. Housed in a Victorian building located within America's most historic square mile, this is "Philadelphia's Great Little Hotel," with 36 designer rooms. Guests are served a complimentary European breakfast and afternoon tea. D, PAC.

Best Western Hotel, Philadelphia NE, 11580 Roosevelt Blvd. (U.S. 1), three miles south of Exit 28 on the Pennsylvania Turnpike; Philadelphia, 19116; 215-464-9500; 800-528-1234. M. Offers 100 guest rooms including four deluxe Jacuzzi suites, nine banquet/meeting rooms, corporate wings, an outdoor pool, a volleyball court, an exercise room and lounge, the *Cabana Bar and Grille* and the *Chocolate Shoppe/Café*. Special packages for Franklin Mills and Sesame Place. D.

Best Western Inn, Route 309 and Exit 26 on the Pennsylvania Turnpike, Fort Washington, 19034; 215-542-7930. M. Close to the Fort Washington Convention Center, this hotel features 106 luxury guest rooms and suites, with all the fun of New Hope not far away. It offers a free Continental breakfast, as well as the *Palace of Asia* restaurant and lounge. There is also an outdoor pool, and full banquet and meeting facilities. *D, CR.*

Best Western, The Inn at King Of Prussia, Route 202, Exit 24 on the Pennsylvania Turnpike; Philadelphia, 19406; 610-265-4500, 800-446-4656. M. Directly across from the King of Prussia Mall and two miles from historic Valley Forge Park, this facility offers 168 large rooms, *Lulu Wellington's* restaurant and bar, an outdoor pool, and Continental breakfast. *D* (SC-AARP cardholders).

Best Western-New Hope, Route 202, New Hope, 18938; 215-862-5221. M. Besides 159 rooms, there are meeting and banquet facilities, as well as a heated, outdoor pool, exercise room and tennis court. Patrons can also enjoy *Friday's* lounge and the *Symphonies Restaurant*. *D, CR, FP.*

BLACK BASS HOTEL, 3744 River Road, Lumberville, 18933; 215-297-5815. M. Located on the Delaware River, this eighteenth-century hotel is the perfect place to really unwind. Seven rooms and suites are decorated in truly historic style, and the restaurant is known for its outstanding American dishes. *PA.*

THE CHESTNUT HILL HOTEL AND RETAIL COMPLEX, 8229 Germantown Ave., Philadelphia, 19118; 215-242-5905 and 800-628-9744. M-E. This stately hotel has been totally renovated and patterned after a European bed-and-breakfast spot. Its 28 rooms include three suites. All are beautifully decorated with early nineteenth-century reproduction furniture. A fine place to stay or have business meetings, with Continental breakfast provided, and dining available in the *Chautauqua*, and *Café Winberie*, and *Pollo Rosso Italian Restaurant*. Enjoy browsing in the quaint shops and Farmer's Market. *PA, D, SC.*

CHRISTOPHER'S ALPINE INN MOTOR LODGE, 650 Baltimore Pike, Springfield, 19064; 610-544-4700. *I.* This motel offers 140 rooms, meeting facilities, a cocktail lounge, and fine dining in the *Central Park* gourmet restaurant.

CLARION SUITES-CONVENTION CENTER, 1010 Race St., Philadelphia, 19107; 215-922-1730, 800-CLARION. M. In the heart of Chinatown, this historic hotel offers 96 suites and the *Silver Palace Restaurant*, featuring a Chinese menu and limited American cuisine. There's a fitness center, meeting and conference space, and limited free parking.

CLUB HOTEL BY DOUBLETREE, 9461 Roosevelt Blvd., Philadelphia, 19114; 215-671-9600; 800-222-8733. M. Located next to

North Philadelphia Airport, the racetracks, and Sesame Place, this Sheraton has 200 deluxe rooms and suites, a domed swimming pool, a restaurant and lounge, and excellent meeting and conference facilities for up to 400 people. *D, CR, SC, G, PAC.*

COMFORT INN AT PENN'S LANDING, 100 N. Columbus Blvd., Philadelphia, 19106; 215-627-7900, 800-228-5150. M. Open since October 1987, this hotel offers 185 rooms, many with waterfront views, as well as three suites. Within walking distance of 50 restaurants, there are no in-house eateries, but rates include a full Continental breakfast. There's a lobby lounge, free parking, and courtesy van service. *FP, SC, CR.*

COVENTRY FORGE INN, Route 23, Coventryville, 19464; 610-469-6222. *I.* Nestled in the rolling hills of Chester County, this lovely 1717 inn offers five tastefully furnished rooms, Continental breakfast on the porch, and fine French dishes in the dining room.

CROWNE PLAZA PHILADELPHIA CENTER CITY, 1800 Market St., Philadelphia, 19103; 215-561-7500. E. Fully renovated guestrooms with every amenity. Frequent guest program. Executive floor with enhanced services and luxuries. Meeting and banquet spaces. *The Elephant* and *Castle Pub and Restaurant,* and the *E & C Espresso Bar.* Convenient to the business and financial districts, the airport, shopping, and tourist, cultural, and historic sites. *D, CR, SC, PA.*

DAYS INN HOTELS
Days Inn, 4200 Roosevelt Blvd., Philadelphia, 19124; 215-289-9200. *I.* There are 116 rooms, Jacuzzis, and free HBO and Continental breakfast. Business, shopping, historical and cultural attractions are nearby. Meeting facilities. *D, SC, CD, G, PAC.*

Days Inn Hotel/Philadelphia International Airport, 4101 Island Ave., Philadelphia, 19153; 215-863-3400. M. Conveniently located off I-95 and adjacent to the airport, and only seven miles from Center City and three miles from the Sports Complex. There are 177 rooms, meeting and banquet facilities that can accommodate up to 100 people, an outdoor pool, a restaurant, lounge, and free airport shuttle. *D, CR, PAC.*

DESMOND HOTEL AND CONFERENCE CENTER, One Liberty Blvd., Malvern, 19355; 610-296-9800, 800-575-1776. *E.* Located 30 minutes from Center City, 10 minutes from Valley Forge, and an hour from Lancaster and Reading, this center provides 201 rooms and nine suites. There is a free Continental breakfast, a restaurant, lounge, deck, indoor pool, fitness center, and jogging trail, as well as tennis and volleyball facilities. *PAC.*

DOUBLETREE HOTEL, Broad and Locust Sts., Philadelphia, 19107; 215-893-1600, 800-222-TREE. *E.* Located along the new Avenue of the Arts, and in the center of the city's museum, cultural, and shopping districts, this 26-story hotel offers 427 rooms and suites. Two floors provide free Continental breakfast and afternoon hors d'oeuvres. There is room service, the *Academy Café,* a bar, health club, indoor pool, roof garden jogging track, and sauna. *PAC.*

ECONOLODGE-PHILADELPHIA INTERNATIONAL AIR-PORT, 600 Route 291, Lester 19029; 610-521-3900. *I.* This budget motel offers 134 guest rooms, a restaurant/lounge, and free airport shuttle service. *D, PA.*

EAGLE LODGE CONFERENCE CENTER AND COUNTRY CLUB, Ridge Pike and Manor Road, Lafayette Hill, 19444; 610-825-8000, 800-523-3000. *E.* Thirty-two meeting rooms and 120 guest rooms. Perfect for corporate or association meetings, with extensive recreational and fitness facilities including the 18-hole Rees Jones golf course. There is a business center, concierge, and computer training room, and it's only 20 minutes from Center City. *PAC.*

EMBASSY SUITES HOTELS
Embassy Suites Hotel, 9000 Bartram Ave., Philadelphia, 19153; 215-365-4500. *E.* At the airport, this hotel boasts five floors of luxury accommodations surrounding an atrium. The suites, which include cycle and boardroom suites, are equipped with microwaves, refrigerators, two telephones, and two TVs. Enjoy the *Atrium Restaurant,* and the bar, complimentary breakfast at the manager's reception, free airport shuttle, indoor pool, exercise facilities, and a billiard room. *PAC.*

Embassy Suites Hotel Center City, 1776 Benjamin Franklin Parkway, Philadelphia, 19103; 215-561-1776; 800-EMBASSY. *E.* The 288 suites in this hotel contain living rooms, kitchen areas, bedrooms, and balconies with spectacular views. The manager's reception offers free breakfast and cocktail. Lunch, dinner, and room service are provided by *T.G.I. Friday's.*

EXECUTIVE MOTOR INN, 675 Baltimore Pike, Springfield, 19064; 610-543-0555. *I.* Here are 82 guest rooms located on Springfield's golden mile. *D.*

The Swann Fountain at Logan Circle on Benjamin Franklin Parkway

G. Widman for the Greater Philadelphia
Tourism Marketing Corporation

FOUR SEASONS HOTEL, One Logan Sq., Philadelphia, 19103; 215-963-1500, 800-332-3442. *E.* The $44-million Four Seasons is another of Philadelphia's deluxe downtown hotels. Overlooking Benjamin Franklin Parkway, it shares a 2 1/2-acre site with a soaring office tower; between the two is a landscaped courtyard accessible from a lobby highlighted by paneled wood, marble, and a fountain. The 365 executive suites and guest rooms are large and magnificently appointed, and offer sweeping views of Logan Square, the Art Museum, and Center City. The *Fountain Restaurant*, also, has a striking view of the Parkway, while the adjacent *Swann Lounge* offers more casual dining and nightly entertainment. Five "boardrooms," one on each of the five guest-room floors, are especially designed for business meetings. The health club features an indoor swimming pool, a whirlpool, saunas, and massage rooms. There is a full-service beauty salon on the premises. *D, FP* (18 and under) *PAC, PA.*

HAMPTON INN PHILADELPHIA INTERNATIONAL AIR- PORT, 8600 Bartram Ave., Philadelphia, 19153; 215-966-1300. *E.* One of the city's newest hotels. Many complimentary amenities. Deluxe continental breakfast, coffee/tea and fresh fruit service, business and fitness centers, and airport shuttle.

HAWTHORN SUITES PHILADELPHIA AT THE CON- VENTION CENTER, 1100 Vine St., Philadelphia, 19107; 215-829- 8300. *E.* A new, 294 unit, all-suite hotel adjacent to the Convention Center. Spacious studio and one-bedroom accommodations with effi- ciency kitchens. Complimentary breakfast.

HILTON PHILADELPHIA AIRPORT, 4509 Island Ave., Philadelphia, 19153; 215-365-4150. *E.* This hotel, within minutes of Philadelphia International Airport, has 331 rooms, including female traveler rooms, two restaurants, and a lounge. It offers an indoor pool, a health spa with saunas, and free HBO. *The Landing Restaurant* and *Players Sports Bar.* Free parking; free airport van service. Full meeting and banquet facilities. *D, FP, PAC, PA.*

HOLIDAY INN HOTELS—The Holiday Inn star shines through- out the Philadelphia area as a symbol of fine accommodations, food, and relaxation facilities. Most offer the same range of services and amenities. Call toll-free 800-HOLIDAY (465-4329).
   Holiday Inn-Airport, 45 Industrial Hwy., Essington, 19029; 215- 521-2400. *M.* Offers 303 rooms, a restaurant, swimming pool, exercise room, free parking, free airport transportation, and meeting and ban- quet facilities. *D, FP, PA,* and *PAC.*

Holiday Inn-City Centre, Eighteenth and Market Sts., Philadelphia, 19103; 215-561-7500. M-E. Completely refurbished from top to bottom, here you will find 445 rooms in the heart of Philadelphia's business and shopping activity. There's also a pool and a restaurant, the *Elephant and Castle*. Full banquet and meeting services are available. D, FP, PAC.

Holiday Inn-City Line, City Ave. at the Schuylkill Expressway, Philadelphia, 19131; 215-477-0200, 800-HOLIDAY. E. This modern high-rise hotel, in the City Line business and media center, has 350 rooms and one restaurant on the premises. *The Glass Tree* offers American family-style dining and buffet-style breakfast seven days a week. There is also a cocktail lounge, *Remy's*, meeting and banquet facilities, a glass-domed, solar-heated swimming pool, and a whirlpool. Fine shopping is within walking distance. Free parking. D, G, CR, FP, PA, PAC (long-term).

Holiday Inn-Express, 120 N. Pottstown Pike, Exton, 19341; 610-524-9000. M. Along with 124 rooms, there is a conference center, meeting rooms, outdoor swimming, and an exercise room. D, SC, CR, PA.

Holiday Inn-Express Midtown, 1305-11 Walnut St., Philadelphia, 19107; 215-735-9300. E. Guests staying in the 164 spacious rooms are offered a free Continental breakfast. There are meeting spaces available, as well as an outdoor pool and free access to *Bally's Total Fitness Center*. D, CR, FP, SC.

Holiday Inn-Fort Washington, 432 Pennsylvania Ave., Fort Washington, 19034; 215-643-3000. M. Here you will find 224 rooms, a restaurant, lounge, and comedy club, as well as an outdoor pool and an arcade. D, G, TA, SC.

Holiday Inn-Independence Mall, Fourth and Arch Sts., Philadelphia, 19106; 215-923-8660; 800-THE-BELL. E. Located in the heart of historical downtown Philadelphia, this Holiday Inn has a pool and 364 rooms decorated in a colonial motif and featuring free Showtime television. Fine cuisine is served in *Benjamin's*, quick meals at *Café Plain and Fancy*, and satellite sporting events in *Reunion Sports Bar*. D, FP, PAC.

Holiday Inn-Lancaster Visitors Center, Route 30 and Greenfield Rd., Lancaster, 17601; 717-299-2551. M-E. Enjoy 189 rooms, indoor and outdoor pools, a fitness center, and banquet and meeting rooms. D, SC, CR.

Holiday Inn-Northeast, 3499 Street Rd., Bensalem, 19020; 215-638-1500. M. Here 4,000 sq. feet of meeting space is available, as well as a lounge and a restaurant. For guests staying in the 117 rooms and two suites, there is an outdoor pool and fitness center. D.

Holiday Inn-Philadelphia Stadium, Tenth St. and Packer Ave., Philadelphia, 19148; 215-755-9500. E. Located almost adjacent to Veterans Stadium and the Spectrum, this hotel offers 238 rooms, meeting and banquet facilities, and free parking. Its *Philly Legends Sports Bar & Grill* is a popular spot, especially following sports events, and the *Jaws Restaurant* has a leisurely atmosphere for breakfast, lunch, and dinner. *D, SC.*

Holiday Inn-Valley Forge, 260 Mall Blvd., King of Prussia, 19406; 610-265-7500. M. Only 100 short steps from the huge King of Prussia Mall, and minutes from Valley Forge National Park, this hotel boasts 225 spacious rooms and 23,000 sq. feet of meeting space. There is a health club and an indoor pool, as well as the *Plaza Food and Spirits* restaurant and lounge. *D, CR, FP, PA.*

Holiday Inn West Chester, 943 S. High St., off Route 202, West Chester, 19380; 610-692-1900. M. This motel offers 141 rooms, free HBO, an outdoor swimming pool, and a café and bar that features fine food. *D, CR, GR, SC.*

THE HOTEL WINDSOR, *E.* 1700 Benjamin Franklin Pkwy., Philadelphia, 19103; 215-981-5678; 877-SUITES9. An all-suite hotel with complimentary amenities, continental breakfast, business and kitchen facilities, fitness center and two on-site restaurants.

HOWARD JOHNSON'S HOTELS

Howard Johnson, 2779 Route 1 N., Trevose, 19053; 215-638-4554; 800-446-4656. For traveling Americans, this pioneer of the motor-lodge concept offers dependable accommodations and dining. Eighty-eight spacious guest rooms, Jacuzzi suites, restaurant, pool, and meeting rooms. Just south of Exit 28 of the PA Turnpike. Minutes from Sesame Place and Franklin Mills Mall. *CR.*

Howard Johnson Airport South, Exit 6 off I-95, Chester, 19013; 610-876-7211. M. Enjoy 117 rooms, a restaurant and lounge, an indoor pool, and exercise facilities, as well as a complete American breakfast and complimentary airport van service. There are also banquet rooms and meeting rooms accommodating 200. *D, SC, FP.*

INN AT PLYMOUTH MEETING, Route 422 and Plymouth Rd., Plymouth Meeting, 19462; 610-825-1980. *I.* This 215-room facility has an outdoor pool, the *White Swan Restaurant* and a lounge, and convenient access to Plymouth Meeting Mall. Catering is available, as well as van transportation. *SC, PA.*

KORMAN SUITES HOTEL AND CONFERENCE CENTER, Twentieth St. near Benjamin Franklin Parkway, Philadelphia, 19130; 215-569-7000. *E.* Gracious rooms and suites with panoramic skyline views. Enjoy the *Tuscan Twenty Restaurant*, complimentary Continental breakfast, and van service. *PAC.*

LATHAM HOTEL, Walnut and Seventeenth Sts., Philadelphia, 19103; 215-563-7474. M. On the National Register of Historic Places, the Latham is a small hotel accented by the finest traditions of Europe. It hosts no conventions and assures the ultimate in personal service, continually upgrading its 139 rooms. From the doorman in his English riding boots to the crystal chandelier in the lobby, the Latham is a delight, with special amenities in each room. The casually elegant *Michel's* is open for breakfast, there's an exercise room to serve you, and there's parking in the nearby garage. *D, PAC, FP.*

LOEWS PHILADELPHIA HOTEL, 1243 Market St., Philadelphia, 19107; 215-627-1200; 800-235-6397. E. A new 585-room luxury hotel close to shopping, touring, the Convention Center, and cultural and historic sites. Business and personal amenities in each room and throughout the hotel.

THE LOGAN INN, Main and Ferry, New Hope, 18938; 215-862-2300. M. Located in the heart of historic New Hope, this 1727 inn is believed to be one of the oldest in the area. In any of the 16 rooms, you will find beautiful antiques and brass beds. Excellent dining is available in the colonial dining room and the greenhouse. During the warm months, there is outdoor dining. *CD.*

MARRIOTT HOTELS—The hotels in the Philadelphia area adhere to the quality in service and fine dining that have forged an excellent reputation for the Marriott chain throughout the world. Call 1-800-228-9290.

Philadelphia Airport Marriott, 1 Arrivals Rd., Philadelphia, 19153; 215-492-9000; 800-682-4087. E. Connected to Terminal B of the airport with 419 attractive rooms, spacious meeting areas, indoor pool, and health club. American cuisine in the *Riverbend Bar and Grille.*

Philadelphia Marriott Hotel, 1201 Market St., Philadelphia, 19107; 215-625-2900; 800-320-5744. E. Conveniently located in downtown Philadelphia, the new Philadelphia Marriott is the biggest thing to hit Philadelphia in years. The 1,200-room hotel features the largest ball-room in the state of Pennsylvania totaling just over 34,000 square feet. Though the hotel is connected via a skybridge to the Pennsylvania Convention Center, it was not designed to be just a convention hotel. The lobby offers intimate warmth which can make any business travel-er or family on vacation feel right at home. In addition to the 1,200 deluxe guest rooms that include 58 luxury suites, the Philadelphia Marriott boasts 124 concierge rooms. Guests will also benefit from an in-house business center offering a range of services including secretar-ial assistance, faxing, photocopying, and notary certification.

From a dining standpoint, the Philadelphia Marriott features a choice of full-service restaurants. *JW's Steakhouse* offers a traditional, appetizing steakhouse menu in a comfortable atmosphere, while *Allie's American Grille and Patio* features a contemporary menu with fun, lighter dishes reflecting today's lifestyles. An All-American sports bar, *Champions,* is complete with your favorite sporting event and light snack. An indoor swimming pool with extensive health club facilities is also available.

Philadelphia Marriott West, Matson Ford Road at Front St., West Conshohocken, 19428; 610-941-5600, 800-237-3639. *E.* Perfect for weekend getaways, this new hotel is on the Liberty Trail, between Historic Philadelphia and Valley Forge National Park. At the crossroads of I-476 and I-76, and near the Main Line, it features the *Regatta Bar and Grille,* concierge guest levels, a heated pool, and exercise facilities.

OMNI HOTEL AT INDEPENDENCE PARK, 401 Chestnut St., Philadelphia, 19106; 215-925-0000. *E.* A luxury hotel located within Independence National Historic Park. Boasts 150 rooms with views of the park, marble bathrooms, and telephones with computer and fax capabilities. Work out in the health club, dine in the *Azalea Restaurant,* and enjoy nightly entertainment in the bar. *PAC.*

PARK HYATT PHILADELPHIA AT THE BELLEVUE, 1415 Chancellor Court (Broad and Walnut Sts.), Philadelphia, 19102; 215-893-1234, 800-233-1234. *E.* Imagine 170 luxurious guest rooms in a magnificently restored historic hotel. Videotape players, phones with dataports, marble bathrooms, free use of adjacent *Sporting Club,* babysitting, gourmet restaurants, afternoon tea, and a cocktail lounge. *PAC.*

PARK RIDGE AT VALLEY FORGE HOTEL, 480 N. Gulph Rd., King of Prussia, 19406; 610-337-1800. *E.* Located next to historic Valley Forge, the vibrant King of Prussia shopping mall, and other attractions, this hotel has 300 rooms, each with a terrace. There's an outdoor pool, a cocktail terrace where drinks and light food can be enjoyed in warm weather, and golf is available on several nearby courses. The special Concierge Floor offers additional services. *D, CR, FP, SC, PAC.*

PENN'S VIEW HOTEL, Front and Market Sts., Philadelphia, 19106; 215-922-7600, 800-331-7634. *E.* A premier boutique hotel overlooking the Delaware. The 40 rooms are exquisitely furnished and some feature fireplaces and Jacuzzis. Italian cuisine is served in the *Ristorante Panorama,* which boasts one of the largest wine bars in the world. Complimentary European breakfast and room service. *PAC.*

PENN TOWERS, Thirty-fourth St. and Civic Center Blvd., Philadelphia, 19104; 215-387-8333, 800-356-PENN. M-E. This 21-story high-rise is located on the University of Pennsylvania campus, next to the Hospital of the University of Pennsylvania, the Civic Center, and the campus of Drexel University. It offers 175 guest rooms and suites, including a concierge level, a grand ballroom that is one of the largest in the area, and 14 meeting rooms that can accommodate up to 500. The *Terrace Restaurant* is informal and friendly, and *I.D.E.A.S.* (Innovative Drinking and Eating Alternatives and Service) is perfect for a quick sandwich or snack. Access to the Penn Children's Center, complimentary van service, and free passes to an area health club. D, PAC.

RADISSON HOTELS
Radisson Hotel Philadelphia Airport, 500 Stevens Drive, Philadelphia, 19113; 610-521-5900. M-E. At the Airport Business Center, this hotel offers 353 rooms, three presidential suites, and 52 mini-suites. It can accommodate banquets of up to 500, and meetings up to 800. There are three boardrooms, an indoor pool, a game room, a restaurant and bar, and airport shuttle service.

Radisson Philadelphia Northeast Hotel, 2400 Old Lincoln Hwy., Trevose, 19053; 215-638-8300; 800-333-3333. M. Ideally located near the variety of things to do in Bucks County, this hotel has 280 rooms, nine suites, a restaurant, lounge, and the *Yellow Jackets Dance Club*. A health club and indoor and outdoor pools are also available. Minutes from Franklin Mills Mall, New Hope, Peddler's Village, and Sesame Place. D, PAC, PA.

RADNOR HOTEL, 591 E. Lancaster Ave., St. Davids, 19087; 610-688-5800; 800-537-3000. E. Located on seven landscaped acres in the heart of Philadelphia's Main Line, the hotel is surrounded by large homes and estates, excellent shopping, eight colleges and universities, and the world headquarters of seven Fortune 500 companies. Its 170 rooms have been beautifully done, as has the cocktail lounge, which has entertainment nightly. Restaurant and full banquet and meeting facilities. *The Valley Forge Golf Club* and indoor-outdoor tennis courts are only minutes away, and the inn has an outdoor olympic pool. Free parking. D, CR, SC, PAC.

RAMADA INNS—This fine chain has distinctive inns in the Philadelphia area. Call toll-free 800-272-6232.

Ramada Inn Airport, 76 Industrial Hwy., Essington, 19029; 610-521-9600. M. A modern high-rise with 305 rooms within minutes of Philadelphia International Airport. In addition to its delightful *Reflections* restaurant and lounge, there is an Olympic-sized heated outdoor pool, a coffee shop, a beauty salon, an exercise room, and nearby tennis courts. Full banquet and meeting facilities, highlighted by the Meadows Ballroom (the largest in Delaware County), can accommodate up to 1,000 people. *D (AP, CR, TA) FP, SC, PAC.*

Ramada Inn Chadds Ford, Routes 1 and 202, Glen Mills, 19342; 610-358-1700. *M.* Located near the historic Brandywine Battlefields, this Ramada features 148 rooms, an outdoor pool, and a ballroom that seats up to 325 for banquets and meetings. *Verino's* restaurant and lounge offers American cuisine with an Italian accent, and a Sunday breakfast buffet. *D, SC, CR.*

THE RITTENHOUSE HOTEL, 210 W. Rittenhouse Square, Philadelphia, 19103; 215-546-9000; 800-635-1042. *E.* An intimate, boutique hotel with lovely rooms offering wonderful views of the square or the city. Adjacent to the business district, it is also within walking distance of shops, galleries, and restaurants. It offers a health club, a business center, room service, and four dining experiences. *PAC.*

THE RITZ-CARLTON, PHILADELPHIA, Seventeenth and Chestnut Sts. at Liberty Place, Philadelphia, 19103; 215-563-1600; 800-241-3333. *E.* A premier hotel located in the heart of the city, within walking distance of museums, theaters, parks, and historic sites. Guests in the 290 guest rooms and suites enjoy room service, in-room massage, a fitness center, a salon, valet parking, and "Ritz-Kids" amenities. There are business services, and a club level with a private lounge and concierge staff. Restaurants include *The Dining Room, The Grill,* and the *Lobby Lounge* which features afternoon tea and daily jazz. Complimentary town car service, as well.

SHERATON HOTELS—These hotels have an international reputation for service and special amenities. Call toll-free 800-325-3535.

Sheraton Bucks County Hotel, 400 Oxford Valley Road, Langhorne, 19047; 215-547-4100. *M-E.* A resort hotel only minutes away from New Hope, with 160 rooms, an indoor pool, a grand Jacuzzi, a health club, and saunas. Enjoy American cuisine in the *BC Bistro.*

Sheraton Philadelphia International Airport Hotel, 4101 Island Ave., Philadelphia, 19153; 215-492-0400; 800-325-3535. *E.* Newly renovated contemporary rooms, meeting spaces, restaurant and lobby. A mile from the airport and 10 minutes from Center City and the sports complex.

Sheraton Rittenhouse Square Hotel, Eighteenth and Locust Sts., Philadelphia 19103; 215-546-9400; 800-325-3535. *E.* A beautiful location for a luxurious hotel. Newly renovated, with 192 rooms and suites, fitness and business centers, a lounge, pub, and restaurant.

Sheraton Society Hill, 1 Dock St., Philadelphia, 19106; 215-238-6000; 888-345-7333. E. 365 rooms including 17 suites adjacent to Independence National Historic Park. Enjoy the four-story atrium lobby, indoor pool, health club, room service, restaurant, and *Wooden Nickel Tavern.* PAC.

Sheraton University City Hotel, Thirty-sixth and Chestnut Sts., Philadelphia, 19104; 215-387-8000. M-E. Adjacent to the University of Pennsylvania and Drexel University, and within walking distance of the Civic Center, this 20-story hotel offers 376 deluxe rooms and special executive suites, the popular *Shula's Steak 2* sports bar, an outdoor pool, and indoor parking. The *Palmaire Ballroom* can accommodate up to 700 people. D, SC, CR, PAC.

Sheraton Valley Forge Hotel and Convention Center, N. Gulph Road and First Avenue, King of Prussia, 19406; 610-337-2000. E. Part of the Valley Forge Convention Plaza which consists of this hotel, the Valley Forge Convention Center, Lily Langtry's Victorian Theatre and Restaurant, and the Parkview Tower Office Building, the hotel is located next to Valley Forge and the King of Prussia shopping mall. The Sheraton Valley Forge is one of the most exciting spots to stay in the area. In addition to 326 deluxe rooms, including the incomparable Fantasy Suites, there are superb facilities for exercise, swimming, volleyball, basketball, handball, squash, racquetball, steam, sauna, and massage. An 18-hole golf course and twin cinemas are nearby. Enjoy gourmet dining in the elegant *Chumley's Steak and Seafood Restaurant* and matchless Las Vegas revues at *Lily Langtry's.* More casual dining can be found in the *Sunflower Café* and *Junior's Deli. Club 92.5 Country Music Saloon* provides entertainment. The Sheraton Plaza Hotel offers 160 more guest rooms, including 70 executive suites. *Bocconcini's Italian Restaurant* and the *Pasta Bar* offer more dining choices. The Valley Forge Convention Center provides 130,000 square feet of space for shows and meetings for up to 6,700 people. D, CR, G, PAC.

SOCIETY HILL HOTEL, Third and Chestnut Sts., Philadelphia,19106; 215-925-1394. M-E. Built in 1832, this lodging served as temporary housing for longshoremen before it became Philadelphia's first bed-and-breakfast hotel. Still the city's smallest hotel (12 rooms), Society Hill Hotel is nestled within Old City and Society Hill, two blocks from Independence Hall. A charming place in the European tradition, it offers personal touches such as fresh-squeezed juice, coffee and tea, and warm rolls with sweet butter in each room in the morning. The rooms themselves have brass double beds with canopies and are always graced by freshly cut flowers. With its stained-glass greenery and jazz, the *Society Hill Bar and Restaurant* is an absolute delight and features a spectacular light menu as well as an outstanding Sunday brunch. Indoor parking nearby.

SUGARLOAF CONFERENCE CENTER, 9230 Germantown Ave., Philadelphia, 19118; 215-242-9100. *E.* Three historic estates have been combined to accommodate professional and corporate groups. The center offers conference and recreational facilities, including tennis courts, swimming pools, a game room, a bowling alley, and nature trails. *PAC.*

SUMMIT INN HOTEL, 351 E. Township Line Rd. (Route 1), Upper Darby, 19082; 215-449-6000. *I.* The Inn offers a panoramic view of a golf course and recently redecorated guest rooms. The Summit is convenient to the Main Line, only six miles from Center City. *FP, SC, G.*

THOMAS BOND HOUSE, 129 S. Second St., Philadelphia, 19106; 215-923-8523, 800-845-BOND. *M-E.* A restored 12-room colonial period guest house, circa 1769, owned by the National Park Service and located within Independence National Historic Park. Breakfast served.

VALLEY FORGE HILTON, 251 W. DeKalb Pike, King of Prussia, 19406; 610-337-1200. *M.* Here you will find luxurious surroundings and 340 rooms near Valley Forge National Historic Park, King of Prussia shopping mall, and Chester County. Its fine restaurants are the *Kobe Steak House* (Japanese hibachi cooking), and *Alexander Café & Lounge* (glass-enclosed on a poolside patio). Its lounge, *Maxwell's*, features live entertainment nightly. There is also an indoor/outdoor pool and a fitness center. *D (CR)* and *PAC.*

WALNUT STREET INN, 1208 Walnut St., Philadelphia, 19107; 215-546-7000; 800-887-1776. *E.* A gracious Victorian inn with 32 spacious guest rooms and suites containing period furnishings surrounding cable TVs. Continental breakfast and discounted indoor parking.

THE WARRINGTON, Route 611, Warrington, 18976; 215-343-0373. *I.* Located in a secluded, wooded area, only 20 minutes from New Hope, this excellent motor lodge has 75 lovely rooms and executive suites, new banquet facilities, and a restaurant. Outdoor pool and meeting facilities. *D.*

WARWICK HOTEL, Seventeenth and Locust Sts., Philadelphia, 19103; 215-735-6000, 800-523-4210. *E.* Opened in 1926, this English Renaissance building just off Rittenhouse Square has become a Philadelphia landmark. Through the years, such luminaries as President Dwight D. Eisenhower, Jack Benny, and Bob Hope have stayed here, and now after multi-million dollar renovations completed in 1994, it is the ultimate in European style and taste. The Warwick's

180 rooms and suites are beautifully furnished and decorated, and the lobby features a barbershop, an apothecary, and fashionable boutiques. The banquet and meeting facilities, led by the Grand Ballroom, can accommodate up to 500 people. Its *Circles off the Square* restaurant is open late, and the concierge is happy to arrange for such amenities as babysitting, flowers, limos, and complimentary use of the beautiful *Panorama* health club. *D.*

THE WAYNE HOTEL, 139 E. Lancaster Ave., Wayne, 19087; 610-687-5000. *E.* This charming Victorian hotel was built in 1906 and over the years was converted to many uses. Around 1985 it was restored as a hotel with 37 rooms, all furnished in Victorian reproductions. A porch typical of the period wraps around the building, and the lobby rooms exude charm. Excellent adjoining restaurant serves complimentary Continental breakfast to guests. *CD, SC.*

WESTIN SUITES PHILADELPHIA INTERNATIONAL AIRPORT, 1 Gateway Center, 4101 Island Ave., Philadelphia, 19153; 215-365-6600. *M.* This hotel, conveniently located near the Philadelphia airport, features 251 two-room suites complete with mini-bar and refrigerator. Extended stay suites offer special amenities. There's the *Atrium Café and Lounge,* an indoor pool, a fitness club, meeting space, and shuttle service to the airport. *D, SC, CR, G, PAC.*

WILLOW VALLEY INN, 2416 Willow St. Pike, Lancaster, 17602; 717-464-2711; 800-444-1714. *M.* These 185 acres of rolling hills in the midst of Amish Country offer fun for the whole family. There are indoor and outdoor pools, a Jacuzzi, a game room, a nine-hole golf course, lighted tennis courts, and a special playground for children. Tours to Pennsylvania Dutch Country. One of the two restaurants is noted for its all-you-can-eat smorgasbord, and in the *Bake Shoppe,* you can watch delicacies being made. *D, PAC.*

WYNDHAM HOTELS
Wyndham Franklin Plaza, Seventeenth and Race Sts., Philadelphia, 19103; 215-448-2000, 800-828-7447. *E.* With its initial venture in the U.S., the Canadian Pacific chain spearheaded new hotel construction in Philadelphia and has scored handsomely with the Franklin Plaza. Now owned by Wyndham Hotels and conveniently located near the city's business, cultural, and historical activity, it offers a near-resort atmosphere of beauty, fine restaurants and lounges, 758 luxuriously appointed rooms, and full banquet and meeting facilities. *Between Friends* features tableside service, while *The Terrace* is a lovely spot to dine just off an airy lobby beneath a 70-foot glass roof. *Clark's*

Uptown, the health club, is one of the city's finest, with an indoor swimming pool, racquetball and squash courts, outdoor handball courts, and an outdoor tennis court surrounded by a jogging track. *D*.

Wyndham Suites Valley Forge, 888 Chesterbrook Blvd., Wayne, 19087; 610-647-6700. *M*. Located near the booming Great Valley Corporate Center, and close to Valley Forge National Park, this 229-suite hotel features *The Town & Country Grill* restaurant and the *Atrium* piano lounge. There's an indoor pool, sauna, Jacuzzi, and exercise room, as well as more than 10 miles of jogging and walking trails. *CR, PAC*.

HOTEL SAFETY

As a public-safety service we include in this chapter the following guidance in case of a hotel fire. All information is taken from a publication of the National Safety Council.

Preliminary precautions start after you check into your hotel. Check the exits and fire alarms on your floor, count the doorways between your room and the exit, keep your key close to your bed and take it with you if you leave your room in case you need to return. If smoke blocks your exit, check the window latches and any adjoining buildings or decks for low level escape.

In case of fire, take your key and crawl to the door. Don't stand; smoke and deadly gases rise. If the doorknob is hot—*do not open*—stay in your room. Then open the window, phone for help, hang a sheet from the window to signal for help, and turn on the bathroom fan. Fill the tub with water, wet towels, and sheets to put around doors if smoke seeps in, and make a tent over your head with a blanket at a partially opened window to get fresh air.

If the doorknob is *not* hot, leave, close the door to your room, proceed to the exit, counting doorways in the dark, and walk down to the ground level. If blocked at lower levels, turn around, walk up to the roof, and keep the roof door open to vent stairwell. Wait for help on the roof. **Do not use elevator. Remember to lie low to avoid smoke and gases.**

ALTERNATIVE LODGING
Bed-and-Breakfast

The British tradition of bed-and-breakfast has become very popular in Philadelphia and its surrounding counties. Townhouses, high-rises, duplexes, and historic homes offer a private guest room with bath and Continental breakfast for a moderate fee. Below are several Reservation Service Agencies that can direct you to the bed-and-breakfast right for you.

Abby's Agency and Guesthouses, Inc., P.O. Box 2137, West Chester, PA 19380; 610-692-4575, 800-950-9130. Specializing in Historic National Register and landmark properties throughout the Brandywine Valley. Rates: $80-$295.

A Bed and Breakfast Connection/Bed and Breakfast of Philadelphia, P.O. Box 21, Devon, PA 19333; 610-687-3565, 800-448-3619. Offering "Gold Medallion Certified" accommodations throughout the Philadelphia region. Rates: $40-$250.

Association of Bed and Breakfasts in Philadelphia, Valley Forge, and Brandywine, P.O. Box 562, Valley Forge, PA 19481-0562; 610-783-7838, 800-344-0123. A selection of 500+ B&B's in Philadelphia and its suburbs with rates ranging from $35-$135.

University City Guest Houses, P.O. Box 28612, 2933 Morris Rd., Philadelphia, PA 19151; 215-387-3731. Rooms and apartments within walking distance of the area's major universities, hospitals, and the Civic Center. Rates: $25-$100.

Campgrounds

The Philadelphia area has a number of campgrounds with facilities ranging from basic water and electrical hook-ups to complete community services.

All-Seasons Resort, Route 10, three miles south of Honeybrook, PA 19344; 717-445-5372. *I-E.* This 149-acre membership campground, with wooded sites, offers everything from putting up your own tent to renting a trailer on the site. Fishing, basketball, volleyball, self-guided tours to Amish Country and Philadelphia, two playgrounds, a game room, and miniature golf. *PA.*

Colonial Woods Family Campground, Lonely Cottage Dr., Upper Black Eddy, PA 18972; 610-847-5808. *I.* Open all year, features boating, fishing, hay rides, hiking, playground, swimming, tennis, miniature golf, and a recreation hall. Shopping in nearby New Hope. Pets allowed on leash.

Mill Bridge Village Campground, one-half mile south of Route 30, east on Ronks Rd., Lancaster, PA 17579; 717-687-8181. *I.* Located in the heart of Lancaster County and on the same site as the quaint Mill Bridge Village, this campground offers fishing, hiking, a country store, and Bingo and line dancing every weekend from Memorial Day through late October. Pets allowed.

Philadelphia/West Chester KOA, Route 162, seven miles west of West Chester, P.O. Box 920P, Unionville, PA 19375; 610-486-0447. *I.* Nineteen acres along the Brandywine River feature canoeing and swimming. Also, game room, TV lounge, and van routes to Philadelphia. Pets on a leash.

Shady Grove Campground, PA Turnpike Exit 21, Rt. 897, P.O. Box 28, Adamstown, PA 19501; 717-484-4225. *I.* Sixty miles from Philadelphia in the "Antique Capital of PA" in Lancaster County. Twenty minutes from Reading and five minutes from the Green Dragon Farmer's Market. Surrounded by Amish farmland, and near gamelands, bass fishing, paddle boating, and miniature golf.

The Greater Valley Forge Picnic and Sports Complex, 157 Game Farm Rd., Schwenksville, PA 19473; 610-667-4187. A 150-acre facility with cabins, used for company picnics, church, school and scout functions, as well as private parties. Swimming, tennis, volleyball, miniature golf, and athletic fields.

Hostels

See STUDENTS in the Special People section.

RESORTS

The Philadelphia area is one of those rare places in which the natural wonders of an ocean and a mountain range are so nearby. Only a little more than an hour's drive from Center City is Atlantic City with its Boardwalk on the sandy beaches of the Atlantic, and, of course, casino gambling. The entire Jersey Shore is a haven for countless Philadelphians and visitors during the summer, with Cape May as one of the most historic resort areas to be found anywhere in the country. In another direction, about a two-hour drive to the northwest, are the beautiful Pocono Mountains, a year-round resort area highlighted by skiing in the winter and a wealth of other activities in the spring, summer, and fall.

Atlantic City

How to Get There

Atlantic City is about an hour and a quarter drive from Center City Philadelphia on the Atlantic City Expressway. New Jersey Transit train (800-AC-TRAIN) and bus service is available, and busing is also provided by the hotel casinos themselves. Air service is provided between Philadelphia International Airport and two airports in the Atlantic City area, Bader Field and Atlantic City International Airport.

Atlantic City Past

A century ago, Atlantic City was *the* resort on the East Coast. In 1870, the city opened the first boardwalk in the world; two years later, it spun the first Ferris wheel. In 1876, it hosted the world's first Easter Parade; in 1893, it produced the first picture postcards (of Atlantic City, of course).

Although Atlantic City had become famous for its Boardwalk, saltwater taffy, and the Miss America Pageant (begun circa 1921), the town began to settle into a slow decline that hit rock bottom in the 1950s. This continued until the late 1970s, when the city rolled the dice on its future with casino gambling.

The Casino Scene

Now, with countless millions of dollars invested in hotel-casinos, Atlantic City is once again alive with visitors and poised to surpass Las Vegas as the gambling capital of the world. Called "The Las Vegas of the East," the city draws hordes of tourists who find it an ideal stopover before or after visits to New York, Washington, and Philadelphia.

Although gambling and the top entertainers that accompanied it provided the impetus for rebirth, Atlantic City also has a host of activities for those whose interests lie outside the casinos. The Boardwalk itself is vibrant, with piers offering shopping, a variety of amusements for youngsters, and hundreds of young artists displaying and selling their work from June to September. Cycling is a must, and bicycles are for rent at convenient locations.

Recreation and Attractions

For sun worshipers, Atlantic City offers a free beach. For anglers, there is excellent deep-sea fishing in the Atlantic and in the bays. Boats for fishing and sightseeing can be chartered from the inlet docks. Golf is available on 14 nearby courses, tennis abounds on numerous indoor and outdoor courts, and there is hiking and canoeing in the nearby Pine Barrens.

In addition to the Miss America Pageant, the Convention Center hosts a boat show, a dog show, and an antique collectors' show among its many special events. It also has huge convention exhibits and one of the world's largest pipe organs. You'll also find thoroughbred horse racing at Atlantic City Race Course, and professional boxing in casino hotel auditoriums.

Shopping For Fun

With crowds flocking to the hotel casinos and other attractions, Atlantic City offers a wide range of quality shopping opportunities. One of the attractions on the Boardwalk is Ocean One, a pier resembling a docked ocean liner replete with portholes, masts, flags, and deck chairs—but actually a shopping mall with stores and shops, restaurants, a mega-arcade, and fast-food eateries. There is more shopping in the casinos themselves and on the avenues, and sprawling shopping malls farther inland.

Eating Out

Atlantic City runs the dining gamut from sidewalk hot dog stands to haute cuisine. Each hotel casino has a top-flight restaurant and various other eateries, but only a block or two away you're sure to find other fine restaurants, usually less expensive, that feature everything from seafood and Italian specialties to Chinese and Mexican food.

Getting Around

Should you drive to Atlantic City, expect to pay from $3-$12 in independent lots. Most casinos offer $2 parking. Jitneys, those little buggies that seat up to 13 people, are a traditional and inexpensive mode of transportation in Atlantic City; you can cover the full length of the city for $1.50. The Boardwalk rolling chairs are a fun way to ride the Great Wooden Way; chair charges range from $5 to $25.

Where to Stay

There are many smaller hotels and motels in Atlantic City that are less expensive than the $100-$200 per night charged in the hotel casinos. Regarding your specific requirements, we suggest you write or call the Atlantic City Convention and Visitors Authority, 2314 Pacific Ave., Atlantic City, NJ 08401; 609-348-7130; 800-BOARDWK; 888-ACVISIT. Website: www.atlanticcitynj.com. Remember, Atlantic City's peak season is the summer; reservations should be made well in advance and rates are the highest.

Listed below are the twelve hotel casinos currently in operation:

Atlantic City Hilton Casino Resort, Boston and the Boardwalk, Atlantic City, NJ 08401; 609-340-7100; 800-257-8677. The Hilton has 800 rooms, seven restaurants, a health club with a Victorian-style indoor pool, and an arcade. The theater seats 2,000.

Bally's Park Place, a Hilton Casino Resort, Park Pl. and the Boardwalk, Atlantic City, NJ 08401; 609-340-2000; 800-225-5977. Bally's has 1,255 rooms, 9 restaurants, a video game room, a pool, and a health spa. Its *Park Cabaret* seats 371.

Caesar's Atlantic City Hotel Casino, 2100 Pacific Ave., Atlantic City, NJ 08401; 609-348-4411; 800-524-2867. Caesar's has 641 rooms, 10 restaurants, an amusement arcade, a beach club, a pool, and a rooftop garden with tennis courts. *Caesar's Circus Maximus* seats 1,100.

The Claridge Casino Hotel, Boardwalk and Park Place, Atlantic City, NJ 08401; 609-340-3400; 800-257-8585. The Claridge has 501 rooms, 6 restaurants, and a health club with a glass-enclosed pool. The *Palace Theater* seats 550.

Harrah's Atlantic City Casino Hotel, 777 Harrah's Blvd., Atlantic City, NJ 08401; 609-441-5000; 800-242-7724. Harrah's has 506 rooms, 244 Atrium Tower Suites, eight restaurants, a glass-enclosed pool, a Nautilus room, deck tennis and shuffleboard, an arcade, a miniature golf course, and a child-care center. *Broadway by the Bay Theatre* seats 850.

Resorts Casino Hotel, 1133 Boardwalk, Atlantic City, NJ 08401; 609-344-6000; 800-336-6378. This, the first casino in Atlantic City, has 670 rooms, 7 restaurants, a beauty parlor, a health club, a glass-domed pool, a sundeck, a rooftop Jacuzzi, and a shopping arcade. *Superstar Theater* seats 1,800.

The Sands Hotel and Casino, Indiana Ave. and Brighton Park, Atlantic City, NJ 08401; 609-441-4000; 800-257-8580. Atlantic City's fourth casino, the Sands has 534 rooms, 5 restaurants, 1 lounge, and a health club with racquetball courts and Nautilus. The *Copa Room* seats 650.

Showboat Casino-Hotel, Delaware Ave. and Boardwalk, Atlantic City, NJ 08401; 609-343-4000; 800-621-0200. The Showboat has 516 rooms, 7 restaurants, the *Big Easy Spa,* a pool, and a bowling center.

Tropicana Casino and Resort, Brighton Ave. and the Boardwalk, Atlantic City, NJ 08401; 609-340-4000; 800-257-6227. As Atlantic City's ninth casino, Tropworld has 1,015 rooms, eight restaurants, a lounge, glass-enclosed elevators, a mall of shops, indoor and outdoor pools, a health club, and a tennis court. The *TropWorld Showroom* seats 1,700.

Trump's Castle Marina Casino Resort, One Castle Blvd., Atlantic City, NJ 08401; 609-441-2000; 800-365-8786. The Castle has 726 rooms and suites, eight restaurants, a health club, a jogging track, a marina, an outdoor pool, and a miniature golf course. The *Crystal Ballroom* seats 1,800.

Trump Plaza Hotel and Casino, Mississippi Ave. and the Boardwalk, Atlantic City, NJ 08401; 609-441-6000; 800-677-7378. This hotel has 556 rooms, 9 restaurants, *The Plaza Spa,* a glass-enclosed pool, and tennis and shuffleboard courts. The *Imperial Ballroom* seats 1,060.

Trump's Taj Mahal Casino Resort, 1000 Boardwalk at Virginia Ave., Atlantic City, NJ 08401; 609-449-1000; 800-825-8786. The Taj Mahal has 1,250 rooms, nine restaurants, four lounges, a health club, an indoor pool, and an exercise room. The *Mark G. Etess Arena* seats 6,000.

Cape May ————————————————————

How to Get There

Regularly scheduled bus service is available from Philadelphia and Atlantic City. If you're driving, follow the Atlantic City Expressway to Atlantic City and head south on Ocean Drive, a total drive of about 40 miles from Atlantic City.

An Overview

Located at the southernmost tip of the New Jersey peninsula, Cape May is a reminder of a century ago when it was one of the most renowned resort areas in the nation and America's oldest seaside resort. If one takes into account the "vacations" of the Lenni Lenape Indians who visited what is now Cape May County to fish and relax in the fifteenth and sixteenth centuries, the resort actually predates the nation itself.

Cape May is now a blend of the best of both the nineteenth and twentieth centuries. Quiet and classic, rooted in solid residential stock, the entire city of Cape May has been designated a National Historic Landmark, and its almost Southern ambiance stands in bold relief to the more hectic atmosphere of some other New Jersey resort areas. With its Victorian architecture of more than 600 authentic nineteenth-century buildings and homes, its small boardwalk, and picture-postcard beach, Cape May is a place for relaxation, strolling or biking through its tree-shaded streets, shopping, sunning, and dining in fine restaurants.

The Atlantic is filled with an overwhelming variety of fish, including bluefish, marlin, fluke, and sea trout. The inland waterways and Delaware Bay to the west offer a variety of different kinds of fishing. Excursion boats and charters operate daily. Crabbing is excellent, too.

Golf, tennis, horseback riding, roller skating, and miniature golf are just a few of the other recreational attractions nearby. You'll also find parks, playgrounds, shuffleboard courts, band concerts, antique car shows, parades, and regattas.

In addition to fine modern and historic lodging in the city itself, Cape May County includes penthouse motel and condo suites, apartments, cottages, bungalows, motels, and efficiency apartments. There are more than 42 privately owned campgrounds with thickly wooded sites for small tents to lakeside trailers and recreational sites with complete hookups.

Prices at Cape May can be high. Rooms in the bed and breakfast inns run from $75-$100 per night. Each house tour costs several dollars, and prices at superior restaurants can add up, too.

For specific information, we recommend you write to The Cape May Welcome Center, 405 Lafayette St., Cape May, NJ 08225, 609-884-9562. For a guidebook, contact the Cape May Chamber of Commerce, P.O. Box 556, 513 Washington St. Mall, Cape May, NJ 08204; 609-884-5508. Website: www.capemaychamber.com.

Pocono Mountains

A two-hour drive northwest of Philadelphia will take you to the breathtaking Pocono Mountains, 2,400 square miles of beautiful scenery with an abundance of recreational activities year-round. For details, see ONE-DAY EXCURSIONS.

DINING

Philadelphia's "restaurant renaissance," which began in the mid-1970s, continues today. Food connoisseurs emerging from the city's restaurants have applauded Philadelphia with kudos generally reserved for the dining establishments of New York and San Francisco.

The wealth and variety of ethnic food available, from Thai food to a range of pastas to mouth-watering French delicacies, make Philadelphia dining a special treat not to be found in many other large cities. The close proximity to the Atlantic Ocean assures one of fresh and inventive seafood dishes in a number of tempting restaurants, and the Delaware River invites waterfront and on-the-water dining. An unusual number of historic buildings now housing eateries add charm and beauty to restaurants of all descriptions throughout this famous old city. Don't forget Philadelphia's own brand of America's favorite food: soft pretzels and cheese steak sandwiches.

There are too many experiences available in and around Philadelphia now, too much excellence, service, variety, and competition for the mediocre to survive. From the elegant to the casual, from old inns to sidewalk and garden cafés, from haute cuisine to neighborhood ethnic, you are assured of satisfying your every dining mood in grand Philadelphia.

Our cost categories based on appetizer, entree, and dessert are:

E	Expensive, over $20 per person.
M	Moderate, $10 to $20 per person.
I	Inexpensive, under $10 per person.

RESTAURANTS BY AREA

BERKS COUNTY
Moselem Springs Inn,
American/Pennsylvania Dutch,
I-M.

BUCKS COUNTY
Black Bass Hotel, American and
Brunches, M.

Cock 'n' Bull, Peddler's Village,
American, E.
El Sombrero, Mexican, I.
Golden Pheasant Inn, French, E.
Hotel du Village, French, M.
Jenny's, American, M.
Mother's Restaurant, Continental,
I-M.

65

Odette's, American, M.
Plumbsteadville Inn, Continental, M.
Sign of the Sorrel Horse, French, M.

CENTER CITY

AOI Japanese Restaurant, Japanese, I-M.
Astral Plane, American, M.
Bookbinder's Seafood House, Seafood, M-E.
Cherry St. Chinese Vegetarian Restaurant, Chinese, I.
China Castle Restaurant, Chinese, I.
China Pagoda, Chinese, I.
Ciboulette, French, E.
Copabanana and Copa Too, Etcetera, I.
Dai i Chi, Japanese, M.
Dante and Luigi's, Italian, M-E.
Deux Cheminees, French, M-E.
Dock St. Brasserie, French, M.
Dr. Watson's Pub, American, I.
Erawan, Thai, M.
The Fountain, International, E.
Friday, Saturday, Sunday, Continental, M.
The Garden, Continental, M.
Happy Rooster, Continental, E.
Hard Rock Café, American, M.
Harry's Bar and Grill, Continental, M.
Hoa Viet, Vietnamese, I.
Ho Sai Gai, Chinese, I.
Imperial Inn, Chinese, I-M.
Irish Pub, American and Irish, I.
The Italian Bistro, Italian, M.
Latimer Deli and Restaurant, Etcetera, I.
Le Bec-Fin, French, E.
Maccabeam, Kosher, I-M.
Marathon Grill, American, I.
Market Fair, at The Gallery at Market East, Etcetera, I.

More Than Just Ice Cream, Etcetera, I.
Morton's of Chicago-Philadelphia, American, M-E.
Mr. J Restaurant, Kosher, I-M.
Palm Restaurant, American, E.
Pikkles Plus, Etcetera, I.
Philippe's Chin on Locust, French, E.
Portofino Restaurant, Italian, M.
Reading Terminal Market, Etcetera, I.
Ristorante La Buca, Italian, M.
Ruth's Chris Steak House, American, E.
Sansom Street Oyster House, Seafood, I-M.
Siam Cuisine, Thai, M.
Singapore (Kosher) Chinese Vegetarian Restaurant, Chinese, I.
South East Chinese Restaurant, Chinese, I.
Spaghetti Warehouse Italian Grill, Italian, I.
Susanna Foo, Chinese, E.
Szechuan China Royal, Chinese, M.
Tang Yean, Chinese, I.
Thai Garden East, Thai, M.
Toto, Italian, M-E.
The Turf Club, American, M.
Warsaw Café, Eastern European, I-M.
Wok Chinese Seafood Restaurant, Chinese, I-M.
Zanzibar Blue, Continental, M.

CENTER CITY—
FAIRMOUNT AREA

Bridgid's, Belgian, E.
Jack's Firehouse, American, M.
London Grill, Continental, M.
North Star Bar, American, I.
Rembrandt's, American, M.
Rose Tattoo Café, International, I-M.
Tavern on the Green, Brunches, I.

tumed staff provide Colonial conversation along with the meals in this recreated eighteenth- century tavern.

Cock 'n' Bull, at Peddler's Village, Rts. 202 and 263, Lahaska; 215-794-4010. *E.* King Henry's Feast and an Evening in the Colonial Kitchen are two dining events at this 30-year-old restaurant. Specialties are Beef Burgundy, chicken potpie, and hot apple dumplings. Lunch, Dinner, Sunday Brunch.

The Columbia Hotel, 148 Bridge St., Phoenixville; 610-933-9973. *M.* Built in 1892, this authentic Victorian hotel presents excellent steaks and seafood. There are four dining rooms, but eating in the dimly lit, paneled barroom is the most fun. Excellent specials include prime rib on the weekend. Lunch and Dinner Mon-Sat, closed Sun.

Dave and Buster's, 325 N. Columbus Blvd., Pier 19 North; 215-413-1951. *M.* Food and games overlooking the Delaware. Great menu along with pocket billiards, shuffleboard, and golf simulators. More than just a meal in the city's largest dining and entertainment venue. Lunch and Dinner.

Dr. Watson's Pub, 216 S. Eleventh St.; 215-922-3427. *I.* Boasts almost 30 years of serving steaks, seafood, wine and beers. Upstairs there are billiards and games, music and entertainment. Lunch, Dinner, Late Snacks.

Fat Tuesday, 431 South St.; 215-629-5999. *I.* Outdoor tables, and live music on Tuesday and Wednesday nights, and a DJ on Friday and Saturday, enliven the fun food and the world's largest selection of frozen specialty drinks. Lunch, Dinner, Late Snacks.

The Hard Rock Café, 1113-31 Market St.; 215-238-1000. *M.* In their own words: "The coolest rock memorabilia you've ever seen, the best food you've ever tasted and the best rock 'n roll you've ever heard."

Houlihan's, several locations, including King of Prussia Mall; 610-337-9522. *I-M.* These popular restaurant-bars offer American and international dishes in a relaxed atmosphere of greenery, antiques, art posters, and soft woods. Lunch and Dinner daily.

Jack's Firehouse, 2130 Fairmount Ave.; 215-232-9000. *E.* Piano and light jazz reverberate off the walls of this 1904 firehouse. American foods are the specialties, with local fish and produce and fresh baked breads. Lunch, Dinner, Sunday Brunch, Late Snacks.

Jefferson House Restaurant, 2519 Dekalb Pike, Norristown; 610-275-3407. *M.* Country dining in this beautiful nine-room Georgian mansion is a delightful experience. The house is surrounded by ten acres that include a duck pond and a springhouse, and the menu is highlighted by such specialties as rack of lamb. Lunch Mon-Fri, Dinner daily, Sun 12-8 pm.

Jenny's, in Peddler's Village, Rt. 202 and Street Rd., Lahaska; 215-794-4020. *E.* Stained glass and cherry woods create an elegant atmosphere to enjoy specialties like Lobster-Crab Sauté and Filet Chesterfield. Lunch, Dinner, Sunday Brunch.

Kansas City Prime, 4417 Main St., Manayunk; 215-482-3700. M. Opened in 1993, this modern American steak house is chef Derek Davis' encore to his stunning success at the "Italifornia"-style Sonoma two doors away. Subtle colors, flowers, and soft jazz create a background for carefully selected and prepared grilled meats and fish. Kobe beef imported from Japan, the most tender and expensive meat in the world, is on the menu, as well as a 27-oz. Cowboy Steak, a 5.5-lb. lobster, double-cut lamb chops, whole Dover sole, and white chocolate bread pudding. Lunch, Dinner, and Late Night Snacks Mon-Sat. Sun Dinner 5 pm-10 pm. Valet parking after 5 pm.

Katmandu, 417 N. Christopher Columbus Blvd.; 215-629-7400. M. Palm trees, white sand beaches, music, food and drink on the waterfront—*Philadelphia's* waterfront. Katmandu serves gourmet food and open-pit barbecue alfresco. Lunch Fri-Sun, Dinner and entertainment nightly. Open year-round.

The Kimberton Inn, Hares Hill Rd. and Kimberton Rd., off Route 113 near Phoenixville; 610-933-8148. M. This 1796 inn offers excellent dining amid crackling fireplaces and a colonial setting accented by a host of antiques. All desserts are homemade. Dinner daily, Brunch Sun.

Liberty Belle Cruises, Penn's Landing, 333 N. Front St.; 215-629-1137. E. Dine in a 600-passenger Mississippi paddle-wheeler during a lunchtime, dinnertime, or moonlight cruise along the Delaware. Tours of Fort Mifflin can be part of the package. Lunch Mon-Sat 12 pm, Dinner Mon-Sat 7-10 pm, Sun Brunch 12:30-2:30 pm, Sun Dinner 4-7 pm, Moonlight Fri-Sat 11:30 pm-2 am. Reservations required.

Marathon Grill, four locations, including 1613 JFK Blvd., across from the Visitors Center; 215-564-4745. I. "Best of Philly" for five consecutive years. Char-burgers, grilled chicken, sandwiches, salads, and pasta. Lunch and Dinner.

The Oak Grill and the Four Dogs at Marshallton, Route 162, West Chester; 610-692-4367. M-E. You'll feel like you're back in the eighteenth century as you dine in the Oak Grill, an impeccably restored example of early federal architecture. The excellent dishes are accompanied by a fine wine list. For more casual dining, try the Four Dogs adjacent to the restaurant. It serves light American fair. Oak Grill: Dinner Wed-Sun. Four Dogs: Lunch and Dinner daily, Brunch Sunday.

Mendenhall Inn, Kennett Pike, Mendenhall; 610-388-1181. M. In the quiet rolling hills of Chester County is this lovely country inn, once an eighteenth-century barn and working mill. It now presents consistently outstanding food, including baked stuffed oysters, South African lobster tail, and calves' liver sauté. There's also a fine selection of imported and domestic wines. Lunch Mon-Sat, Dinner daily, Sun Brunch.

Montserrat (see NIGHTLIFE Bars).

Morton's of Chicago—Philadelphia, One Logan Square; 215-557-0724. *M-E.* "Best of Philly" 1993 and "Best Steakhouse in Philadelphia 1994." This classic steakhouse specializes in aged prime steaks, veal chops, and lobster. Relaxed, sophisticated atmosphere. Lunch Mon-Fri, Dinner daily.

North Star Bar (see NIGHTLIFE Cabarets, Dinner Theater, and Supper Clubs).

Odette's, South River Rd., New Hope; 215-862-2773. *M.* Built in 1794 and once a tavern for travelers on the Delaware Canal, Odette's offers superior American cuisine. Lunch and Dinner daily, Brunch Sun.

Omni Galaxy Grill, at the Franklin Institute, Twentieth St. and Benjamin Franklin Pkwy.; 215-448-1355. *I.* Healthy helpings of science along with sandwiches, salads, soups, and appetizers from the counter. Lunch and Dinner.

Omni Hotel's Azalea Restaurant, Fourth and Chestnut Sts.; 215-925-0000. *M.* This is the only restaurant that overlooks Independence Park. Enjoy contemporary American cuisine that uses locally produced ingredients. Breakfast, Lunch, Dinner.

Palm Restaurant, 200 S. Broad St.; 215-546-7256. *E.* More than 60 years of serving 24-oz. prime rib, 18-oz. steaks, 5-lb. lobsters, and home-made cottage fries. Lunch and Dinner.

Rembrandt's, Twenty-third and Aspen Sts.; 215-763-2228. *M. Philadelphia Magazine* voted this restaurant's romantic dining "Best of Philly." Enjoy the modern cuisine and the skyline view to an accompaniment of live jazz. Lunch, Dinner, Sunday Brunch.

Ruth's Chris Steak House, 260 S. Broad St.; 215-790-1515. *E.* Award-winning "Best of Philly" restaurant for steaks, lobster, seafood, potatoes, vegetables, and salad. Lunch and Dinner. Open daily.

Seven Stars Inn, Ridge Rd. and Route 23W, Phoenixville; 610-495-5205. *M-E.* Few who come to this 1736 inn for dinner leave without remnants of their meals to nibble on later. Portions are large and the food is simply too good to leave behind. Among the most popular selections are the surf and turf, lobster tail, and prime rib, and all are served with a choice of two of the seven fresh vegetable dishes. Dinner Tue-Sun.

Society Hill Hotel, 301 Chestnut St.; 215-925-1919. *I.* Inexpensive and creative dining, a cozy jazz piano bar, and the "Classiest Outdoor Café" (*Philadelphia Magazine*). Lunch, Dinner, and Late-Night Snacks daily, Sunday Brunch.

Spirit of Philadelphia, board at The Great Plaza at Penn's Landing; 215-923-1419. *M-E.* Your waiters and waitresses will entertain you with a musical revue, while you cruise the Delaware. Lunch, Dinner, Sunday Brunch. Reservations required.

The Terrace, Route 1, Chadds Ford; 610-388-6771. *I-M.* This restaurant, built at a cost of $3 million, has been a welcome addition to the world-famous splendor of Longwood Gardens. A self-service café that resembles a country market, the Terrace serves hot and cold soups, salads, sandwiches, and a special of the day. The dining room offers American regional fare that includes local produce and fresh trout when available. Lunch and Tea daily, Dinner when the garden is open late.

333 Belrose Bar and Grill, King of Prussia Rd. and 333 Belrose Lane, Radnor; 610-293-1000. M. Upscale contemporary décor. Sophisticated American cuisine. A blend of American, Asian, Caribbean, Italian, and Mexican influences. Open-air patio. Lunch Mon-Fri, Dinner daily, Brunch Sun.

T. G. I. Friday's. Multiple locations including 1776 Benjamin Franklin Pkwy.; 215-665-TGIF (8443). I. Relaxation and fun in an American bistro. Breakfast, Lunch, Dinner and Late Night.

The Turf Club, Seventeenth and Market Sts.; 215-639-9000; and other locations. M. Wager on national horse racing while you enjoy full-course meals and cocktails. Lunch, Dinner, Sunday Brunch.

United States Hotel Bar and Grill, 4439 Main St., Manayunk; 215-483-9222. M. This restaurant features a raw bar, New York strip steak, blackened Louisiana redfish, etc. Lunch Mon-Sat, Dinner daily.

Valley Green Inn, Springfield Ave. and Wissahickon Creek, Chestnut Hill; 215-247-1730. M. You won't be able to resist the charm of this eighteenth-century inn located along the picturesque paths of Fairmount Park. Tempting hot dishes are especially satisfying on the dining porch in fair weather but they can also be enjoyed inside, where George Washington and Lafayette once dined on their way to Germantown. Lunch and Dinner daily, Brunch Sun.

The White Dog Café, 3420 Sansom St.; 215-386-9224. M. Contemporary American cuisine with farm-fresh ingredients in the heart of University City. Old favorites are combined with innovative dishes for an eclectic mix in a country inn atmosphere. Breakfast, Lunch, Dinner, and The Black Cat gift shop, too.

Belgian

Bridgid's, 726 N. Twenty-fourth St.; 215-232-3232. E. Specialties like Belgian crab cakes, Duck Chambord, and Bouillabaisse Ostendaise distinguish the modern and traditional cuisine of this Belgian restaurant near the Art Museum. There's seafood, too, and Belgian beers to enjoy near the fireplace. Lunch, Dinner, Sunday Brunch.

Cuvee Notre Dame, 1701 Green St.; 215-765-2777. M. Belgian cuisine in an indoor and outdoor café. Lunch, Dinner, Sunday Brunch. Open daily.

Chinese

Cherry Street Chinese Vegetarian (Kosher) Restaurant, 1010 Cherry St.; 215-923-FOOD (3663). *I.* Informal candlelight dining near the Convention Center, featuring vegetarian, macrobiotic, and Pritikin menus. 11:30 am-11 pm daily.

China Castle Restaurant, 939 Race St.; 215-925-7072. *I.* Authentic Cantonese Chinese cooking. Lunch Mon-Sat, Dinner daily.

China Pagoda, 1508 Sansom St.; 215-567-8863. *I.* Cantonese and Hunan specialties. Box lunches and free delivery to hotels. Lunch and Dinner.

Dragon Inn (Kosher), 7628 Castor Ave.; 215-742-2575. *I-M.* Authentic Chinese cooking, as well as rib steaks, and hot dogs and fries for the kids. The atmosphere is friendly, the décor Oriental, and the servings huge. They'll wrap the leftovers. Sun-Thu 11:30-9, Sat nights between October and April. Call for details.

Ho Sai Gai I, 1000 Race St.; 215-922-5883, **Ho Sai Gai II,** Tenth and Cherry Sts.; 215-925-8384. *I.* Also at three other locations. These highly acclaimed Chinatown restaurants rank among Philadelphia's finest. The décor in Ho Sai Gai II is more elaborate than that of its predecessor, but the food at both is consistently top-flight and a little more innovative than you'll find elsewhere in the area. You can choose from Szechuan, Mandarin, and Taiwanese soups, and from among the entrees, a spectacular dish called "Seven Stars Around the Moon" (lobster, tenderloin beef, chicken, and roast pork sautéed in Chinese vegetables and surrounded by fried jumbo shrimp). A fine selection of vegetarian dishes, including superior stir-fries, are available too. Lunch and Dinner Mon-Sat.

Hu-Nan, 47 E. Lancaster Ave., Ardmore; 610-642-3050. *I.* This award-winning restaurant shuns the stir-fry dishes for the more sophisticated and complex, and the results are a stylish Chinese eatery. It specializes in the peppery cuisine of China's Hu-Nan region; the shrimp, with scallions and peppers in a sherry sauce, is like none other. Lunch Mon-Fri, Dinner daily.

Imperial Inn, 146 N. Tenth St.; 215-627-5588. *I-M.* For 25 years, this quality restaurant has offered a splendid selection of Szechuan, Mandarin, and Cantonese dishes. Lunch and Dinner daily, Sunday Brunch.

Peking-Tokyo Restaurant, Granite Run Mall, Routes 1 and 352, Media; 610-566-4110. *I.* Two locations and two-time winner of "Best of Philly." Unlike most shopping center Chinese restaurants, here you'll find dashes of haute cuisine with the more familiar Chinese-American favorites, and authentic Japanese cuisine, too. Among the more creative specialties are shark's fin soup, beef sinews, and Peking duck. Lunch and Dinner daily.

Singapore (Kosher) Chinese Vegetarian Restaurant, 1029 Race St.; 215-922-3288. *I.* Buddhist, Hindu, and Muslim vegetarian recipes. Fat-free cooking. Free delivery in Center City. Lunch and Dinner.

South East Chinese Restaurant, 1000 Arch St.; 215-629-1888. *I.* Located near the famous Chinese arch, this Cantonese and Szechuan establishment also offers macrobiotic, Pritikin, and vegetarian menus. Mon-Thu 11:30 am-11 pm, Fri-Sat until midnight, Sun until 10 pm.

Susanna Foo, 1512 Walnut St.; 215-545-2666. *E.* Six-time winner of the "Best of Philly" award, this beautiful restaurant is run by chef/owner Susanna Foo, who received the 1997 James Beard Best Chef Mid-Atlantic Region award. Lunch, Dinner, Sunday Brunch, Late Snacks.

Szechuan China Royal, 727 Walnut St.; 215-627-7111-2. M. Elegant but cozy, and you can have your favorite dishes delivered free of charge to most Center City hotels. There's also a comfortable bar and lounge. Lunch and Dinner.

Tang Yean, 220 N. Tenth St.; 215-925-3993. *I.* A Chinese health food restaurant with no MSG or oil. Fresh vegetables, chicken, seafood, and rice. Late Lunch and Dinner daily.

Wok Chinese Seafood Restaurant, 1613 Walnut St.; 215-751-9990. *I-M.* Dishes from Szechuan, Mandarin, and Hunan cuisine represented. Lunch Mon-Sat, Dinner daily.

Continental

Chadds Ford Inn, Routes 1 and 100, Chadds Ford; 610-388-7361. M. This historic inn has been satisfying customers since 1736, and the splendor of the surrounding countryside is now captured by the Wyeth paintings that adorn the walls. Among the more popular dishes are bay scallops in sherry sauce and heavy cream, veal Oscar, and roast duck a la maison. Lunch and Dinner daily, Sunday Brunch.

Crier in the Country, Route 1, Baltimore Pike, Glen Mills; 610-358-2411. *E.* Continental cuisine elegantly served in a restored, candlelit Victorian mansion. You can even escape here to a bed and breakfast weekend. Dinner Tue-Sun, Champagne Sunday Brunch.

Dilworthtown Inn, Route 202 at Brinton's Bridge Rd. and Old Wilmington Pike; 610-399-1390. M. Built in 1758 and now authentically restored, this inn presents fine Continental and French cuisine that includes such dishes as crab imperial, filet mignon, and roast duckling. All are enhanced by an excellent wine list. Candlelight Dinners daily.

Friday, Saturday, Sunday, 261 S. Twenty-first; 215-546-4232. M. Everything in this tiny rowhouse restaurant has been done with care and imagination. The décor is intimate yet casual, with the tapestry ceiling, mirrors, and reflected candlelight. The freshest ingredients are used in dishes you'll select from the blackboard menu, and it won "Best of Philly" for its wine value. Breakfast and Lunch, Mon-Fri, Dinner daily.

The Garden, 1617 Spruce St.; 215-546-4455. M. This townhouse restaurant, with a popular outdoor garden for summer dining, has forged a well-deserved reputation for great food. The interior dining rooms are decorated with charm and warmth, and the award-winning menu offers outstanding versions of steak tartare, veal medallion with ginger, roast duckling a l'orange, and breast of chicken. All are prepared with the utmost care. Lunch and Dinner Tue-Fri.

General Warren Inn, West Old Lancaster Highway, Malvern; 610-296-3637. M. Soft candlelight glows amid the crystal in this gracious inn that dates back to 1745. Dine on such favorites as veal Oscar Warren Tavern, rack of lamb, Caesar salad prepared for two, and a wide range of homemade pastries that include French chocolate ice cream with walnut crust. Bed and breakfast accommodations, too. Lunch and Dinner Mon-Sat.

General Wayne Inn, 625 Montgomery Ave., Merion; 610-664-5900. M. This is a national historic restaurant that has been serving up hearty food since 1704. Turn back the clock and let the chef lavish you with one of his special seafood dishes. Lunch and Dinner Tue-Sun, Brunch Sunday.

The Guard House Inn, 953 Youngsford Rd., Gladwyne; 610-649-9708. M. Built in 1790 as a post office, this structure was later a hotel and a bar. Now a restaurant, the Guard House serves superior cuisine in a log-cabin setting of old cedar and oak. Among the specialties are calves' liver with sage butter and bacon, medallions of veal in mushroom cream, and roasted farmhouse duckling with orange or pepper sauce. Dinner Mon-Sat.

Happy Rooster, 118 S. Sixteenth St.; 215-563-1481. E. An elegant bistro with an eclectic menu of American, Continental, and Russian specialties, and the best stocked bar in the city. Mon-Sat 11:30 am-1:30 am.

Harry's Bar and Grill, 22 S. Eighteenth St.; 215-561-5757. E. There's an upstairs dining room and another dining room downstairs, each with its own bar. Eighteenth-century oil paintings of thoroughbred racehorses and hunting scenes grace the walls, providing a clubby atmosphere for those dining on the homemade pastas and aged beef. Lunch and Dinner Mon-Fri.

Jethro's, First and Ruby Sts., Lancaster; 717-299-1700. M. The décor is very simple, plywood-paneled walls and sparse furnishings, but you'll find some outstanding dishes arriving at tables graced with crisp linen and flowers. Dinner Mon-Sat.

London Grill, 2301 Fairmount Ave.; 215-978-4545. M. Conveniently located across the street from the Art Museum, this cozy spot provides friendly service, sophisticated dishes, and, from Wednesday through Saturday nights, live entertainment. Lunch Sun-Fri, Dinner daily, Late Snacks, Sunday Brunch.

Monte Carlo Living Room, 150 South St.; 215-925-2220. E. This is easily one of the most exquisitely decorated restaurants in Philadelphia, with glass chandeliers and imported lace and crystal on the tables. An elegant club is upstairs. The menu features fishermen's baskets of lobster, salmon, and piettro, along with Dover sole in champagne sauce, veal, baby lamb chops, and steak. Dinner daily.

The Moshulu, Pier 34, 735 S. Columbus Blvd.; 215-923-2500. E. Dine and dance on a luxuriously restored 100-year-old sailing ship—the only restaurant-sailing ship in the world. Top it off with a magnificent view of the river and the city skyline. Lunch, Dinner, and Sunday Brunch.

Mother's Restaurant, 34 N. Main St., New Hope; 215-862-9354. I-M. After you've wandered through the quaint shops on Main Street, you'll find the comfortable surroundings and friendly service of this restaurant most inviting. In addition to the contemporary indoor dining room, there's also a lovely outdoor garden where you can dine in the warm months. Don't leave without some homemade goodies from the bakery and delicatessen. Lunch and Dinner daily.

94th Aero Squadron, 2750 Red Lion Rd.; 215-671-9400. M. Many of you will find this restaurant a delightful place in which to dine, especially if you love aviation. The original headquarters for the 94th Aero Squadron features World War I memorabilia and offers a panoramic view of the Northeast Airport. While you dine on a fine selection of Continental dishes, you'll also enjoy listening to the activity going on in the control tower. Dinner daily, Sunday Brunch.

Plumbsteadville Inn, Route 611 at Stump Rd., Plumbsteadville; 215-766-7500. M. The four dining rooms of this old inn are subtly decorated in a colonial motif, accented by a glowing fireplace and gleaming chandeliers. The Continental and American cuisine is excellent, and the lounge presents entertainment weekends. Lunch and Dinner Tue-Sun, Brunch Sun.

Samuel's, Spread Eagle Village, Lancaster Ave. and Eagle Rd., Wayne; 610-687-2840. M-E. This lovely restaurant has the ambiance of a French country inn with its blazing fireplace, shining copper pots hanging from the mantle, and fresh flowers on the tables. The cuisine is as delightful as the surroundings and includes fresh herbs on fresh fish and pasta. Live jazz Friday and Saturday. Lunch Mon-Sat, Dinner daily, Sunday Brunch.

Thomas', 4201 Main St., Manayunk; 215-483-9075. M. An eclectic Continental menu and a 100-year-old bar. Lunch Mon-Fri, Dinner daily, Sunday Brunch.

Ulana's (see NIGHTLIFE Music for Listening and Dancing).

William Penn Inn, Route 202 and Sunnytown Pike, Gwynedd; 215-699-9272. M. In a colonial inn that dates back to 1714, the Mayfair dining room and the Seafood Tavern offer 35 different entrees and more than 150 wines. The portions are the he-man variety and include country-style roast rack of lamb, filet mignon, pork cutlet and lobster tail, and other specialties. Lunch Mon-Sat, Dinner daily, Brunch Sun.

Zanzibar Blue, 200 S. Broad St., 215-732-5200. M. A fashionable dining room and a fine jazz club. Dinner, Sunday Brunch.

Eastern European

Warsaw Café, 306 S. Sixteenth St.; 215-546-0204. I-M. This friendly restaurant prepares superior versions of such hearty cuisine as borscht, German vegetable salad, beef stroganoff, sauerbraten, stuffed cabbage leaves, and Norwegian strudel (chicken, vegetables, almonds, raisins, and herbs in a light pastry crust). It's the only Eastern European restaurant in Pennsylvania. Lunch and Dinner Mon-Sat.

English

Dickens Inn, Head House Square, 421 S. Second St.; 215-928-9307. M. Dining in the historic 1788 Harper House is like dining in an old English pub. The cuisine is typically British, including Beef Wellington, rack of lamb, and of course, Yorkshire pudding. The outstanding desserts are fresh from the downstairs bakery. The Main Tavern, Sportsman's Bar, and Rigger Bar sell imported ales, and the new Café Bar specializes in espresso, cappuccino, and flavored coffees. Lunch and Dinner daily.

French

Ciboulette, 200 S. Broad St. (at The Shops at the Bellevue); 215-790-1210. E. An excellent and exquisite French Provencal menu. Winner of "America's Top Table Award" from Gourmet, and the "Award of Excellence" from the Wine Spectator. Lunch and Dinner.

Coventry Forge Inn, Route 23, Coventryville; 610-469-6222. M. For more than a quarter-century, this carefully maintained eighteenth-century inn has served basic French cuisine with an emphasis on freshness and simplicity. Dine on the enclosed porch in the summer or enjoy the cozy, romantic atmosphere the fireplaces lend the dining rooms in the winter. Hot cream watercress soup is a favorite, as well as the excellent rack of lamb. A fine selection of wines is available. The inn also offers colonial lodging in a quiet, rural setting. Tue-Fri, Dinner Tue-Sat.

Deux Cheminees, 1221 Locust St.; 215-790-0200. *E.* Located in a splendid Frank Furness townhouse, Deux Cheminees has earned a four-star rating. It was named one of the 30 best restaurants in America by Conde Nast Traveler, and Philadelphia's top restaurant by *Money Magazine.* Dinner.

Dock Street Brasserie, Eighteenth and Cherry Sts.; 215-496-0413. *I.* Take a brewery tour and try fresh beers and ales from Philadelphia's only full-grain brewery, while you enjoy a French menu and great wine list. There's a billiard room, too, and live music Friday and Saturday. Lunch, Dinner, Late Snacks.

Golden Pheasant Inn, 763 River Rd. on Route 32 in Erwinna, Bucks County; 610-294-9595. *E.* Romantic dining is available in this lovely 1857 country inn. French dishes are served in three dining rooms, including the Greenhouse, a glass-enclosed solarium, also outdoors on the canal. Dinner Wed-Sun, Sunday Brunch.

Hotel du Village, North River Rd. and Phillips Mill Rd., New Hope; 215-862-5164. *M.* Here you'll find the delightful combination of traditional French cuisine served in an atmosphere of an old English manor house. The delicious dishes include lamb chops with green herbs, sole in curried butter, and filet with artichoke heart and choron sauces. Dinner Wed-Sun.

The Inn at Historic Yellow Springs, Art School Rd., Chester Springs; 610-827-7477. *M-E.* This country inn was once a fashionable eighteenth-century resort. Much effort has been made to retain its historic appearance while creating intimate dining areas in an elegant, country atmosphere. An innovative selection of French gourmet dishes are served daily. Dinner Tue-Sun, Sunday Brunch.

La Fourchette, 110 N. Wayne Ave., Wayne; 610-687-8333. *M.* This cozy, candlelit spot specializes in nouvelle cuisine and seafood and is a favorite of the Main Line crowd. Dinner daily, Sunday Brunch.

Le Bec-Fin, 1523 Walnut St.; 215-567-1000. *E.* More than 30 years ago, this restaurant was the first to introduce Philadelphians to superior French cuisine. Now it is one of Philadelphia's finest restaurants, having received a host of awards, and some national critics believe it is the best French restaurant in the East. What is incredible about Le Bec-Fin is that, under the endless quest for perfection by owner George Perrier, it somehow gets a little better every year. Enhanced by its Louis XVI atmosphere, sophisticated, warm, intimate, the service is as polished as the crystal. Lunch and Dinner. Prix fixe. Classic guitar music Friday and Saturday.

Philippe's Chin on Locust, 1614 Locust St.; 215-735-7551. *E.* French-Eurasian Continental cuisine. Lunch and Dinner daily. Sunday Brunch.

Provence, 379 Lancaster Ave., Haverford; 610-896-0400. M. South of France cuisine is served in this unusual, casual café. The décor is sparse, however, the portions are anything but. A lot of care and imagination go into everything on the menu. Afterwards, top off your meal with one of the scintillating desserts. Lunch Mon-Sat, Dinner daily, Sunday Brunch.

Sign of the Sorrel Horse, Old Bethlehem Rd., Quakertown; 215-230-9999. E. There are no distractions here, just superior French dishes prepared to meet the most discriminating taste. Located in the serene countryside of Quakertown, this restaurant presents an array of tantalizing dishes and daily specials. Dinner Wed-Sun.

Taquet, 139 E. Lancaster Ave., Wayne; 610-687-5005. M-E. This charming Victorian restaurant, in the historic Wayne Hotel, serves contemporary French cuisine at its best. Lunch Mon-Sat. Brunch Sun. Dinner daily.

Vicker's Tavern, Gordon Dr. and Welsh Pool Rd., Lionville; 610-363-7998. E. This is a nineteenth-century farmhouse where pottery was once manufactured. Now carefully restored, it houses five cozy dining rooms that present creative French and Continental cuisine that includes lobster tail in champagne sauce, quail with chestnut stuffing, and tournedos with artichokes and Bearnaise sauce. Lunch Mon-Fri, Dinner Mon-Sat.

Greek

South Street Souvlaki, 509 South St.; 215-925-3026. I-M. Once a takeout gyro and ice-cream stand, this restaurant now specializes in Greek and Middle Eastern dishes for takeout or eating on the premises. The menu changes frequently, but there's always moussaka and a wide range of Greek pastries, seafood, lamb, and chicken dishes. Lunch and Dinner daily.

Indian

New Delhi Indian Restaurant and Sweets, 4004 Chestnut St.; 215-386-1941. M. Bring your own drinks to the lunch or dinner buffets with Tandoori specialties. Mon-Thu 5:30-9:30, Sat-Sun noon-4.

International

The Fountain, One Logan Sq.; 215-963-1500. E. Elegance prevails in this restaurant in the Four Seasons Hotel, where pastel marble and gleaming brass are graced by windows with a magnificent view of

Benjamin Franklin Parkway. Dishes from an international menu are carefully prepared and beautifully presented. Breakfast, Lunch, and Dinner daily. Brunch Sun.

Judy's Café, Third and Bainbridge Sts.; 215-928-1968. *I-M.* This friendly neighborhood bistro attracts a regular clientele with hearty meals at prices that can't be beat. Dinner daily.

Knave of Hearts, 230 South St.; 215-922-3956. *M.* For the romantically inclined, this is the perfect place to woo that special person. Soft candlelight flickers throughout, and there's a glass-enclosed garden in the back. It won't take long to discover that a lot of imagination has gone into the dishes on the small but varied menu. Lunch and Dinner daily, Sunday Brunch.

The Palladium Restaurant and the Gold Standard, 3601 Locust Walk; 215-387-DINE (3463). *M.* Restored red oak paneling is highlighted by leaded glass windows, a warm fireplace, a friendly bar area, and an outdoor cafe. Downstairs you'll find the 200-seat Gold Standard cafeteria, and upstairs, the Palladium Restaurant. The same menu is offered on both levels, and it includes a delightful collection of international dishes. Lunch Mon-Fri, Dinner daily.

The Restaurant School, 4207 Walnut St.; 215-222-4200. *I.* This charming restaurant offers the opportunity to watch future chefs displaying their culinary talents. The school has received considerable acclaim for its interesting assortment of dishes, many of which are prepared at tableside, and the menu is constantly changing. Dinner Tue-Sat.

Roller's, 8705 Germantown Ave., Chestnut Hill; 215-242-1771. *I.* Perched on the top of Chestnut Hill is this small café, well known for its interesting dishes. The menu is forever changing, and if you're in a rush, takeout is available at Roller's Market, right next door. Lunch Tue-Sat, Dinner Tue-Sun, Sunday Brunch.

Rose Tattoo Café, Nineteenth and Callowhill Sts.; 215-569-8939. *M-E.* Five dining rooms and two bars feature international and American dishes with an emphasis on seafood. Lunch Mon-Fri, Dinner Mon-Sat.

Tiramisu, 528 S. Fifth St.; 215-925-3335. *E.* Roman/Jewish cuisine, including chicken, pasta, and seafood, followed by homemade desserts. Lunch, Dinner, Late Snacks.

Irish

Downey's, Front and South Sts.; 215-625-9500. *M.* This is an Irish spot so authentic that the downstairs bar, before it wound up here, was once part of a bank in Dublin. The hours are great (meaning late) and the food matches. In addition to a magnificent oyster bar which is laden with the freshest of seafood, you'll find a menu filled with such hearty delights as super sirloin steaks, green pasta with scallops in cream sauce, duckling with green peppercorn sauce, and of course, Irish stew. Lunch and Dinner daily, Brunch Sun. Light snacks. Live entertainment.

Irish Pub (see NIGHTLIFE Bars).

Italian

Cent'Anni, 770 S. Seventh St.; 215-925-5558. *I-M.* In the old American-Neapolitan tradition, here you'll find red-checked table-cloths, a warm and cozy atmosphere, and a wide selection of seafood, pastas, and chicken dishes served in healthy portions. Dinner daily.

Dante and Luigi's, 762 S. Tenth St.; 215-922-9501. *I-M.* The room is like an old-world parlor, the food is exceptional, and this is the oldest Italian restaurant in America. Check out the calamari. Open Tue-Sun.

Felicia's, 1148 S. Eleventh St.; 215-755-9656; 800-587-9190. M. Italian cuisine with an abundance of veal and pasta dishes and ricotta cheesecake for dessert. Tue-Fri noon-10:30, Sat 3:30-10:30, Sun 4-10.

Frankie's Seafood Ilaliano, Eleventh and Tasker Sts.; 215-468-9989. M. An Italian family restaurant specializing in veal chops, salmon, broiled swordfish, and tuna Sicilian. Lunch and Dinner.

The Italian Bistro, 211 S. Broad St.; 215-731-0700. M. Wood-fired brick ovens and rotisseries produce delectable Italian cuisine. Satellite Italian music adds spice and flavor. Lunch and Dinner.

La Famiglia, 8 S. Front St.; 215-922-2803. M. Some say this is the city's finest authentic Italian restaurant. Mamma and Papa Sena fashion their dishes from personal recipes they gather each year in Italy. An exceptional Milanese appetizer combines mozzarella cheese and Italian ham, breaded in cornbread and eggs. The wine list is one of the most extensive in Philadelphia. Lunch Tue-Fri, Dinner Tue-Sun.

La Grolla Trattoria, 782 S. Second St.; 215-627-7701. M. La Grolla translated into English means "cup of friendship," a traditional phrase from the Northern Alps. In this quiet, elegant, formal dining room, the cuisine of North Italy is served. Dinner Mon-Sat, Brunch Sun.

Lamberti's Cucina, Second and Walnut Sts.; 215-238-0499. M. Dine indoors, or alfresco on the deck. Interesting wine and pasta. Lunch and Dinner.

Mama Yolanda's, 746 S. Eighth St.; 215-468-1273. M. This charming Italian restaurant has become a popular spot, noted for its excellent veal, chicken, seafood, and pasta with homemade sauces. Dinner Tue-Sun.

Marabella's, 1700 Benjamin Franklin Pkwy.; 215-981-5555. M. A contemporary Italian restaurant in the museum district, featuring innovative cuisine in an upbeat setting. Try an assortment of homemade pasta, grilled seafood, or veal chops, specialty pizzas, salads, or sandwiches. Desserts are sinful. Lunch and Dinner daily.

Marra's, 1734 E. Passyunk Ave.; 215-463-9249. *I.* As Philadelphia's oldest Italian restaurant, this family-owned dining spot has 73 years of experience in preparing homemade pasta, veal, chicken, and seafood dishes. The hot brick oven also produces a delectable thin-crust pizza that proves to be an ideal companion to a selection from the extensive list of imported beers and wines. Lunch and Dinner Tue-Sun.

Moonstruck, 7955 Oxford Ave., Fox Chase; 215-725-6000. M. There is much to look forward to at this Italian restaurant—the mirrored, airy atmosphere, the small chic bar, and Northern Italian dishes prepared and served to perfection. Dinner daily.

Portofino Restaurant, 1227 Walnut St.; 215-923-8208. M. Central and Northern Italian cuisine served here, with daily specials. Luxury dining at moderate prices. Lunch Mon-Fri, Dinner Mon-Sat.

Ralph's, 760 S. Ninth St.; 215-627-6011. *I.* Dining at this family-operated restaurant has been a Philadelphia tradition since 1900. All the Italian dishes, especially the veal, linguini, and chicken varieties, are exceptional, especially when accompanied by the homemade pastas. And it must be said—the mussels are a must. Lunch and Dinner daily.

Ristorante LaBuca, 711 Locust St.; 215-928-0566. M. This cozy restaurant features regional Italian cuisine and Old World service in a softly lit dining room with brick and stucco walls. Free garage parking after 5 pm. Lunch and Dinner.

Saloon Restaurant, 750 S. Seventh St.; 215-627-1811. M. This is a most attractive restaurant, with its carved-wood molding and paneling, antiques, stained glass, and white-tiled floors. The whole-wheat pasta with crabmeat is a rare treat and the fettuccini Alfredo certainly is a credit to its name. However, the Saloon's reputation has been forged by its treatment of steaks, sirloins, and filet mignon. Lunch Tue-Fri, Dinner Mon-Sat, Entertainment Wed-Sat.

Savona, 100 Old Gulph Rd., Gulph Mills; 610-520-1200. *E.* Developed by dynamic restaurateurs Evan Lambert and Andrew Feinstein, Savona is off the beaten track but worth the trip. Housed in an elegantly restored historic stone inn that dates back to 1763, this restaurant quickly became one of Philadelphia's most highly regarded dining destinations when it opened in 1997. Terra cotta floors, saffron walls, and fragrant flowers and greenery provide an authentic Mediterranean feel designed by co-owner Sabine Filoni. The cuisine is the genius of her husband and co-owner, Dominique Filoni, and is a sophisticated fusion of French artistry with the Italian passion for flavor. The dishes have a Mediterranean touch that transports one to the woods and gardens of Southern France where Dominique developed his passion for cooking. He shines in the use of fresh herbs—the pan-seared foie gras with peach basil sauce is like a little piece of heaven. The service is formal and sterling in its quality, as is the extensive wine cellar. All of this has made Savona the only Philadelphia recipient of the Five Star Diamond Award by the American Academy of Hospitality. Dinner Sun-Thu 5:30-10 pm; Fri and Sat to 11 pm.

Sonoma, 4411 Main St., Manayunk; 215-483-9400. M. Derek Davis' "Italifornia" restaurant in Manayunk was named the hottest spot in Philadelphia by *Philadelphia Magazine*. Downstairs is an open kitchen with a wood-burning stove, floor-to-ceiling windows, and an outdoor patio herb garden. The second floor greenhouse, with its 20-foot ceilings, skylights, and view of the Manayunk Bridge, houses the famed vodka bar with 80 varieties of the drink displayed on ice. The menu includes salads, pastas, homemade breads and desserts, and specialties from the grill, such as the superb honey-lavender hickory-roasted salmon. Lunch, Dinner, and Late Snacks daily. Sunday Brunch. Valet parking after 5 pm.

Spaghetti Warehouse Italian Grill, 1026 Spring Garden St.; 215-787-0784. I. Italian fast food (no long waits), including pasta, Parmigiana, and a 15-layer lasagna. Take-out and group menus. Lunch and Dinner.

Stephen's Bella Cucina, City and Haverford Aves.; 610-896-0275. M. This Italian spot has been a hit ever since its doors opened. The stylish Main Line crowd loves the quality and ample portions on its menu. Lunch and Dinner daily.

Toto, 1407 Locust St.; 215-546-2000. M-E. Northern Italian dishes prepared and served with flair in one of the prettiest restaurants in the city. Across the street from the Academy of Music. Dinner daily.

Towne House, Baltimore Pike and Veteran's Square, Media; 610-566-6141. M. Italian plus. Families have been known to fill Babe D'Igazio's ten dining rooms for his homemade pasta, large salads, and Italian and seafood specialties. He also offers prime rib of beef and a 2 1/2-pound Porterhouse steak, both of which rank among the largest in town. Lunch Mon-Sat, Dinner daily.

Triangle Tavern, Tenth and Reed Sts.; 215-467-8683. I. This neighborhood restaurant and bar is the epitome of South Philadelphia Italian food, fun, and festivity. It specializes in pasta, pizza, mussels, and antipasto salads. Local bands, musicians, and singers Friday and Saturday nights. Lunch and Dinner daily.

Villa Strafford, 115 Strafford Ave., Wayne; 610-964-1116. M-E. Fine Italian and American cuisine. Served in elegant surroundings on Philadelphia's Main Line. Lunch Mon-Fri, Dinner Mon-Sat.

Japanese

AOI Japanese Restaurant, 1210 Walnut St.; 215-985-1838. *I-M.* Sushi, shrimp tempura, and beef teriyaki. Lunch and Dinner.

Le Champignon-Tokio, 122 Lombard St.; 215-922-2515. M. The atmosphere is Japanese and French, with candlelight, flowers, wine, and sake. The menu is mixed, too, with French, Japanese, and Thai selections. Lunch, Dinner, Late Snacks, and a bed and breakfast option, too.

Dai i Chi Japanese Steak House, 234 N. Tenth St.; 215-625-3912. M. Karaoke, as well as sushi, sukiyaki, and teppanyaki style cooking.

Hikaru, Three locations including 607 S. Second St.; 215-627-7110. M. Take your shoes off in the tatami room and enjoy sushi or sukiyaki. Five time winner of "Best of Philly." Lunch Mon-Fri, Dinner daily.

Kawabata, 2455 Grant Ave.; 215-969-8225. *I-M.* Kimono-clad waitresses serve from an authentic Japanese menu. The sushi bar features more than 20 varieties of fresh fish. Lunch Mon-Fri, Dinner daily.

Meiji-En, Pier 19, Christopher Columbus Blvd. at Callowhill St.; 215-592-7100. *E.* A teppanyaki-style grill room, main dining room, sushi bar next to a waterfall, cocktail lounge, and the best waterfront views in the city. Live jazz Friday and Saturday nights and at "Philly's Best" Sunday Brunch. Lunch, Dinner, Sunday Brunch.

Kosher

Hatikva, 7638 Castor Ave.; 215-725-5200. M. Kosher Mediterranean and American cooking. Friendly service, tasty selection. Call for details.

Hillel House at the University of PA, Irv's Place, 202 S. Thirty-sixth St.; 215-573-7596. *I-M.* Cafeteria-style casual dining. Lunch, Mon-Thu 11:30-1:30. Dinner Mon-Thu 5:30-8:00. Dinner after synagogue services Friday night and Saturday lunch by special arrangement through Kosher Dining at U of P, 215-898-7013.

Holyland Pizza, 8010 Castor Ave.; 215-725-7444. *I-M.* Pizza, falafel, salads, pasta, fish platters. Very informal and fun. Tue, Wed, Thu, Sun, 11-9. Saturday nights between October and April. Call for details.

Jerusalem Kosher Restaurant, 6410 Ventnor Ave., Ventnor, NJ; 609-822-2266. M. A family-run restaurant serving Middle Eastern specialties in a friendly, welcoming atmosphere. Call for hours.

Maccabeam, 128 S. Twelfth St.; 215-922-5922. *I-M.* Satisfying Israeli, Middle Eastern, and American menu. Mon-Thu 11-8, Fri 11-3, Sun 12-8.

Maxim's, Sawmill Village Shopping Center, 404 Rt. 70 E, Cherry

Hill, NJ; 856-428-5045. M. Mediterranean and American cuisine in a friendly, family-owned establishment. Call for hours.

Mr. J Restaurant and Bakery, 1526 Sansom St.; 215-568-2448. I-M. "Home cooking at its best," say the ads. Mediterranean and American cuisine. Shabbat dinners available, too. Call for hours.

Shalom Pizza, 7598 Haverford Ave., Overbrook; 215-878-1500. I-M. Pizza every which way, plus Middle Eastern specialties, sandwiches, and platters. Delivery available. Call for hours.

Simi's Place, 300 Levering Mill Rd., Bala Cynwyd; 610-949-9420. I-M. Deli, burgers, Philly-steaks, and buckets of wings and things. Friendly atmosphere. Call for hours.

Time Out—Falafel Kingdom, 9846 Bustleton Ave.; 215-969-7545. I-M. The ads say this restaurant serves "award-winning, authentic Israeli/Middle-Eastern cuisine" and vegetarian salads. Call for hours.

Mexican

Binni & Flynn's (see NIGHTLIFE Bars).

El Sombrero, 1046 Bustleton Pike, Feasterville; 215-357-3337. I. This no-frills, family-run restaurant serves truly authentic Mexican dishes. But expect to wait, for each is cooked to order with the finest of ingredients, and the ultimate takes a little time. Along with the traditional guacamole, nachos, and burritos, try the fish house soup or the pierna al horno (roast pork in succulent gravy). Lunch Thu-Fri, Dinner daily.

Mexican Post, 104 Chestnut St.; 215-923-5233. I. Enjoy fajitas and eight flavors of margaritas in a casual, friendly atmosphere. Lunch, Dinner, Late Snacks. Open daily.

Paloma Mexican Haute Cuisine, 6516 Castor Ave.; 215-533-0356. M-E. Upscale Mexican dining. Dinner Tue-Sun.

Zocalo, Thirty-sixth and Lancaster Ave.; 215-895-0199. M. The only handmade corn tortillas in town, along with great margaritas, all the Mexican favorites, patio dining and free parking. Lunch and Dinner.

Moroccan

Marrakesh, 517 S. Leithgow, just off South St.; 215-925-5929. M. Dining in Marrakesh is truly a unique experience; you sit close to the floor on pillowed benches and are served on revolving brass circles. Eating Moroccan style means using the fingers of your right hand; your hands will be cleansed with warm water poured from a brass kettle. A typical dinner starts with a nibbling of three vegetables, three salads, some breads, and bastilla, a pastry filled with eggs and poultry. Then comes lemon chicken, skewered lamb, and couscous tinged with the flavor of zucchini, turnips, and a nice hot sauce. Dinner daily. Belly dancers available.

Pennsylvania Dutch

Good 'n Plenty Restaurant, East Brook Rd., Route 896, Smoketown; 717-394-7111. *I-M.* In this old farmhouse, sect ladies whip up family-style Pennsylvania Dutch meals of pork, chicken, and beef with sauerkraut and rich egg noodles. The platters are passed around and you eat as much as you want. Lunch and Dinner Mon-Sat.

Groff Farm, RD 3, Mount Joy; 717-653-2048. M. This working farm was once the home of Betty and Abe Groff. Now it is one of the best places to eat in Lancaster County. In the Early American farmhouse that has been converted into a series of small dining rooms, you'll enjoy robust, a-la-carte or family-style meals that include country ham, Chicken Stoltzfus (chicken with tiny bits of pastry in thick gravy), and prime rib. Seconds are encouraged, and after the bean soup embellished with chunks of ham, the fresh, steamed vegetables, homemade breads and butter, and whatever you choose for your main course, you'll depart filled to the brim. Dinner Tue-Sat.

Moselem Springs Inn, Routes 222 and 662 in Fleetwood, between Reading and Allentown; 610-944-8213. M. Built more than 130 years ago as a place for food, drink, and lodging for travelers headed to and from Philadelphia, this inn has retained an atmosphere of an era gone by. The dining rooms are graced with flickering fireplaces; you'll love the tasty meats from the smokehouse in the back, the fresh vegetables, homemade breads, and dark butter. Pennsylvania Dutch, contemporary, and traditional fare. Dinner Tue-Sun, Brunch Sun.

Seafood

Bookbinder's Seafood House, 215 S. Fifteenth St.; 215-545-1137. M-E. The fourth generation of Bookbinders, Sam and Richard, continue to operate the more than 100-year-old family business that long ago became an institution in Philadelphia. In an atmosphere of oak panelling, nautical chandeliers, and captain's tables, the menu boasts live Maine lobsters up to 3-4 pounds in size, super fresh oysters, clams and jumbo shrimp, and a variety of fresh fish dishes. The mussels in red sauce are truly special. Also, don't hesitate to order from Booky's selection of prime meats; they are first-rate. Lunch and Dinner daily.

Chart House, 555 S. Christopher Columbus Blvd. at Penn's

Landing; 215-625-8383. *E.* Indoors or on the patios, enjoy views of the Delaware and fresh seafood, steaks, a salad bar, and an oyster bar. Dinner and Sunday Brunch.

DiNardo's, 312 Race St.; 215-925-5115. *I-M.* Winner of "Best of Philly" award 11 times. The menu includes most of the usual seafood favorites, along with custom cut steaks, chicken, and pasta, but practically everyone comes to roll up their sleeves and dig into the trays brimming with steamed Louisiana crabs. You can thank the DiNardo family for the super seasoning and sauces. Open daily.

Flying Fish Seafood Restaurant, 8142 Germantown Ave., Chestnut Hill; 215-247-0707. *M.* This is a casual but elegant restaurant featuring seafood and luscious desserts. Lunch Tue-Sat, Dinner Mon-Sat.

Old Original Bookbinder's, 125 Walnut St.; 215-925-7027. *M-E.* Dining here has been a Philadelphia tradition since it was opened in 1865. All done up in mahogany, antiques, and tables laden with superior seafood, this is where the locally important and out-of-town famous go to dine (and be seen). Seven rooms, each different, seat a total of 1,000 customers. Start with the peerless snapper soup, then move on to a menu that includes live Maine lobster, crabmeat, oysters, shrimp, and clams. The sole, scrod, swordfish, and bluefish are tops, broiled to perfection. Lunch and Dinner daily.

Philadelphia Fish & Company, 207 Chestnut St.; 215-625-8605. *I-M.* This restaurant specializes in mesquite grilling, and the desert hardwood that burns so hot brings out the best of flavors in the seafood and chicken served here. Order from the blackboard and then watch your meal being grilled in the kitchen through the large picture window. Lunch and Dinner.

Sansom Street Oyster House, 1516 Sansom St.; 215-567-7683. *I-M.* The emphasis is strictly on the seafood here, not the décor—it has a "Best of Philly" oyster bar. The floors are bare and the walls are "decorated" by a collection of oyster plates, some of them antique. All the clams and oysters are shucked on the premises and can be bought individually. In addition to the raw delights of the oyster bar, succulent clam and oyster stews, broiled and fried fish, and shellfish platters are available. Lunch and Dinner.

Snockey's Oyster and Crab House, Second and Washington Sts.; 215-339-9578. *I-M.* This family-owned restaurant has been preparing the specialty of the day, oyster stew soup, since 1912. Other seafood favorites are made with lobster, shrimp, clams, and mussels. Lunch and Dinner daily.

Thai

Erawan, Twenty-third and Sansom Sts.; 215-567-2542. M. Classic and authentic Thai food. The degree of spiciness is suited to your palate. Lunch and Dinner daily.

Sala Thai, 700 S. Fifth St.; 215-922-4990. I. Authentic Thai cuisine, including Angel Wing, Satay, and Thai pizza. There's a take-out market, too. Breakfast, Lunch, Dinner.

Siam Cuisine, 925 Arch St.; 215-922-7135. M. Surrounded by an elegant atmosphere, this "Best of Philly" restaurant offers a unique blend of dishes from Thailand. Some of its specialties include fried fish cakes and Thai beef salad, along with an assortment of exotic desserts. Lunch Mon-Sat, Dinner daily.

Thai Garden East, 101 N. Eleventh St.; 215-629-9939. M. Award-winning cuisine, including steamed dumplings, Cho Chee duck, and Kanon Being. Lunch and Dinner.

Vietnamese

Hoa Viet, 1022 Race St.; 215-592-8540. I. Specialties include lobster cooked in beer, French steak, and King of the Sea hot and sour soup. 9:30 am-10 pm.

Saigon Restaurant, 935 Washington Ave.; 215-925-9656. I. Le Hop and his wife operate this restaurant beneath their rowhouse home, preparing excellent meals with fresh ingredients and vegetables from the nearby Italian Market. Their curry dishes, a Vietnamese beef soup called "pho," and their spring rolls are out of this world. Lunch and Dinner Wed-Mon.

ETCETERA

The Bourse, Independence Mall, between Fourth and Fifth Sts.; 215-625-0300. I. The Food Court of this historic merchant's exchange building has a dozen fast-food eateries that feature international as well as local specialties. Choose from Philadelphia's own cheese steaks, sandwiches from Bain's, soups, salads, and more. Desserts? Try a fabulous sundae. It's all to be enjoyed along the open-air balconies. Mon-Sat 10 am-6 pm, Sun noon-6 pm.

Copabanana, 344 South St.; 215-923-6180, and **Copa Too,** 263 S. Fifteenth St.; 215-735-0848. I. These Center City cantinas serve great burgers, Tex-Mex, fiery Spanish fries, and fresh margaritas. Lunch and Dinner daily.

Country Club Restaurant and Pastry Shop, 1717 Cottman Ave.,

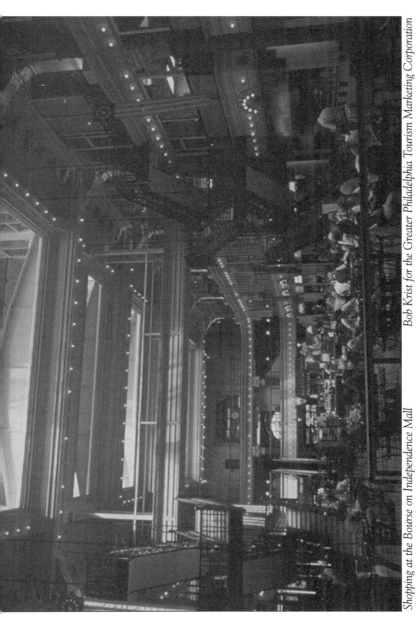

Shopping at the Bourse on Independence Mall Bob Krist for the Greater Philadelphia Tourism Marketing Corporation

Northeast Philadelphia; 215-722-0500. *I*. A landmark diner with famous baked goods, at least five varieties of chicken daily, brisket, blintzes, matzo ball soup, etc. Open 24 hours Fri and Sat, 7 am-1 am other days.

Famous Fourth Street Delicatessen, 700 S. Fourth St.; 215-922-3274. *I*. This Philadelphia institution for more than 70 years is still "famous" for its Jewish specialties—blintzes, corned beef, and chopped herring sandwiches, as well as for its knishes and kugels. The chocolate chip cookies are a must. Mon-Sat 7:30-6, Sun 7:30-4:00.

The French Bakery and Café, 8624 Germantown Ave. (rear), Chestnut Hill; 215-247-5959. *I*. Continental breakfast and light lunches featuring croissant sandwiches, quiches, and soups. A neighborhood hangout. Open daily 8:30-4:30.

Hymie's Merion Delicatessen and Restaurant, 342 Montgomery Ave., Merion; 610-664-3544. *I*. For 30 years this award-winning deli has been serving a loyal following with generous portions of homemade cabbage and matzo ball soup, blueberry, cheese, and cherry blintzes, and lox and bagels. The roast turkey and chicken are specialties, too. Daily 7 am-10 pm, Fri-Sat until 11 pm.

Latimer Deli and Restaurant, 255 S. Fifteenth St.; 215-545-9244. *I*. All entrees are homemade, including turkey, brisket, roast beef, whitefish salad, quiche, kugel, etc. Daily dinner specials. Daily 8 am-10 pm.

LeBus, 3402 Sansom St.; 215-387-3800. *I*. Located in University City and other locations, this restaurant has the best muffins and corn-bread in town. Also, soups, salads, and pasta dishes. Light Breakfast, Lunch, and Dinner daily.

Market Fair, at The Gallery at Market East, 9th and Market Sts.; 215-925-7162. *I*. Here you'll find 40 eateries and sit-down restaurants in the nation's largest urban enclosed shopping center. They serve everything from Chinese and Mexican foods to clams and pizza. Mon, Tue, Thu, Sat 10 am-7 pm, Wed, Fri 10 am-8 pm, Sun noon-5 pm.

Melrose Diner, 1501 Snyder Ave.; 215-467-6644. *I*. Started in 1932, this 24-hour Philadelphia institution is now serving good, old-fashioned American food to an average of 3,000 people per day! All the fresh ingredients for the dishes on the standardized menu are weighed to the fraction; consequently, there's consistent excellence from week to week with such winners as the bean and vegetable soup, lamb stew, roast chicken, crab cutlets, and ever-popular apple pie. The Melrose Diner may be strictly "diner" in décor, but with the exception of Christmas Eve and Christmas Day, it's always open with wholesome, hearty food. Open 24 hours.

More Than Just Ice Cream, 1119 Locust St.; 215-574-0586. *I*. This place caters to the entire family with much more than just ice cream. Using the freshest ingredients, Kay, the owner, whips up quiches and chili daily, and for dessert has apple cobbler, apple pies, and pumpkin pies that are out of this world. Hot loaves of honey bread also are on sale. Mon-Fri 10 am-12 pm, Sat-Sun to 12:30 am.

Mulberry Market, 236 Arch St. (across from the Betsy Ross House); 215-592-8022. *I.* A grocery and deli within the Historic Square Mile. Platters, salads, sandwiches, hoagies, desserts, beer. Breakfast, Lunch, and Dinner daily.

Pat's King of Steaks, 1301 S. Ninth St.; 215-468-1546. *I.* This is another Philadelphia institution where, 24 hours a day, people from all walks of life line up for the thinly sliced beef on fresh rolls, doused with hot melted cheese. "Philadelphia cheese steaks" originated with Pat's, and you can get them "wid" or "wid'out" onions. How good are they? Well, rumor has it that Sinatra sent his chauffeur up from Atlantic City to pick up a limousine-full. 24 hours. Closed Christmas Day and New Year's Day.

PhilaDeli, 410 South St.; 215-923-1986. *I.* Everything you'd expect to find in a Jewish-style delicatessen, including the generous portions. A great beer selection, too. Breakfast, Lunch, Dinner, Sunday Brunch, and box lunches.

Pikkles Plus, 1801 Market St.; 215-751-1914. *I.* Fresh cooked turkey every day and all fresh deli selection. Center City lunch crowd. Sun-Fri 7-3:30, Sat 8-3:30.

Pizzeria Uno, 511 S. Second St.; 215-592-0400. *I.* This is a fun, bustling spot with a saloon decor where you'll find no less than ten varieties of deep-dish pizza along with an interesting selection of sandwiches, salads, soups, and drinks. Sun-Thu 11:30 am-1 am, Fri-Sat until 2 am.

Reading Terminal Market, Twelfth and Arch Sts.; 215-922-2317. *I.* Built in 1892, this bustling marketplace, now on the National Register of Historic Places, is across the street from the new Pennsylvania Convention Center. It houses approximately 80 merchants, most selling produce, meat, fish, groceries, and a veritable smorgasbord of over-the-counter delights. Clearly, the challenge here is choosing from Amish specialties, country cooking, or an international array that includes French, Italian, Mexican, Middle Eastern, Indian, and Asian dishes. The Terminal also provides a beer garden. Mon-Sat 8 am-6 pm. The Amish merchants are open Wed-Sat.

CAFETERIAS

Ben's, at the Franklin Institute, Twentieth St. and Benjamin Franklin Pkwy.; 215-448-1200. *I.* Enjoy nutritional all-American sandwiches, salads, soups, hot dogs, and hamburgers along with a healthy helping of science. Breakfast and Lunch.

The Gold Standard (see DINING, International—The Palladium Restaurant).

Museum Café, at the University of Pennsylvania Museum of Archaeology and Anthropology, Thirty-third and Spruce Sts.; 215-898-4089. *I*. Fresh, homemade foods surrounded by history and archeology. Breakfast and Lunch.

The Terrace (see DINING, American).

BRUNCHES

Sunday brunch can be enjoyed in many restaurants and interesting locations throughout the Philadelphia area. Some are to be found amid the scenic beauty of rolling hills, old barns, creeks, and streams; others are conveniently located near historic sights, museums, and seasonal activities. Some may have a harpist or a jazz quartet playing in the background, while others are loads of fun for the whole family.

With variety as our criterion, we have selected a number of restaurants for Sunday brunch in and around Philadelphia, and have included some that do not already appear in our regular dining section. You may wish to call in advance for any changes in times and format. Also, remember that in Pennsylvania, alcoholic beverages cannot be served until 1 pm. on Sunday.

Black Bass Hotel, 3744 River Rd., Lumberville; 215-297-5770. M. The champagne brunch is a lovely experience in this historic inn on the Delaware River. From 1-3 pm.

The Four Dogs, 1300 West Strasburg Rd.; West Chester; 610-692-5702. M. The a-la-carte menu features simple, quality preparations. From 11 am-3 pm.

Friday's, 4000 City Ave.; 215-878-7070. *I*-M. The Sunday menu here is highlighted by Belgian waffles, quiches, puffed pancakes, croissants, and eggs benedict. Special price on champagne. From 11 am-1 pm.

Lily Langtry's, 1160 First Ave., King of Prussia; 610-337-2000. *I*. This Las Vegas dinner theater features an all-you-can-eat buffet with egg dishes, bacon and link sausages, Swedish meatballs, chicken, homemade baked goods, pancakes, hash browns, and a large assortment of salads. Matinee (and Dinner) shows.

Meiji-En, Pier 19, Christopher Columbus Blvd. at Callowhill St.; 215-592-7100. *E*. Enjoy live jazz and the best waterfront views in the city while dining in this Japanese-American restaurant on "Philly's Best" Sunday Brunch.

The Moshulu, Pier 34, 735 S. Columbus Blvd.; 215-923-2500. *E*.

Brunch while gazing at a magnificent view of the river and the city skyline. Bask in this luxuriously restored 100-year-old sailing ship—the only restaurant-sailing ship in the world.

Ship Inn, Lancaster Ave. at Ship Rd., Exton; 610-363-7200. *I.* In this turn-of-the-century tavern enjoy a variety of homemade breads, egg and chicken dishes, and sumptuous desserts. From 10 am-2 pm.

Society Hill Hotel, Third and Chestnut Sts.; 215-925-1919. *I.* Inside or outside of Philadelphia's first bed-and-breakfast hotel you can partake of a fixed price menu that includes eggs benedict, egg dishes, Belgian waffles, and homemade breads along with a Bloody Mary or Mimosa. From 11:15 am-2:15 pm.

Sunnybrook Partners, East High St., Pottstown; 610-326-6400. *I.* Sunday brunch is a festive occasion in this 20-acre countryside setting. The huge, high-quality servings include eggs scrambled on an open grill, spare ribs, salads, and a lavish selection of desserts. The giant theater organ adds to the congenial atmosphere, 9:30 am-1:30 pm.

Tavern on the Green, Twenty-first and Green Sts.; 215-235-6767. *I.* This cheery, plant-filled restaurant offers a dozen entrees that include crabmeat benedict, Mexican ranch-style eggs, crepe du jour, deep fried brie, and eggs. Super fresh salads and excellent desserts will accent your visit. From 11:30 am-3 pm.

PERFORMING ARTS

With its world-famous orchestra and ballet, its opera company, the Curtis Institute, and such landmarks as the Academy of Music and the Forrest, Merriam, and Walnut theaters, Philadelphia's roots in the performing arts are well established. Philadelphia's music is a great tradition. So is its dance. With theater soaring on the wings of such groups as the Arden Theatre Company, the People's Light and Theater Company, and the Wilma Theatre Company, the city's entire performing arts scene has come alive with innovation, diversity, and creativity. And with the establishment of The Avenue of the Arts, extending for miles from North to South Broad Street, with the Apollo of Temple at one end and the soon-to-be-completed Regional Performing Arts Center near the other, the city's cultural community can only strengthen and grow. The reaction has been extraordinary; audiences are rising with unbridled applause, media critics can't say enough good things about what they're seeing and, perhaps most revealing of all, a great number of Philadelphia's finest talents in music, dance, and theater are staying home to perform.

PERFORMING ARTS BY AREA

BUCKS COUNTY
Bucks County Playhouse, Theater

CENTER CITY
Academy of Music, Music
Academy of Vocal Arts, Opera
Collegiate and Archdiocesan Choirs, Vocal
Concerto Soloists of Philadelphia, Music
The Curtis Institute of Music Recitals, Music
Forrest Theater, Theater
Lord and Taylor Organ Concerts, Music

Mellon Jazz Festival, Music
Mendelssohn Club of Philadelphia, Vocal
Merriam Theater, Theater
Neighborhood Concerts, Summer Concerts
Pennsylvania Ballet, Dance
Philadelphia Boys Choir and Men's Chorale, Vocal
Philadelphia Chamber Music Society, Music
Philadelphia Classical Guitar Society, Music
Philadelphia Clef Club of Jazz and Performing Arts, Music

Philadelphia Dance Company,
Dance
Philadelphia Orchestra, Music
Philadelphia Singers, Vocal
Philadelphia Theatre Company,
Theater
Philly Pops, Music
Plays & Players, Theater
Prince Music Theater, Summer
Concerts
Regional Perfoming Arts Center,
Dance, Music
Savoy Company, Opera
Singing City, Vocal
Temple University Theaters,
Theater
University of the Arts, Dance,
Music
Walnut Street Theatre, Theater
Wilma Theatre, Theater

CHESTER COUNTY
The People's Light and Theatre
Company, Theater
Savoy Company, Opera

DELAWARE COUNTY
Hedgerow Theater, Theater
The Media Theatre for the
Performing Arts, Theater
Tower Theater, Music
Villanova Theater, Theater

FAIRMOUNT PARK
Mann Center for the Performing
Arts, Summer Concerts
Robin Hood Dell East, Summer
Concerts

LANCASTER COUNTY
American Music Theatre, Music

LEHIGH COUNTY
Pennsylvania Shakespeare Festival,
Theater

MONTGOMERY COUNTY
Cheltenham Center for the Arts,
Theater
Keswick Theater of Performing
Arts, Theater
Philadelphia Folk Festival, Summer
Concerts
Philadelphia Folksong Society,
Vocal

NORTHEAST
The Settlement Music School,
Music, Dance

NORTH PHILADELPHIA
Apollo of Temple, Music
Freedom Theater, Theater
Temple University Boyer College of
Music, Music
Temple University Theaters,
Theater

NORTHWEST
Bach Festival of Philadelphia,
Music
Delaware Valley Opera Company,
Opera
LaSalle College and Music Theater,
Theater
The Settlement Music School,
Music, Dance
Summer Opera Festival, Summer
Concerts

OLD CITY—SOCIETY HILL
The Arden Theater Company,
Theater
New Market Cabaret Theatre,
Theater
Opera Company of Philadelphia,
Opera
Painted Bride Art Center, Theater
Philomel, Music
Relache, Music
Society Hill Playhouse, Theater

SOUTH PHILADELPHIA
First Union Complex, Music
Mummers Bands, Summer Concerts
The Settlement Music School,
    Music, Dance

UNIVERSITY CITY
Annenberg Center, Theater
Drexel University, Division of
    Performing Arts, Music, Theater,
    Dance
International House, Dance, Music
Mandell Theater, Theater
Pennsylvania Pro Musica, Vocal

University of Pennsylvania Music
    Department, Music, Vocal

WATERFRONT
Blockbuster-Sony Music
    Entertainment Center, Music
Penn's Landing, Summer Concerts

WEST PHILADELPHIA
Bushfire Theatre, Theater
Group Motion Multi Media Dance
    Theater, Dance
Settlement Music School, Music,
    Dance

DANCE

Drexel University, Division of Performing Arts, Thirty-second and Chestnut Sts.; 215-895-ARTS. Fine performances by the Dance Ensemble and the Marion Tonner Ballet in the Mandell Theater.

Group Motion Multi Media Dance Theater, 3500 Lancaster Ave.; 215-928-1495. Formed in West Berlin in 1962, this group came to the United States six years later after performing and touring in Germany. Now performing extensively in colleges and theaters on the East Coast, and with engagements abroad, its emphasis is on dance accented by live and taped electronic instrumental music, films, slides, video tapes, and lighting. Studio performances throughout the year with weekly workshops open to the public.

International House, 3701 Chestnut St.; 215-387-5125. This international/intercultural residential and cultural center at the University of Pennsylvania presents concerts, dance programs, and exhibits throughout the year. In May, the center presents the Philadelphia Festival of World Cinema.

The Painted Bride Art Center, 230 Vine St.; 215-925-9914. Cutting edge dance, music, theater, poetry, performance and fine art are presented at this nonprofit venue. The Center strives to mount positive multicultural programs and to highlight the ability of the arts to inspire, heal, and effect social change.

Pennsylvania Ballet, 1101 S. Broad St.; 215-551-7000. This nationally acclaimed company performs both classical and contemporary ballet. Its Shirley Rock School of the Pennsylvania Ballet trains new artists, and The Off-Center Ballet is a wing of the company that concentrates on new works by leading contemporary American choreographers. The Academy of Music became the Ballet's permanent home starting with the 1984-85 season. Seven subscription series are offered, and the company performs an annual holiday production of "The Nutcracker."

Philadelphia Dance Company, 9 N. Preston St.; 215-387-8200. Founded in 1970 and known more informally as "Philadanco," this outstanding African-American company specializes in classical ballet and modern dance forms. It maintains a year-round schedule of performances in Philadelphia and on tour.

Regional Performing Arts Center. (See MUSIC.)

Settlement Music School. (See MUSIC.)

University of the Arts, Broad and Pine Sts.; 215-717-6000. Founded in 1870, the University has built an outstanding reputation for training performing artists. Free annual concerts in chorus, jazz, dance, opera, and orchestral music are held in the fall and spring at the Drake Theater and Laurie Wagman Hall.

MUSIC

Academy of Music, Broad and Locust Sts.; 215-893-1935. Academy Charge: 215-893-1999. Built in 1857, the Academy is the only surviving European-style opera house in America, and is the oldest auditorium in the United States still in use in its original form and for its original purpose. The Academy is the official home of the Philadelphia Orchestra until it moves to the new Regional Performing Arts Center in 2001. Its magnificent interior of crimson, cream, and gold, as well as its matchless acoustics, have been the setting for the world's finest concerts, recitals, opera, and ballet. Among the legends that have performed at the Academy, often with the Philadelphia Orchestra, are Paderewski, Caruso, Mahler, Rachmaninoff, Horowitz, Rubinstein, and Cliburn. The Academy has also been home for the Pennsylvania Ballet, the Philly Pops, and the Opera Company of Philadelphia. Named a National Historic Landmark in 1963, it has been the site of speeches by numerous presidents and such orators as Susan B. Anthony and Mark Twain. Available for tours (see SIGHTS).

American Music Theatre, 2425 Lincoln Hwy. East, Lancaster; 717-397-7700. This is a magnificent, new 1,600 seat theater in Pennsylvania Dutch country. Original musical productions as well as famous names are presented here.

The Apollo of Temple, One Apollo Center, 1776 N. Broad St.; 215-204-2400. This exciting new venue at Temple University on the Avenue of the Arts hosts concerts, shows and family entertainment. It is also home to Temple University basketball.

Bach Festival of Philadelphia, 8419 Germantown Ave.; 215-247-4020. Tickets: 247-BACH. Started in 1976 by Michael Korn as a local

Academy of Music on Broad Street, "Avenue of the Arts"   *Greater Philadelphia Tourism Marketing Corporation*

celebration of beautiful music, this has evolved into a major festival that has attracted capacity audiences and critical acclaim. Music director Dennis Schmidt presents up to six concerts a year performed by international artists specializing in solo, ensemble, and orchestral presentations of Johann Sebastian Bach's music. Performances are held at area churches, colleges, and art galleries.

Blockbuster-Sony Music Entertainment Center, One Harbor Blvd., Camden, NJ; 609-365-1300. Known as the E-Centre, this new 25,000 seat outdoor venue is a prime entertainment mecca for the Delaware Valley. Directly across the Delaware River from Penn's Landing, it can be reached by crossing the Ben Franklin Bridge or by riding the Riverlink Ferry. Everything from classical music to rock and roll is presented here.

Concerto Soloists of Philadelphia, 338 S. Fifteenth St.; 215-545-5451. Modeled after the orchestras of Bach and Mozart, this renowned chamber orchestra specializes in a wide range of baroque and classical music. Under the direction of Marc Mostovoy, who founded the soloists in 1964, it performs concerts at the Walnut Street Theatre and the Holy Trinity Church on Rittenhouse Square, as well as on national and international tours.

The Curtis Institute of Music Recitals, 1726 Locust St.; 215-893-7902. Founded in 1924, this highly respected music school is one of the superior training grounds for the musical elite, endowing all its students with full-tuition scholarships. Free concerts, including opera and chamber music, are presented by the students every Monday, Wednesday, and Friday during the school year. Other concerts and special events are always scheduled.

Drexel University, Division of Performing Arts, Thirty-second and Chestnut St.; 215-895-ARTS. Professional musicians have formed a resident orchestra at Drexel University since 1964. Annual concerts, some of them free, are held in the Main Hall or in Mandell Theater on campus.

First Union Complex, Pattison Place, Broad St. and Pattison Ave.; 215-336-3600. This home of the Flyers and the Sixers is also host to exciting mega-concerts.

International House. (See DANCE.)

Lord and Taylor Organ Concerts, Thirteenth and Market Sts.; 215-241-9000. These free concerts are presented every shopping day on the largest organ in the world, which overlooks the Grand Court of Lord and Taylor's department store. Concerts at 11:30 am and 5:30 pm, Mon-Sat.

Philadelphia Chamber Music Society, 135 S. Eighteenth St.; 215-569-8587. The Society showcases renowned international artists, as well as outstanding young concert soloists and ensembles. From

October to May, concerts are performed at the Pennsylvania Convention Center and at Centennial Hall at the Haverford School.

Philadelphia Classical Guitar Society, 2038 Sansom St.; 215-567-2972. The Society has provided the finest in guitar concerts and workshops for Philadelphia since 1968. Monthly concerts from September to May, and meetings at the IPSO Café.

Philadelphia Clef Club of Jazz and Performing Arts, 738 S. Broad St.; 215-893-9912. This nonprofit organization is jazz heaven—a place to preserve, promote, and present jazz. Training and workshops are offered along with performances in the 250-seat theater. There are also a members' lounge, gift shop, library, and catering facilities available for rent.

Philadelphia Orchestra, Broad and Locust Sts.; 215-893-1900 and 893-1930. From its first concert on November 16, 1900, the Philadelphia Orchestra has been heralded as one of the finest orchestras to be found anywhere. Over the years, more than a few experts have called it "the greatest orchestra in the world." It was the first American symphony orchestra to make a recording (1917) and now boasts more than 500 long-playing albums to its credit. It was also the first orchestra to be featured in films (1937) and on television (1948), and the first to perform in the People's Republic of China. Under the direction of Wolfgang Sawallisch, who succeeded the brilliant Riccardo Muti and the legendary Eugene Ormandy, the Orchestra performs at the Academy of Music from September through May until its 2001 move to the Regional Performing Arts Center. A series of free concerts are held at the Fredric R. Mann Music Center in Fairmount Park in June and July.

Philly Pops, 400 Market St.; 215-923-7600. This orchestra combines symphonic and popular music with outstanding guests. Performances are at the Academy of Music, and directed by Peter Nero.

Philomel, 240 S. Third St.; 215-574-0523. The oldest group of its kind in Philadelphia, six to twelve musicians perform a series of concerts in Greater Philadelphia area churches, colleges, and art centers, using all original or reproduction Baroque period instruments.

Regional Performing Arts Center, Broad and Spruce Sts. 215-732-7900. Scheduled to open in 2001, this magnificent 2,500-seat venue on the Avenue of the Arts will be a state-of-the-art concert hall and theater. It will be home to the world-famous Philadelphia Orchestra and host other local, national, and international arts groups.

Relache, the Ensemble for New Contemporary Music, 715 S. Third St.; 215-574-8246. This Philadelphia-based ensemble has received considerable recognition for its contemporary music. It performs from September to May at the Philadelphia Arts Bank and at Drexel University's Mandell Theater.

The Settlement Music School, 416 Queen St.; 215-336-0400. Founded in 1908, Settlement Music School is the largest community arts school in the country. At locations in Germantown, Jenkintown,

Northeast, South and West Philadelphia, the school provides 6,000 students with high quality music and dance instruction, regardless of their age, background, or ability to pay. The five Settlement Music School branches also serve as host to numerous performances and master classes throughout the year, including weekly student and faculty recitals, chamber orchestra concerts, and a contemporary music concert series.

Temple University Boyer College of Music, Rock Hall, Broad St. and Cecil B. Moore Ave.; 215-204-8307. On the Avenue of the Arts, this venue hosts concerts, recitals, and classes by and for students, faculty, and guest artists.

Tower Theater, Sixty-ninth and Ludlow Sts.; Upper Darby; 610-352-2887. This theater features Electric Factory concerts in jazz, folk, and rock. Don't forget that the Factory also brings such concerts to the Spectrum, Veteran's Stadium, TLA, the Mann Music Center, the Academy of Music, the First Union Complex, the Blockbuster-Sony entertainment Center, and the Hershey Park Complex.

University of Pennsylvania Music Department, Performance Ensembles, 201 S. Thirty-fourth St.; 215-898-6244. The University presents a full concert season each academic year featuring performances by its instrumental, vocal, and early music ensembles, as well as professional ensembles and soloists. The repertoire is classical and modern and includes works by faculty composers. Students, faculty, staff, and residents of the Philadelphia area are welcome to audition. The concerts are held in the Irvine Auditorium for a modest admission charge. The groups include:

Ancient Voices, an a capella chorus—Middle Ages and Renaissance music

Baroque Ensemble—Baroque chamber music

Chamber Singers, about 12 skilled singers—madrigals, chansons, and part-songs

Choral Society, about 100 voices—major classical works

Madrigal Singers—lighter music of the Renaissance

Penn Chamber Music Society

Recorder Ensemble—Renaissance consort music

University Symphony Orchestra

University Wind Ensemble

University of the Arts. (See DANCE.)

Opera

Academy of Vocal Arts, 1920 Spruce St.; 215-735-1685. In operation for almost 60 years, this tuition-free opera school and presenting company offers numerous recitals and master classes throughout the season. The recitals and operas are presented in the AVA's nationally renowned Helen Corning Warden Theater and at other locations.

Delaware Valley Opera Company, 1731 Chandler St.; 215-725-4171. Performing throughout the year, this company presents concerts, one-act operas, recitals by various members, and full-scale operas with orchestra. Performances at the opera company's outdoor theater and the Paul D. Osimo Theater near Hermitage Mansion in Roxborough. Feel free to bring lawn chairs and blankets (see Summer Concerts).

Opera Company of Philadelphia, 510 Walnut St.; 215-928-2100. International stars present grand opera in Philadelphia's only grand opera company. Performances are at the Academy of Music and super-titles are provided with every performance.

The Savoy Company, P. O. Box 59150, Philadelphia 19102; 215-735-7161. Founded in 1901, this is the second oldest Gilbert and Sullivan company in the world. At the Academy of Music in May, at Longwood Gardens in June, and other times and locations. Website: www.savoy.org.

Summer Concerts

Mann Center for the Performing Arts, Fifty-second St. and Parkside Ave.; 215-546-7900. This pastoral setting is the site of concerts by the Philadelphia Orchestra in June and July and by other top entertainment in August. To purchase reserved, sheltered seating for Orchestra concerts, call 215-893-1999. Seating for 4,000 is also obtainable on the grassy slopes and bleachers. In addition, you can receive free lawn tickets, when available, for only a $2 service charge, by calling the above ticket number. Bring a blanket or deck chairs and picnic on the grass. Box suppers and refreshments are available at intermission. The August portion of the program is devoted to pop concerts, ballet, theater, and opera.

Mellon Jazz Festival, for information contact Mellon PSFS, 215-553-3668 or 553-4684. For 10-12 days in June, throughout the Philadelphia region, the festival offers top-notch groups playing big-band swing, small-group hard bop, and other jazz styles. Among the artists who have performed in this festival are Sonny Rollins, McCoy Tyner, Archie Shepp, and Miles Davis.

Mummers Bands, Mummers Museum, Second St. and Washington Ave.; 215-336-3050 and 467-1315. From May through September, weather permitting, the Mummers play and strut for free in all their glory every Tuesday night at 8 pm in the Museum's parking facilities. Please bring your own chairs. Refreshments available.

Neighborhood Concerts, Fairmount Park Commission; 215-685-0000. Free concerts are sponsored by the park during July and August. Bring blankets and snacks and enjoy. Call for details.

Penn's Landing, Christopher Columbus Blvd. and Spruce St.; 215-922-2FUN. Website: www.pennslandingcorp.com. Something is happening every summer weekend on the waterfront—concerts, parades of tall ships, ice cream bashes, fitness fun-fests, maritime days, fantastic fireworks, etc. Various festivals are held throughout the summer and include a wealth of ethnic foods, exhibits, music, and dancing. And for kids, Sundays are free "fun-days" from 2-4 pm. Join in the festival atmosphere.

Philadelphia Folk Festival, 7113 Emlen St.; 215-242-0150, 800-556-FOLK. For three days and nights in late August, this festival offers international folk music performers and groups in concerts and workshops. There is also camping out, folk dancing, and special programs for children held at Old Poole Farm, Schwenksville.

Prince Music Theater, 1412 Chestnut St.; 215-569-9700 and 972-1000. It has been called "America's leading showcase for new and adventurous music theater," and is devoted to music theater in all forms, including opera, musical comedy, drama, cabaret, and experimental works.

Robin Hood Dell East, East Fairmount Park; 215-685-9560. In July and August the Dell features top stars in music and dance in a series of low-cost, Department of Recreation concerts.

Summer Opera Festival, Hermitage Mansion, Henry Ave. and Hermit Lane, Roxborough; 215-725-4171. Bring a blanket or a lawn chair and enjoy these operas at the outdoor Paul D. Osimo Theater on acreage surrounding the Hermitage in Fairmount Park. The Delaware Valley Opera Company stages three productions on Saturday nights throughout the summer.

Vocal

Collegiate and Archdiocesan Choirs, 222 N. Seventeenth St.; 215-587-3696. These choirs perform independently and together in concerts and special liturgies at the Cathedral-Basilica and elsewhere in the Philadelphia area.

Mendelssohn Club of Philadelphia, 1218 Locust St.; 215-735-9922. Founded in 1874 by William W. Gilchrist, this nationally recognized choral ensemble stages four programs a year in a series of subscription concerts in the Philadelphia area. The avocational chorus has performed with the Philadelphia Orchestra, is directed by Alan Harler, and welcomes new members.

Pennsylvania Pro Musica, 225A S. Forty-second St.; 215-222-4517. Founded in 1968, this is the oldest professional soloist, choral, and orchestral performing organization in Pennsylvania. It stages 10-12 concerts per year at the First Reformed Church, featuring fine classical and pre-classical music. Dedicated to original research, promotion, publication, performance, and exegesis of fine music, it also offers lectures, panel discussions, and concert previews.

The Philadelphia Boys Choir and Men's Chorale, 225 N. Thirty-second St.; 215-222-3500. A select group of 100 boy and 35 adult male singers, this 30-year-old group has received national and international recognition for its White House appearances, performances with Luciano Pavarotti and the Philadelphia Orchestra, and a Bob Hope television special from Peking, China. Directed by Robert G. Hamilton, the choir performs music primarily by American composers, as well as classical, spiritual, and folk music. It has traveled 700,000 miles to every major continent in the world, performing in 13 languages for royalty, heads of state, and millions of people.

Philadelphia Folksong Society, 7113 Emlen St.; 215-242-0150. The Society presents monthly formal concerts, followed by informal gatherings of performers and members of the audience. Other annual events include the Philadelphia Folk Festival in August, the Spring Thing in May, and the Fall Fling in October.

The Philadelphia Singers, 1211 Chestnut St., Suite 200; 215-751-9494. This ensemble of 30 professional singers, directed by David Hayes, and founded in 1972, performs more than 200 works from every part of the choral repertoire. The singers have established a tradition of performing special programs in unusual locations, such as the "Music from San Marco" program in the Great Stair Hall of the Philadelphia Museum of Art, and Handel's "Samson" in Temple Shalom. Its Christmas performances of Handel's "Messiah" in local churches have become a local institution.

Singing City, 1634 Sansom St.; 215-569-9067. As Philadelphia's world-famous community choir, this 100-voice group combines a tradition of musical excellence with human service by singing at hospitals, senior citizens' centers, and often on city streets. It continues to draw critical acclaim.

University of Pennsylvania Music Department. (See MUSIC.)

THEATER

Annenberg Center, University of Pennsylvania, 3680 Walnut St.; 215-898-6791. This four-theater performing arts center is one of the most exciting in Philadelphia, offering a variety of entertainment. From October to April, the Center sponsors a series of plays selected from Broadway and from America's leading theater companies.

Classicals, musicals, and premieres are held in the Zellerbach Theater and the Annenberg School; national artists and local groups present dance, music, and plays in the Studio Center and the Harold Prince Theater. In May, the Center offers the Philadelphia International Theatre Festival for Children.

Arden Theatre Company, 40-50 N. Second St; 215-922-8900. Native Philadelphians form the majority in this company. The innovative company has presented numerous world and Philadelphia premieres on its intimate 175-seat Acadia Stage and its 300-seat Mainstage Theatre. It is dedicated to "telling the greatest stories by the greatest storytellers of all time."

Bucks County Playhouse, 70 S. Main St., New Hope; 215-862-2041. Located in a former gristmill built in 1790, this is the official State Playhouse of Pennsylvania, and stages productions from April through December. It has featured such stars as Helen Hayes, Walter Matthau, and George C. Scott performing in plays by Noel Coward, Tennessee Williams, and George Bernard Shaw. It now looks much as it did when it was first converted into a playhouse in 1939.

Bushfire Theatre of Performing Arts, Fifty-second and Locust Sts.; 215-747-9230. Founded in 1976, this community-based company is committed to nurturing local playwrights, and providing classes in all aspects of theater.

Cheltenham Center for the Arts, 439 Ashbourne Rd., Cheltenham; 215-379-4660. This charming community theater founded in the 1930s seats 150 people and presents semi-professional actors and actresses with professional goals. The plays dare to be different and include Agatha Christie's mysteries and children's productions.

Drexel University, Division of the Performing Arts, Thirty-second and Chestnut Sts; 215-895-ARTS. The Drexel Players stage three spirited mainstage performances annually in the Mandell Theater. A number of student dance and musical concerts are also performed.

Forrest Theater, 1114 Walnut St.; 215-923-1515. Named after the legendary actor Edwin Forrest (1806-1872), the Forrest presents four to five Broadway productions each year. Originally opened as a movie house, it now seats 1,800 and has featured top stars in such smash hits as "Annie," "The Phantom of the Opera," "Cats," and "Les Miserables."

Freedom Theatre, 1346 N. Broad St.; 215-765-2793. Founded in 1966, the Freedom continues to provide performing arts training and/or employment for gifted inner-city residents. Under the direction of Walter Dallas, it has received critical acclaim for its energy and creativity, and was cited by the John F. Kennedy Center for the Performing Arts as one of the nation's best African-American theaters. Located in the old mansion of the nineteenth-century stage actor Edwin Forrest, the theater also performs at area colleges, schools, libraries, churches, hospitals, and prisons.

Hedgerow Theatre, 64 Rose Valley Rd., Wallingford; 610-565-4211. Formed in the 1920s, this 134-seat theater has a resident company of professionals from across the country. A wide variety of performances unfold in the playhouse which was originally built as a grist mill in 1840 and later used as a bobbin mill.

Keswick Theater of Performing Arts, 291 Keswick Ave., Glenside; 215-572-7650. The 1,300-seat Keswick, a historic landmark designed by Horace Drumbauer (designer of the Art Museum), used to be a vaudeville stop for Fanny Brice, the Marx Brothers, and Stepin Fetchit. Now it's a performing arts center with plays, dance concerts, and variety shows.

LaSalle College and Music Theater, 146 W. Laurel St.; 215-951-1375. Founded in 1962, this college-sponsored professional theater thrives on youthful exuberance, colorful sets, costumes, and highly professional choreography rather than on "name" performers. The Masque Theater of LaSalle offers fall and spring productions and holds student drama workshops.

Mandell Theater, Drexel University, Thirty-third and Chestnut Sts.; 215-895-ARTS. Since the early 1970s, this theater has offered a number of presentations in the performing arts. Its main stage has productions by students and faculty. Professional dance companies also use the theater for major productions.

The Media Theatre for the Performing Arts, 104 E. State St., Media; 610-566-6700 and 891-9820; 800-568-7771. A magnificent 1927 English Renaissance theater, showcasing Broadway shows and other performing arts. Dining in the Crystal Room is optional.

Merriam Theater, 250 S. Broad St.; 215-875-4800 and 732-5446. The 1,668-seat Merriam belongs to the University of the Arts, one of only a handful of fully accredited private performing arts colleges in the nation. It presents professional musicals, dramas, and touring companies, and draws upon the student body for a wide range of concerts, musical events, dance, and theater.

New Market Cabaret Theater, 415 S. Second St; 215-627-9801 and 925-3769. In Society Hill, this 300-seat theater offers off-Broadway hits, concerts, bands and dancing. There's also catering available for 500.

Painted Bride Art Center, 230 Vine St.; 215-925-9914. The center features professional and experimental performances in music, dance, theater, and poetry, as well as a regular series of jazz, chamber, and folk music. There are also appearances by Philadelphia-area and nationally recognized artists, as well as exhibits of unusual art in all forms of media.

Broad Street, "Avenue of the Arts"

Bob Krist for the Greater Philadelphia
Tourism Marketing Corporation

Pennsylvania Shakespeare Festival, Labuda Center for the Performing and Fine Arts, at Allentown College, 2755 Station Ave., Center Valley; 610-282-3192. Top-level staging and acting of works by the Bard and other playwrights in a state-of-the-art theater on a pastoral campus.

The People's Light and Theatre Company, 39 Conestoga Rd., Malvern; 610-644-3500. One of the most attractive regional theaters in the country, People's Light offers a main stage subscription series. It also operates an Outreach program, taking live professional productions to non-traditional audiences.

The Philadelphia Theatre Company, 1714 DeLancey St.; 215-735-0631 and 568-1920. This professional theater company is Philadelphia's only resident theater directed toward producing contemporary American plays. Its performances are held at the historic Plays & Players Theater near Rittenhouse Square.

Plays & Players, 1714 Delancey St.; 215-735-0630. This club, founded in 1911, presents at least four main attractions a year, along with a Children's Theater and Children's Theater Workshop Series. The theater hall, purchased in 1922, is listed in the National Register as a historical monument.

Society Hill Playhouse, 507 Eighth St.; 215-923-0210. Having celebrated its thirtieth anniversary, this is Philadelphia's original professional off-Broadway theater. The playhouse is devoted to contemporary American and European works. It has presented hundreds of area premieres and developed and encouraged many performers, technicians, and playwrights. It offers a full-service bar, and dinner/theater packages with restaurants on South Street.

Temple University Theaters, Temple University, Thirteenth and Norris Sts., 215-204-1122. This is one of only a handful of collegiate companies in the United States with a membership in the League of Professional Theater Training Programs. All of Temple's culturally diverse shows are produced, directed, and performed by students and faculty. Productions are staged at the Tomlinson and Randall Theaters on the main campus, Thirteenth and Norris Sts., and at Stage Three, 1619 Walnut St., on the Center City campus.

Villanova University Theatre, Ithan and Lancaster Aves., Villanova University; 610-645-4760 and 645-7474. An October-April program of semi-professional productions is staged in the Vasey Theatre on the Villanova campus. Contemporary and classic world plays are presented.

The Walnut Street Theater, Ninth and Walnut Sts.; 215-574-3550. Open since 1809, this historic landmark playhouse is the oldest theater in continuous use in the English-speaking world and has premiered countless plays that went on to Broadway and worldwide acclaim. The

1,052-seat mainstage theater produces significant dramatic, comic, and musical works; the two studio theaters present new and experimental works; and the theater school offers theatrical training.

The Wilma Theatre, Broad and Spruce Sts.; 215-546-7824. Founded in 1973 this theater mounts a variety of exceptional productions including world premiere drama, original works, and multimedia presentations. The 300-seat state-of-the-art theater is on the Avenue of the Arts.

Dinner Theaters

(See NIGHTLIFE, Cabarets, Dinner Theaters, and Supper Clubs.)

NIGHTLIFE

With the revitalization of Center City, the opening of the Convention Center, the awakening of the waterfront, and the launching of the Avenue of the Arts, nightlife in Philadelphia has taken off. In a city where the question used to be "Should we go out?" the question has now become "Which place tonight?" From lavish nightclubs to intimate piano bars, from Irish pubs to throbbing jazz spots, from comedy houses and cabarets to Las Vegas revues, Philadelphia's night spots are alive with unprecedented energy, quality, and yes, sheer fun.

For the young—or the young-at-heart—or the curious, Philadelphia's South Street can be considered a nightlife entity in itself. Not only is it home to dozens of restaurants, bars, and comedy clubs, but it is the place to stroll, to gawk at some of the more bizarre Philadelphians, and to shop in some oddball boutiques that stay open until the wee hours. Check the Dining section for many entertainment spots already listed.

NIGHTLIFE BY AREA

BUCKS COUNTY
Comedy Cabaret, Comedy
Comedy Works, Georgine's Restaurant, Comedy
Golden Plough Inn, Music for Listening and Dancing
Paso Doble Ballroom, Music for Listening and Dancing
Peddler's Village Murder Mystery Dinner Theater, Cabarets, Dinner Theaters, and Supper Clubs

CENTER CITY
Circles Off The Square, Warwick Hotel, Bars

Doc Watson's Pub, Bars
Frank Clements, Bars
The Irish Pub, Bars
J.J.'s Grotto Restaurant, Music for Listening and Dancing
Park Hyatt Philadelphia at the Bellevue, Music for Listening and Dancing
Polly Esther's Nightclub, Music for Listening and Dancing
Roxy Screening Rooms, Film
Social Club, Music for Listening and Dancing
Zanzibar Blue, Music for Listening and Dancing

112

CENTER CITY— FAIRMOUNT AREA

North Star Bar, Cabarets, Dinner Theaters, and Supper Clubs
Philadelphia Museum of Art, Film

CENTER CITY—PARKWAY

Academy of Natural Sciences, Film
Free Library of Philadelphia, Film
Four Seasons Hotel, Music for Listening and Dancing
Mace's Crossing, Bars
Tuttleman's IMAX Theater, Film

CHESTER COUNTY

Binni & Flynn's, Bars

MAIN LINE AREA AND CITY AVENUE

Comedy Cabaret, Comedy
Friday's, Bars
Radnor Hotel, Music for Listening and Dancing

MONTGOMERY COUNTY

Bennigan's, Bars
Lily Langtry's Showroom and Victorian Restaurant, Cabarets, Dinner Theaters, and Supper Clubs
Shadows, Sheraton Valley Forge Hotel, Music for Listening and Dancing
United Artists King of Prussia Stadium 15 and IMAX Theatre, Film

NORTHEAST PHILADELPHIA

Comedy Cabaret, Comedy

NORTHWEST PHILADELPHIA

Campbell's Place, Bars
Chestnut Hill Hotel, Bars
McNally's Tavern, Bars

OLD CITY—SOCIETY HILL

Brasil's Restaurant and Nightspot, Music for Listening and Dancing
Café Sassafras, Bars
Dickens' Inn Tavern, Bars
Khyber, Music for Listening and Dancing
President's Room, Old Original Bookbinder's, Bars
Ritz 5, Film
Society Hill Hotel, Bars
Tin Angel, Music for Listening and Dancing

QUEEN VILLAGE AND SOUTH STREET

Copabanana, Bars
Downey's, Bars
Monte Carlo Living Room, and the Primavera, Music for Listening and Dancing
MontSerrat American Bistro, Bars
Mystery Café Dinner Theater at Bistro Romano, Cabarets, Dinner Theaters, and Supper Clubs
Ulana's, Music for Listening and Dancing

SOUTH PHILADELPHIA AND AIRPORT

Philly Legends Sports Bar and Grille, Music for Listening and Dancing

UNIVERSITY CITY

Cavanaugh's, Cabarets, Dinner Theaters, and Supper Clubs
International House Film and Folklife Center, Film

WATERFRONT

Baja Beach Club, Music for Listening and Dancing

Dave & Buster's, Bars
Deco Nightclub, Music for Listening and Dancing
Egypt Nightclub, Music for Listening and Dancing
Katmandu, Music for Listening and Dancing

Rock Lobster, Bars
Spirit of Philadelphia, Cabarets, Dinner Theaters, and Supper Clubs
Warmdaddy's, Music for Listening and Dancing

See WATERFRONT listings in DINING section for descriptions of numerous other exciting clubs.

Bars

Bennigan's, 160 N. Gulph Rd., King of Prussia; 610-337-0633. Several locations. These friendly spots offer a happy hour from 5-7 pm.

Binni & Flynn's Cantina, Gateway Shopping Center, Wayne; 610-293-0880. Southwest cantina bar and restaurant where you can enjoy nachos, burritos, enchiladas, and tacos. Entertainment Wed-Sat.

Café Sassafras, 48 S. Second St.; 215-925-2317. Enjoy a typical French bistro where Philadelphians gather around an original bar that's more than 100 years old. The menu is highlighted by gourmet hamburgers, spinach salads, and onion soup.

Campbell's Place, 8337 Germantown Ave.; 215-242-2066. The upstairs cozy bar ranks among Philadelphia's best with soups, sandwiches, and homemade desserts. Come well-dressed.

Chestnut Hill Hotel, 8229 Germantown Ave.; 215-247-7570. Relax to piano music in the Chestnut Grill and Lounge. Tue-Sun.

Circles Off The Square, Seventeenth and Locust Sts.; 215-790-7785. This inviting restaurant and bar is in the Warwick Hotel.

Copabanana, Fourth and South Sts.; 215-923-6180. A fun spot, as the name suggests, with an island theme; three bars, two downstairs, one up, and a fine selection of Mexican food.

Dave & Buster's, Pier 19, 325 N. Columbus Blvd.; 215-413-1951. In their own words: "Over 70,000 square feet of great food and great fun." A playground for grown-ups with state-of-the-art electronic simulators and lively music. Lunch and dinner.

Dickens' Inn Tavern, 421 S. Second St.; 215-928-9307. This authentic Old English pub (separate from the well-known restaurant) offers a wide selection of imported beers and ales. Menu features Shepherd's Pie, beefeater sandwiches, and fish and chips served in English newspapers. Dart board, of course.

Doc Watson's Pub, 216 S. Eleventh St.; 215-922-3427. This rustic, woodsy saloon has three floors with a bar on each level and offers 32 domestic and imported beers. Music and games can be enjoyed on the second floor nightly. The complete menu features daily and weekly specials.

Downey's, Front and South Sts.; 215-625-9500. This is a very popular place for the after-work crowd. Downstairs is a rustic bar (it used to be in a Dublin bank) with walls covered with newspaper pages of historic significance. Upstairs, in the lovely brass and mahogany dining room, piano and guitar music can be heard nightly, and a strolling string ensemble can be enjoyed on Saturday nights and at Sunday brunch. (See DINING.)

Frank Clements, 224 S. Fifteenth St.; 215-985-9600. Here's an interesting little saloon, dating from the 1920s, where Center City businessmen provide their own entertainment.

Friday's, 4000 City Line Ave.; 215-878-7070. Friday's is pleasantly cluttered with woodsy atmosphere, stained glass, tile ceiling, catering to the after-work crowd. Happy hour with free buffet 4-7. Sunday Brunch.

The Irish Pub, 2007 Walnut St.; 215-568-5603. St. Patrick's Day is always celebrated in this pub. Stained glass, posters, and maps of Ireland enhance the walls. The menu features corned beef and cabbage, Irish stew, and pork chops, along with imported beers.

Mace's Crossing, 1714 Cherry St.; 215-564-5203. At this popular little spot on the Parkway, the after-work crowd likes to unwind. While the sun is setting, enjoy a drink on the small outdoor patio.

McNally's Tavern, 8634 Germantown Ave.; 215-247-9736. Since 1921, this has been a casual, friendly spot known for its scrumptious sandwiches. Outside, look for the green door. Inside, ask for the "Schmitter." Foreign and domestic beers on tap.

MontSerrat American Bistro, 623 South St.; 215-627-4224. This attractive, woodsy bar and restaurant is known for the large selection of food at reasonable prices, and the award-winning desserts. Outdoor café, and Sunday Brunch with chamber music. Lounge features live jazz.

President's Room, 125 Walnut St.; 215-925-7027. The bar in Old Original Bookbinder's is one of the finest in Philadelphia. Enjoy the drinks while you scan the antiques.

Rock Lobster, on the Delaware at Vine St.; 215-627-ROCK. Philadelphia Magazine says you'll find "The most convivial mix of people, the best food and the most fun." There's a happy hour and live music to accompany the upscale lunch and dinner served in a casual outdoor atmosphere.

Society Hill Hotel, Third and Chestnut Sts.; 215-925-1394. The first bed-and-breakfast hotel in Philadelphia features a modern, good-looking bar. There's lots of carved wood, stained glass, and flowers, with large windows overlooking Independence Park. Popular drinks are made with freshly squeezed citrus juices. Jazz piano Tuesday through Saturday night and also during Sunday brunch.

Cabarets, Dinner Theaters, and Supper Clubs

Cavanaugh's Restaurant, 119 S. Thirty-ninth St.; 215-386-4889 and 662-5000. See an entertaining show along with the excellent food.

Lily Langtry's Showroom and Victorian Restaurant, North Gulph Rd. & First Ave., King of Prussia; 610-337-LILY. Located in the Sheraton Valley Forge, Lily's presents a highly energetic Las Vegas revue and variety show. There are lavish production numbers and much changing of costumes in a Victorian atmosphere of hand painted skylights, glittering chandeliers, and balconies. Lunch or dinner is served before the show. Tue-Sat.

Mystery Café Dinner Theater at Bistro Romano, 120 Lombard St.; 215-238-1313. Musical comedy productions on Fridays and Saturdays. Call for details.

North Star Bar, Twenty-seventh and Poplar Sts.; 215-684-0808. This cabaret has music, comedians, poets, and lots of fun. Original, live music Wed-Sat with local legends and national touring groups. The spot is also known for its chili served in bread bowls.

Peddler's Village Murder Mystery Dinner Theater, Rts. 202 and 263, Lahaska; 215-794-4010. From July to September you can enjoy a hearty country buffet together with a spine-tingling show.

Spirit of Philadelphia, docks at The Great Plaza at Penn's Landing; 215-923-1419. A revue is performed by your waiters and waitresses while you cruise the Delaware. There are also two dance bands.

Comedy

Comedy Cabaret. Multiple locations including: Best Western Hotel, 11580 Roosevelt Blvd; 215-676-5653. Montgomery Grill, 261 Montgomery Ave., Bala Cynwyd; 610-664-4451. Poco's, 625 Main St., Doylestown; 215-345-5653. Comedy entertainment with open mike nights and star searches.

Comedy Works, 1320 Newport Rd., Bristol; 215-741-1661. Located in Georgine's Restaurant, the shows are Friday and Saturday nights. Dinner is optional.

Music for Listening and Dancing

Baja Beach Club, 939 N. Delaware Ave.;215-928-9979. A wild place to party.

Brasil's Restaurant and Nightspot, 112 Chestnut St.; 215-413-1700. As its name suggests, the music is Latin, reggae, and Cuban.

Deco Nightclub, Spring Garden Plaza, Front and Spring Garden Sts.; 215-923-6001. An upscale after-hours club for music and dancing. Call for membership information.

Egypt Nightclub, 520 N. Christopher Columbus Blvd.; 215-922-6500. Spirited dancing on a bi-level dance floor.

Four Seasons Hotel, One Logan Square; 215-963-1500. The Swann Lounge offers piano and dancing on Friday and Saturday nights.

Golden Plough Inn, Peddler's Village, Rt. 202 & Street Rd., Lahaska; 215-794-4004 and 794-4020. Jazz piano bar and other live entertainment Fri and Sat at Jenny's Restaurant.

J.J's Grotto Restaurant/Jazz Club, Twenty-first and Chestnut Sts.; 215-988-9255. Live jazz Tue-Sat nights.

Katmandu, Pier 25, 417 N. Columbus Blvd.; 215-629-1101. Live music and nightly DJs. The dancing is "Best of Philly."

Khyber, 56 S. Second St.; 215-238-5888. British pub-style eating and drinking spot with entertainment nightly. Features aggressive rock and new wave. You've got a choice of more than 100 kinds of beer and imported wine.

Monte Carlo Living Room, and the Primavera, Second and South Sts.; 215-925-2220. Situated above what may be the most handsomely appointed restaurant in town, the Monte Carlo Living Room is one of the city's most exclusive night spots, and one of its most expensive. Dance on imported Italian marble and stroll on carpets that seem like velvet. There's also a balcony, smoked mirrors, glass ceilings, and comfortable sofas. For a less expensive alternative, visit the pleasurable Primavera.

Park Hyatt Philadelphia at the Bellevue, 1415 Chancellor Court at Broad and Walnut Sts., 215-893-1234, 800-233-1234. There's live piano and much more on the weekends.

Paso Doble Ballroom, 4501 New Falls Rd., Levittown; 215-547-2311. Those who want to show off their dancing talents will love this large ballroom and its live band music. For those who may require a few tips, dance lessons are available.

Philly Legends Sports Bar & Grille, Tenth and Packer Ave.; 215-755-9500. Located in the Holiday Inn Philadelphia Stadium, and has over 40 TVs and dancing, too.

Polly Esther's Nightclub, 1201 Race St.; 215-851-0776. Right behind the Convention Center, this is an authentic 1970s and '80s club with a "Saturday Night Fever" lit up dance floor, a Brady Bunch wall, and DJs taking requests all night.

Radnor Hotel, 591 E. Lancaster Ave., St. Davids; 610-688-5800. Live entertainment and dancing on Friday evenings.

Shadows, Sheraton Valley Forge Hotel, Route 363, King of Prussia; 610-337-2000. This dazzling nightclub with its special lights, sound system, and sunken dance floor features dancing from Wednesday through Saturday nights.

Social Club, 2009 Sansom St.; 215-564-2277. Located above the Academy of Social Dance, this place is open to the public 9-11:30 pm Thursday nights, featuring disco, Latin, slow dance, and waltzing to the sound system.

Tin Angel, 20 S. Second St.; 215-928-0978. Above Serrano restaurant in Old City, this is the place for anyone who loves folk music and wants to do some serious listening.

Ulana's, 205 Bainbridge; 215-922-4152. Ulana's is a unique multistory Queen Village bar, restaurant, and club. Continental cuisine in the dim and cozy restaurant downstairs, and after dinner, go upstairs for the dancing. Occasional music on weekends.

Warmdaddy's, 4 S. Front St.; 215-627-2500. An upscale club with live music. "The #1 blues club on the East Coast."

Zanzibar Blue, 200 S. Broad St.; 215-732-5200. You'll find big name performers here and live jazz every night.

Film

Following a nationwide trend, there is a growing interest in films in exciting Philadelphia. The following list offers the best schedules for repertory cinema, foreign film, and classics.

International House Film and Folklife Center, 3701 Chestnut St.; 215-387-5125. Neighborhood Film/Video Project: A showcase of works produced by independent filmmakers along with a series of foreign films. Guest speakers often appear with their movies, and occasionally a workshop is staged with the film program. Philadelphia Film Festival of World Cinema: A citywide 12-day festival each May, screening over 100 films from around the world.

Ritz 5, 214 Walnut St.; 215-925-7900. This theater presents quality first-run foreign films. Classy clientele, extremely comfortable seats.

Roxy Screening Rooms, 2023 Sansom St.; 215-923-6699. Two screening rooms of 132 seats each. Limited runs of obscure films and revivals, and more commercial movies.

Special films and series are presented at the following centers:

Academy of Natural Sciences, Nineteenth St. and the Parkway; 215-299-1000. Throughout the year the Academy's 425-seat auditorium presents motion pictures and animated cartoons relating to animals, the history of dinosaurs, and nature. Free with admission. Check newspapers for times and schedules.

Free Library of Philadelphia, Central Library on Logan Square, Nineteenth and Vine Sts., and at branches; 215-686-5322. A series of free films is shown on an irregular basis at 2 pm Sunday in the Montgomery Auditorium except during summer. Topics vary and include everything from MGM musicals to aviation, foreign movies, and travel. Regional libraries also present a free film series. Check newspapers for times and schedules.

Philadelphia Museum of Art, Van Pelt Auditorium, Twenty-sixth St. and the Parkway; 215-763-8100. Special movies are often shown in conjunction with the current exhibitions. Children's films are shown occasionally on Sundays.

Tuttleman IMAX Theater, at the Franklin Institute, Twentieth and Benjamin Franklin Pkwy.; 215-448-1111. Tickets: 215-448-1254. A mind-boggling four-story wrap-around theater, showing Omnimax movies: Spectacular science films about people, animals, nature, the environment, and space. Futures Center and Omniverse Theater are open Mon-Wed 9:30-5, Thu-Sun until 9.

United Artists King of Prussia Stadium 15 and IMAX Theatre, Mall Blvd., across from The Plaza at King of Prussia; 610-222-UAUA. IMAX on a giant five-story screen and blockbuster films on 15 wall-to-wall curved screens.

SIGHTS

As the birthplace of the American democratic process, Philadelphia is without question one of the most historic cities of the United States, a city flourishing with names like Washington, Jefferson, and Franklin as if these men were old and trusted friends, which in fact they once were. From stately Independence Mall to historic Germantown, from battle-scarred Old Fort Mifflin to the haunting Brandywine Valley and the rolling meadows of Valley Forge, Philadelphia with its surrounding counties is *the* place where the United States began, and an omnipresent reminder of when, why, and how.

While many visitors come in search of the nation's roots—in the historic buildings, churches, mansions, homes, and museums (there are more than 90 museums in Philadelphia alone)—they invariably discover much, much more than was originally expected. Among these new discoveries are the parks and arboretums, the wildlife refuges and bird sanctuaries, colonial plantations and homesteads, excellent zoos and amusement parks, even a nineteenth-century ironmaking community meticulously restored.

One of Philadelphia's strongest attributes is its wealth of sights, many of which are free or available at a very nominal fee. To see the following six of the most popular attractions at a discount price, purchase the City Pass for $29.50 for adults: (lower price for seniors and youths): Philadelphia Museum of Art, Franklin Institute Science Museum, Philadelphia Zoo, Academy of Natural Sciences, Independence Seaport Museum, and the New Jersey State Aquarium. The Pass can be purchased at any of the six locations and is valid for nine days. For more information, contact the Visitor's Center at 215-636-1666; 800-537-7676.

Below we have listed as many historic, interesting, intriguing, and varied sights as space permits. Since there may be slight changes in the individual schedules or hours, we recommend that you call in advance of your visit.

Please note: In addition to the sights listed below, you will find the Independence Park area and many more attractions in our walking tours, Metro and Main Line/Brandywine Valley driving tours, and one-day excursions. Historic Germantown and Historic Places of Worship are in separate sections of this chapter.

120

SIGHTS BY AREA

BERKS COUNTY
Daniel Boone Homestead
Hopewell Furnace

BUCKS COUNTY
Andalusia

CENTER CITY
Academy of Music
African-American Historical and
 Cultural Museum
American-Swedish Historical
 Museum
Arch St. United Methodist Church
The Atheneum of Philadelphia
Atwater Kent Museum
The Balch Institute for Ethnic
 Studies
Civil War Library Museum
Congregation Rodeph Shalom
Eastern State Penitentiary
Edgar Allen Poe House
Historical Society of Pennsylvania
Library Company of Philadelphia
Mutter Museum
The National Shrine of St. John
 Neumann
Rosenbach Museum and Library
Shoe Museum

CENTER CITY AND
THE PARKWAY
Academy of Natural Sciences
Franklin Institute Science Museum
Free Library of Philadelphia
Please Touch Museum

CHESTER COUNTY
Chester County Historical Society
Historic Yellow Springs
Swiss Pines Garden

DELAWARE COUNTY
Brinton 1704 House
Caleb Pusey House
Chanticleer, a Pleasure Garden
Colonial Pennsylvania Plantation
Franklin Mint Museum
John Chad House
John Heinz National Wildlife
 Refuge at Tinicum
Newlin Mill
Thomas Massey House
Tyler Arboretum

LANCASTER COUNTY
Hershey Park

MONTGOMERY COUNTY
Clifton House
Elmwood Park Zoo
Graeme Park
Highlands Historical Society
Hope Lodge
Mill Grove
Morgan Log House
Peter Wentz Farmstead

NORTH PHILADELPHIA
Wagner Free Institute of Science

NORTHEAST PHILADELPHIA
Pennypack Environmental Center
Ryerss Museum and Library

NORTHWEST PHILADELPHIA
Historic Germantown, separate
 section
Morris Arboretum
Schuylkill Nature Center for
 Environmental Education

OLD CITY—SOCIETY HILL
Arch St. Meeting House

Betsy Ross House
Christ Church
Congregation Mikveh Israel
Historic Old St Augustine's
    Catholic Church
Historic St. George's Methodist
    Church
Lights of Liberty
Mother Bethel A.M.E. Church
National Museum of American
    Jewish History
Old First Reformed Church
Old Pine Presbyterian Church
Old St. Joseph's Church
Pennsylvania Hospital
Philadelphia Vietnam Veteran
    Memorial
Society Hill Synagogue
St. Mary's Church

St. Peter's Church
Welcome Park

QUEEN VILLAGE
Gloria Dei Old Swedes Church
Queen Village, description

SOUTH PHILADELPHIA
Fort Mifflin
Mario Lanza Institute and Museum
Mummers Museum

SOUTHWEST PHILADELPHIA
Bartram's Gardens

UNIVERSITY CITY
University Museum of Archaeology
    and Anthropology

Academy of Music, Broad and Locust Sts.; 215-893-1935. CH. The official home of the Philadelphia Orchestra from 1900 until its twenty-first-century move to the new Performing Arts Center, the "Grand Old Lady of Locust Street" celebrated its 140th anniversary on January 23, 1997. Since most of the $250,000 that was raised to build the Academy was used in the magnificent crimson, gold, and cream interior, the exterior was left "plain like a market house" so that a marble front might one day be added. It never was, however, because through the decades the mellowed brick brownstone and cast-iron exterior became most representative of historical Philadelphia. There are one-hour afternoon tours of this Registered National Historic Landmark (see PERFORMING ARTS).

Academy of Natural Sciences, Nineteenth St. and Benjamin Franklin Parkway; 215-299-1000. CH. Founded in 1812, this is the oldest natural history and science research museum in the country. It exhibits animals in their natural habitat. The bird, fish, and plant collections are among the most comprehensive in the world, including bird specimens that were used as models by Audubon. Plant specimens were gathered by Lewis and Clark during their explorations of the West. Thomas Jefferson's own fossil collection even found a home here. Visitors are always fascinated by the exhibit of the 65-million-year-old dinosaur. The Academy also features Outside-In, a nature museum designed especially for children. Those ages 12 and under can try to lift a meteorite, find dinosaur footprints in a slab of pre-historic rock, and crawl through a fossil cave. The Academy's division of education also presents live animal "Eco-Shows."

African-American Historical and Cultural Museum, Seventh and Arch Sts.; 215-574-0380. CH. This is the world's most comprehensive museum of the African-American past, tracing the roots of black history, art, and culture from Africa to the United States. Five galleries are filled with maps, masks, hairstyles, model slave ships, art, and sculpture; the Fine Arts gallery features a wealth of graphics, oils, and watercolors. Tue-Sat 10 am-5 pm, Sun 12-5 pm.

American Swedish Historical Museum, 1900 Pattison Ave.; 215-389-1776. CH *(children under 12 NCH when accompanied by an adult).* Modeled after a seventeenth-century Swedish manor house, the museum is located on land that was settled by the Swedes prior to Penn's arrival in 1682. It has 14 galleries of materials depicting 300 years of Swedish contributions to American life that include early glass, textiles, paintings, drawings, and etchings. Many of the rooms are accented by the finest in twentieth-century Swedish architecture. Library, gift shop. Tue-Fri 10 am-4 pm, Sat-Sun noon-4 pm.

Andalusia, north of Philadelphia, on the Delaware River, Andalusia; 215-245-5479. CH. This was the first mature Greek Revival mansion in America, and is one of the best known country estates from Philadelphia's Federal period. Built in 1795, it was later occupied by Nicholas Biddle, director of the Second Bank of the United States. Members of the Biddle family still live here. Hours by appointment.

The Atheneum of Philadelphia, 219 S. Sixth St.; 215-925-2688. NCH. Named for the classical Greek goddess of wisdom, The Atheneum was founded in 1814 by members of The American Philosophical Society and is housed in a National Historic Landmark building that was called "the handsomest edifice in the city" when it opened in the mid-nineteenth-century. As the first major structure in America to be built in the Italianate Revival style, it was authentically restored to its former grandeur in 1975. It maintains an independent research library specializing in nineteenth-century social and cultural history. Guided tours Mon-Fri 10:30 am and 2 pm.

Atwater Kent Museum, 15 S. Seventh St.; 215-922-3031. CH. This handsome marble building is Philadelphia's own history museum, depicting everyday life in the city through its 300 years of existence. Displays include antique working clocks, hammers and saws, political posters, sunbonnets, train tickets, toys, guns, swords, ship models, even cigar store Indians. Wed-Mon 10 am-4 pm.

The Balch Institute for Ethnic Studies, 18 S. Seventh St.; 215-925-8090. CH. Founded in 1971, this museum and library explores the history of immigration and the melding of more than 100 ethnic cultures in the United States. Documents, clothes, household goods, and other artifacts reveal what immigrants brought and how and where they lived after arriving. You can sit on a genuine Ellis Island bench while learning about the millions of immigrants who sat on such benches before you. "Discovering America: The Peopling of Pennsylvania," is on permanent display, and "Do Your Own Heritage" is an interactive video display that allows you to learn more about your roots. Museum Tue-Sat 10 am-4 pm, Library Mon-Sat 9 am-5 pm.

Bartram's Garden, Fifty-fourth St. and Lindbergh Blvd.; 215-729-5281. CH. Started in 1728 by John Bartram, a Quaker, this is the oldest botanical garden in the nation. Encouraged to pursue his botanical interests by Benjamin Franklin and James Logan, Bartram later traveled extensively, returning with seeds and roots that he planted in his garden, observed, propagated, and shipped abroad. In 1765 King George III appointed him a Royal Botanist. Bartram's former home also is on the 27-acre property, which is ideal for picnicking. House tours: April-December Wed-Sun noon-4 pm; January-March Wed-Fri. Grounds are free and open 9 am-4 pm daily. The garden can be reached by taking the #36 trolley from City Hall.

Betsy Ross House, 239 Arch St.; 215-627-5343. *Voluntary contributions*. This two-story Colonial home is where Betsy Ross lived and where she is credited with sewing the nation's first flag. Tue-Sun 10 am-5 pm and holiday Mondays.

The Brinton 1704 House, 1435 Oakland Rd., south of Dilworthtown, Chester County; 610-399-0913. CH. In the rolling hills of the Brandywine Valley, this is one of the most authentic restorations in the state. It was built in 1704 by William Brinton, based on his memories of medieval English architecture. Inventories taken at his death in 1751 provided his descendants with the authentic basis upon which this restored Quaker house is furnished. Open Sat and Sun, May-September, noon-5 pm.

The Caleb Pusey House, 15 Race St., Upland; 610-874-5665. CH. This is the last remaining house in Pennsylvania William Penn is known to have visited. His good friend, Caleb Pusey, was Pennsylvania's first historian, and also managed the Chester Mills, a saw and grist mill set up by Penn and his partners. Pusey built this house in 1683. It is now completely restored. On the 12 acres there is also a 1790 log house, an 1849 schoolhouse museum, a gift shop, and picnic tables. May-September Tue, Thu, Fri, Sat, 10 am-4 pm.

Chanticleer, a Pleasure Garden, 786 Church Rd., Wayne; 610-687-4163. CH. A botanical garden to soothe the soul, featuring perennials, containers, vegetable gardens, woodlands and wildflowers. April-October Wed-Sat 10 am-5 pm.

Chester County Historical Society, 225 N. High St., West Chester;

Reflections of the Betsy Ross House in Old City

Bob Krist for the Greater Philadelphia Tourism Marketing Corporation

610-692-4800. CH. This museum and library has an extensive collection of more than 50,000 examples of furniture, textiles, metals, and ceramics reflecting history of the area. Extensive printed materials, manuscripts, and genealogical data ideal for family research are also available. Mon-Fri, Sat, 9 am-5 pm. Groups by appointment.

Civil War Library and Museum, 1805 Pine St.; 215-735-8196. CH. This is a recognized national research center for the Civil War. Among its highlights are two life masks of Lincoln, a dress uniform and presentation sword of Gen. Ulysses S. Grant, flags, guns, uniforms, and relics from the War Between the States. Tue-Sat 11 am-4:30 pm.

Clifton House, 473 Bethlehem Pike, Fort Washington; 215-646-6065. NCH. Located in the heart of the Whitemarsh encampment area, this house stands on the site of the original Sandy Run Inn, where the cold, hungry men of Washington's army once stayed in the tavern's common room. The tavern burned down in 1802, was rebuilt, burned down again in 1852, was rebuilt again and named Clifton House for the steep cliff that was in back of it at the time. Its museum is one of the finest small museums and historical libraries in Pennsylvania. It was on the three nearby hills that the Continental Army watched over British-occupied Philadelphia from November 2 to December 11, 1777, prior to its march to Valley Forge. Museum first and third Sun of the month 2-4 pm, Library Wed 2-4 pm and 7-9 pm. Closed July and August.

The Colonial Pennsylvania Plantation, in Ridley Creek State Park off Route 3, three miles west of its intersection with Route 252 in Newtown Square; 610-566-1725. CH. Watch an eighteenth-century farmer and his helpers go about daily chores on this "Living History Farm," where the original acres date back to a patent by William Penn's commissioners. The farmhouse, springhouse, store, barns, even the horses, cattle, sheep, and pigs, are much the same as they were in the 1770s. April-November Sat-Sun 10 am-5 pm. Group tours Tue-Fri by reservation. Call for details about the Colonial Craft Fair.

Daniel Boone Homestead, Route 82, just north of Route 422, Birdsboro; 610-582-4900. CH. Though he's most identified with the settling of the West, Daniel Boone, son of Quaker parents, was born in a log house here in November 1734. At the time, this area of Berks County was on the fringes of the wilderness, and it was here that Boone learned to hunt, trap, and shoot. Sometime in the eighteenth century, the log house was replaced by the two-story stone structure that has been carefully restored to its original flavor. Tue-Sat 9-5, Sun noon-5.

Edgar Allen Poe House, 532 N. Seventh St.; 215-597-8780. NCH. The famed poet and writer enjoyed his most productive and contented years in Philadelphia, where he lived from 1838 to 1844. It was here that he resided in 1843 with his wife Virginia, and her mother, Mrs. Clemm, writing "The Black Cat," "The Tell Tale Heart," and "The

Gold Bug." It was in Philadelphia that Poe achieved his greatest success as an editor and critic. Of Poe's several homes in Philadelphia, this is the only one that survives, and Congress has selected the site as the nation's memorial to him. Winter hours: Wed-Sun 9 am-5 pm, except Christmas Day and New Year's Day.

Eastern State Penitentiary, Twenty-second St. and Fairmount Ave.; 215-236-3300. *CH.* This used to be home to the likes of Willie Sutton and Al Capone, but today it's a prison museum and site of special tours, performances and events. It was designed innovatively in the 1820s when prison reformers believed solitary confinement would lead to rehabilitation—not insanity, as it did in many cases—and it became a much-copied model before it finally locked its gates in 1971. Call for hours. Children under seven cannot be admitted.

Elmwood Park Zoo, Harding Blvd., Norristown; 610-277-3825. *CH.* If you've been touring the sites and battlefields of Valley Forge, this will provide an ideal break for the children. It's clean and friendly, with paths leading past cages housing all kinds of favorite animals, including monkeys and lions. There's a reptile house, an aviary, and a petting zoo. Daily 10 am-4 pm. Extended weekend and summer hours.

Fort Mifflin, Island Ave. and Fort Mifflin Rd. near Philadelphia International Airport; 215-492-1881. *CH.* It was in 1772 that the British began to build this fort, but it was the Continental Army that completed it in 1776 under the direction of Benjamin Franklin. The British then won back the fort after seven weeks of fierce fighting, during which more than 250 patriot soldiers were killed. Twenty years after the war, Fort Mifflin was rebuilt. During the Civil War, the fort served as a prison for military deserters, and was an active military installation until 1959. Now a National Historic Landmark, the fort is operated by the Atwater Kent Museum and contains such vivid reminders of the Revolution as cannons, officers' and soldiers' quarters, and their arsenal. Outside is one of the oldest houses in Philadelphia, built by a Swedish settler in the 1660s. After being scarred by cannon fire during the attack on the fort during the Revolution, it was dubbed the "Cannonball Farmhouse." Tours, uniform and weapon demonstrations, soldier life programs. Open April-November. Wed-Sun 10-4. Weekdays by reservation only.

The Franklin Institute Science Museum, Twentieth St. and Benjamin Franklin Parkway; 215-448-1200. *CH.* Founded in 1824 and named for Benjamin Franklin, the Institute consists of four parts: Science Center and Fels Planetarium; Mandell Futures Center; Tuttleman Omniverse Theater; Benjamin Franklin National Memorial. You can walk through a human heart or play the world's largest pinball machine. The Institute pioneered the use of computer exhibitions, becoming the nation's first push-button museum of science and

Benjamin Franklin Memorial at the
Franklin Institute Science Museum

Greater Philadelphia Tourism
Marketing Corporation

technology. From the beginning, the Institute included a 350-ton Baldwin locomotive, and now it includes airplanes, helicopters, and space capsules. Under the dome of Fels Planetarium, one is introduced to the mysteries and wonders of the universe, in particular the sun, moon, and stars. Multimedia shows are presented daily, and several public shows are given each year. The Omniverse Theater, with its four-stories-high screen, presents Imax movies that rush you through rapids and shoot you to the moon. The museum is also the site of the Benjamin Franklin Memorial, dedicated in 1938, and, in 1972, designated by Congress as the official national memorial to Franklin. In honor of the museum's 175th anniversary in 1999, it installed "Franklin—He's Electric," a must-see, 5,500-square foot permanent interactive display, highlighting Franklin's multitude of achievements in the fields of optics, agriculture, meteorology, medicine, astronomy, engineering and electricity. Science Center: Open daily 9:30-5. Futures Center and Omniverse Theater, Mon-Wed 9:30 am-5 pm, Thu-Sun 9:30 am-9 pm. Call for prices and show hours. The Institute offers restaurants, shops, and a parking garage.

The Franklin Mint Museum, Route One, Franklin Center, Media; 610-459-6168. *NCH.* This is the world's largest private mint, producing limited edition coins, medals, and objects in honor of world figures and events. The museum features a remarkable range of art in precious metals, bronze, pewter, crystal, and porcelain, as well as books, recordings, graphics, jewelry, and furniture, also original works by Wyeth, Rockwell, and other renowned artists. The highlight is watching the mint's manufacturing process in various mediums, and chances are you'll be able to watch a craftsman making a Franklin Mint collectible on the spot. The omnipresent film describes the art of minting from start to finish. Mon-Sat 9:30 am-4:30 pm, Sun 1-4:30 pm.

Free Library of Philadelphia, Central Branch, Logan Square; 215-686-5322. *NCH.* Designed by Julian Abele, this is a replica of the Ministry of Marine on the Place de la Concorde in Paris. More than 6 million books, magazines, newspapers, recordings, and other materials are housed here. Among its treasures are the world's largest collection of automated history, the world's largest collection of orchestral scores, and Philadelphia's largest collection of children's books. Its Rare Book department features, among a myriad of stunning collections, original manuscripts and first editions of works by Charles Dickens and Edgar Allen Poe. There are daily tours. On Sunday afternoons, the Library presents films, concerts, lectures, and children's programs. The exhibits in the main lobby change regularly.

Graeme Park, One-half mile west of Route 611 on County Line Rd., Horsham; 215-343-0965. *CH.* William Keith erected the buildings on this lovely rural setting in 1721-22, not so much for a residence as for a place to manufacture alcohol (he called it "Fountain Low"). Eventually he fell into conflict with the Penn family, which had appointed him Provincial Governor. After they removed him from office in 1726, Keith lived here briefly before returning to England. Dr. Thomas Graeme, a respected Philadelphia physician, bought the property as a country estate and entertained a great deal. His daughter Elizabeth, however, emerged as a tragic and controversial figure; according to legend, her ghost still walks the estate at night. Tours of the Keith House: Wed-Sat 10 am-4 pm, Sun noon-4 pm. In June, the park hosts Living History Day.

Hershey Park, Exit 20 on the Pennsylvania Turnpike, then follow the signs; 800-HERSHEY. CH. This is the centerpiece of the town which rose around Milton Snavely Hershey's chocolate factory. Started by Hershey shortly after the turn of the century as an amusement park for his employees, it now includes 87 acres, virtually in the center of town, with 8 theme areas, 36 rides, and 5 entertainment centers. Its four roller coasters are among the scariest in the nation. The 11-acre Zoo America features more than 200 North American animals, birds, and reptiles, and the Aqua Theater has performances by dolphins and sea lions. Adjacent to the park is Hershey's Chocolate World, where a tour highlights the history and manufacture of Hershey's chocolate, and the Hershey Museum, which features exhibits and artifacts from early Americana and serves as a tribute to the man who started it all. Open from mid-May to mid-September; call for specific times and prices.

Highlands Historical Society, 7001 Sheaff Lane, Fort Washington; 215-641-2687. CH. Built by Anthony Morris in 1796 as a "country house for entertaining," the Highlands were visited often by Morris's friends, among them Presidents Madison, Monroe, and Jefferson. Morris is credited with introducing Madison to the widowed Dolly Todd. The handsome Georgian house and the beautiful gardens surrounding it have since been faithfully restored. Office open daily 9 am-4 pm. By appointment only.

Historical Society of Pennsylvania, 1300 Locust St.; 215-732-6201. CH. There is a veritable gold mine of Pennsylvania history here, including the most comprehensive research library anywhere in the state, the largest collection of genealogical works, portraits, and scenes of the colonial period by great artists, and the largest and most important historical manuscript collection in private hands in the United States. The manuscript collection includes the voluminous archives of the Penn family, maps, prints, and drawings of the Pennsylvania scene. There is also fine Philadelphia silver and furniture, and many other fascinating items once the property of the Penn, Franklin, Washington, and Jefferson families. Tue, Thu, Fri, Sat, 10 am-4:45 pm, Wed 2-8:45 pm.

Historic Yellow Springs, off Route 113, east of its intersection with

Route 401, Chester Springs; 610-827-7414. *NCH* (donations accepted). Started in 1722 as a popular colonial spa with lodging at the inn and baths in the iron, sulfur, and magnesium mineral springs, Yellow Springs and the inn ultimately became the only Revolutionary War hospital commissioned by the Continental Congress. It later became a spa once more, then an orphanage, then the summer campus of the Pennsylvania Academy of Fine Arts and a motion picture studio until 1974. The entire village is on the National Register of Historic Places and features an elegant restaurant. The inn was remade into a hotel. Self-guided walking tour, artwork, spring craft show, fall antique show. Daily 9 am-4 pm.

Hope Lodge, 553 Bethlehem Pike, Whitemarsh; 215-646-1595. *CH.* This beautiful home in the finest Georgian tradition was built in 1750. It was occupied by Samuel Morris, a successful grist mill operator who died here in 1770, and was in the middle of various military operations during the Revolutionary War. It is named for the Hope banking family, which purchased the home in 1784. Tours: Wed-Sat 9 am-4 pm, Sun noon-4 pm.

Hopewell Furnace, Route 345, six miles south of Birdsboro; 610-582-8773. *CH.* As a magnificent restoration of this ironmaking community between 1820 and 1840, Hopewell Village brings back the time when it was famed for its stoves, pig iron, domestic and farm implements, and the cannon, shot, and shell it made for the Continental Army during the Revolutionary War. Mark Bird, who built Hopewell in 1771, was an ardent patriot who served as a colonel in the militia. Among the restored structures are the ironmaster's house, charcoal house, village barn, tenant houses, blacksmith shop, the church, and furnace. Of special interest: sheep shearing in May; "Living History" program July to Labor Day, in which employees in period costumes demonstrate the manufacturing, cooking, and domestic skills once used in this National Historic Site. Daily 9 am-5 pm.

John Chad House, Route 100 just north of Route One, Chadds Ford; 610-388-7376. *CH.* Built in 1726, this charming stone building was the home of ferryman/farmer/tavern keeper John Chad, after whom Chadds Ford was named. It has since been restored, and aromatic baked goods emerge from the beehive oven every Saturday and Sunday. Open May to September, Sat and Sun, noon-5 pm. Tours available. For tours at other times, call for an appointment.

John Heinz National Wildlife Refuge at Tinicum, Eighty-sixth St. and Lindbergh Blvd.; 215-365-3118. *NCH.* One of the largest tidal, freshwater marshes in the state of Pennsylvania, and visited by more than 275 species of birds, numerous turtles, and an abundance of wildlife, Tinicum is an outdoor delight. There are walking trails, an observation tower, and a 500-foot boardwalk through the marsh. It all goes back to the seventeenth century, when the Swedes, Dutch, and English diked and drained part of the marsh for grazing. Now migratory birds use the area as a resting and feeding spot during their flights in the spring and fall. Daily 9 am-4 pm, guided walks from the Visitors Center. Schedule available.

Library Company of Philadelphia, 1314 Locust St.; 215-546-3181. *NCH.* Benjamin Franklin founded this library in 1732, when its first books were brought from England. It is now the oldest circulating library in the nation, and contains 300,000 books. It is highlighted by such historical minutiae as the metal box in which members placed requests for books to be imported, Thomas Jefferson's personal copy of his first published book, and Lewis and Clark's guidebook for their expedition in 1804. Mon-Fri 9 am-4:45 pm.

Lights of Liberty, PECO Energy Liberty Center, Sixth and Chestnut Sts.; 877-GO-2-1776 or 215-LIBERTY. Website: www.lightsofliberty.org. *CH.* Don't miss this spectacular addition to the historic sights at Independence Mall. Wearing surround-sound headsets and following a costumed Liberty Leader, groups take an interactive tour of America's most historic square mile after dark, participating as Colonial times and the Revolution come to life. The faces of historic buildings light up with five-story moving 3-D images and special effects, while the headsets produce voices, sound, and the glorious music of the Philadelphia Orchestra. The headsets are programmed for various languages, and there's even a Whoopi Goldberg version of the tour for children. Call for hours, admission prices, and reservations.

Mario Lanza Institute and Museum, at the Settlement Music School, 416 Queen St.; 215-468-3623. *NCH.* The museum is a tribute to the great tenor who was born and raised in South Philadelphia. A large bust of the singer made by one of his fans in Hungary is on display, as are numerous photographs, gold records, personal items from his wallet, and newspaper and magazine articles recounting his thrilling yet tragic story. Recordings of Lanza's greatest hits provide background music. The museum is sponsored by the Mario Lanza Institute, which provides outstanding young talents with scholarships to the Settlement Music School, where Lanza received his early musical education. Vintage films are shown daily. Mon-Sat 10 am-3:30 pm. Closed Sat, July and August.

Mikveh Israel Cemetery, Spruce St. between Eighth and Ninth; 215-922-5446 (Congregation Mikveh Israel). *NCH.* Through the gates, you get an excellent view of the cemetery that was founded in 1738 by Nathan Levy on ground he acquired from William Penn. Among those buried here are Levy, whose ship brought the Liberty Bell to Philadelphia, Haym Salomon, one of the major financiers of the Revolutionary War, 21 veterans of the Revolution, and Rebecca Gratz, who helped establish the Hebrew Sunday School Society in 1838, and the Jewish Foster Home and Orphan Asylum in 1855. Open by appointment. Call Mikveh Israel Synagogue.

Mill Grove: The Authentic Audubon Home and Wildlife Sanctuary, Audubon Rd., west of Route 363, Audubon; 610-666-5593. *NCH.* This beautiful 130-acre estate, whose mansion (circa 1762) is the only true Audubon home still standing in America, was owned for 17 years by John James Audubon's father, a French sea captain. In 1804 the father brought his son here to supervise the estate, and it was while he roamed the wooded hills along the Perkiomen Creek and the Schuylkill River that the young Audubon gained his first impressions of American birds and wildlife. The estate is now a wildlife sanctuary with miles of trails, feeding stations, nesting boxes, and trees and shrubs attractive to birds. The mansion serves as a museum with all the major works of the world-famous naturalist, artist, and author on display. Tue-Sat 10 am-4 pm, Sun 1-4 pm.

Morgan Log House, 850 Weikel Rd., one block west of Route 363, Towamencin Township; 215-368-2480. *CH.* Built in 1695 by Daniel Boone's maternal grandparents, Edward and Elizabeth Morgan, the log house has been completely restored and is furnished with antiques from the Philadelphia Museum of Art, the Dietrich Foundation, and the Finklestein Collection. After standing virtually unnoticed for almost 300 years, it is now on the National Register of Historic Places. Tours: April-December, Thu, Sat, Sun, 10 am-6 pm. Fridays, Memorial Day to Labor Day, 6-8 pm. Other times by appointment.

Morris Arboretum, 100 Northwestern Ave., between Stenton and Germantown Aves.; 215-247-5777. *CH.* The Morris Arboretum brought to Philadelphia an institution modeled after the great British botanic gardens—the Royal Botanic Gardens of Edinburgh and Kew, and of Cambridge and Oxford Universities. Administered to by the University of Pennsylvania, this 92-acre estate is alive with 3,500 varieties of exotic and native shrubs and trees. It is particularly noted for its conifers, hollies, and azaleas, while winter accents the many evergreens and the tropical Fern House. April-October, Mon-Fri 10 am-4 pm, Sat, Sun, 10 am-5 pm.

Mummers Museum, 1100 S. Second St. at Washington Ave.; 215-336-3050. *CH.* Designed as a permanent display of Philadelphia Mummery, its history, and traditions, this museum is filled with memorabilia representing the pageantry of the famed New Year's Day parade. The parade's roots date back to pre-colonial times, and it is all evident here. Tue 9:30 am-9:30 pm. Wed-Sat 9:30 am-5 pm, Sun noon-5 pm. Free outdoor String Band concerts, Tue at 8 pm, May-Sept.

Mutter Museum, at the College of Physicians of Philadelphia, 19 S. Twenty-second St.; 215-563-3737, ext. 41. *CH.* Named for Dr. Thomas

Dent Mutter, who gave his unique collection of specimens and models to the College of Physicians of Philadelphia in 1858, the museum of medical anomalies contains a host of skeletons, surgical instruments, and medical lore that includes a seventh-century B.C. prescription tablet from Assyria. Gracing the walls of the 1909 English Renaissance building are artwork and sculpture busts by Thomas Eakins, Charles Wilson Peale, Thomas Sully, and William Rush. A garden of medicinal herbs adjoins the College Hall. Mon-Sat 10 am-4 pm, Sun noon-4 pm.

National Museum of American Jewish History, 55 N. Fifth St., Independence Mall East; 215-923-3811. CH. This is the only museum in the United States that is devoted exclusively to the role of Jewish people in the growth and achievements of America. A permanent exhibit is "Creating American Jews," with a smaller gallery featuring changing exhibits. The Museum is attached to Congregation Mikveh Israel, the oldest synagogue in Philadelphia and second oldest in America. Tours available. Gift shop with magnificent Jewish artwork. Mon-Thu 10 am-5 pm, Fri 10-3, Sun noon-5 pm. Closed Sat.

National Shrine of St. John Neumann, St. Peter the Apostle Church, Fifth St. and Girard Ave.; 215-627-3080. NCH. Saint John Neumann was the first American to be canonized by the Roman Catholic Church, the father of parochial education in America, and the fourth bishop of Philadelphia. This is his final resting-place; his body lies in a glass casket. Tue-Fri 10 am-4 pm, Sat 10 am-5 pm, Sun 1-5 pm.

Newlin Mill Park, S. Cheney Rd. off Baltimore Pike, seven miles west of Media; 610-459-2359. CH. This lovely property, which has grown to 150 acres from the original 3 1/2, contains the mill, the stone house, log cabin, blacksmith shop, and picnic tables in the woods for a pleasant day in the country. Ponds are stocked with trout, and fishing can be enjoyed for a fee, without a license. Three miles of paths wind through ancient trees. Nathaniel Newlin, a Quaker who emigrated from Ireland in 1683, built the mill in 1704. The house was built in 1739. Daily 9 am-dusk. For reservations to the picnic grove, call in advance. Office hours: daily 9-4, weekends 9-5.

Pennsylvania Hospital, Eighth and Spruce Sts.; 215-829-3971. NCH. This is the nation's oldest hospital, founded in 1751 by Benjamin Franklin and Dr. Thomas Bond. The Great Court features a gallery of portraits of the hospital's most famous men as well as colonial medical instruments and a library of rare books. There's also America's first surgical amphitheater, built in 1804 and last used in 1868. The History of Nursing Museum contains a wealth of materials tracing the development of the nursing profession. Mon-Fri 9 am-5 pm, by reservation only.

Pennypack Environmental Center, 8600A Verree Rd. near Bloomfield Ave.; 215-685-0470. NCH. The center offers 150 acres of hiking trails, with maps for self-guided walks. It is also a nature sanctuary with exhibits of local wildlife. Daily 9 am-5 pm. Hours vary, but the trails are always open. A bulletin board shows the trails and lists activities.

Peter Wentz Farmstead, Shearer Rd. off Route 73, Worcester; 610-584-5104. *NCH (donations accepted)*. This restored colonial mansion was used by George Washington before and after the Battle of Germantown and is one of the top ten tourist attractions in Pennsylvania. Based upon research, the structure is *exactly* as it was in 1777—from the bright mortar between the stones of the main house to the crisp contrast between black and white shutters. The farm includes typical eighteenth-century crops and animals, a reception center with interpreters in authentic costumes, the barn that was built in 1744, 14 years before the main house, and an orchard of apples, peaches, and pears. Tue-Sat 10 am-4 pm, Sun 1-4 pm. Groups by reservation.

Philadelphia Vietnam Veteran Memorial, Christopher Columbus Blvd. & Spruce St.; 215-636-1666. *NCH*. Dedicated in 1987 and noted for its architecture, this memorial honors the 642 Philadelphians who died during the Vietnam War.

Please Touch Museum, 210 N. Twenty-first St.; 215-963-0667. *CH*. This museum is designed specifically for children seven years and younger. It is also ideal for handicapped children 12 and under. Some of the exhibits have Braille signage. Here, the arts, sciences, technology, natural sciences, and cultural subjects are offered with an accent on sound, and on watching and petting small animals, crawling and climbing, and acting out fantasies in masks, costumes, and uniforms, as well as with puppets. Daily, 9-4:30.

Queen Village, south of Head House Sq. in Society Hill. This neighborhood is Philadelphia's oldest, originally settled in the early 1600s by the Swedes but quickly taken over by the English who made it their own. Now a neighborhood of many old homes that have been faithfully restored, Queen Village is also the site of Gloria Dei, or Old Swede's Church, at Swanson and Christian Streets. Opened in 1700, it is the oldest church in Philadelphia.

Rosenbach Museum and Library, 2010 Delancey Pl.; 215-732-1600. *CH*. This museum has earned world-wide recognition for its priceless books and manuscripts, which include the *Bay Psalm Book*, the first Bible printed in the Western Hemisphere, James Joyce's manuscript of *Ulysses,* and the manuscript of Chaucer's *Canterbury Tales*. It has the only known first copy of Benjamin Franklin's *Poor Richard's Almanac* and a letter sent to Stalin by Franklin Roosevelt and Winston Churchill. Also included are superior collections of silver, furniture, porcelain, and works of art, including artwork by author/illustrator Maurice Sendak, all initiated by the brothers Rosenbach, Philip, and Dr. A.S.W., and displayed in an elegant nineteenth-century townhouse. Tours. Tue-Sun 11 am-4 pm.

Ryerss Estate, Cottman and Central Aves.; 215-745-3061. *NCH.* The estate offers a jewel of a museum and library with a tower that has a stunning view of the Philadelphia skyline. The hilltop mansion was built in 1859 as the country home of Joseph Waln Ryerss, a wealthy Philadelphia merchant. In 1978, it was restored by architects specializing in the Victorian period, and it stands as a tribute to their expertise. Museum Sat and Sun 1-4 pm, Library Fri-Sun 10 am-5 pm. Tours of the entire estate by appointment.

Schuylkill Nature Center for Environmental Education, 8480 Hagy's Mill Rd., Upper Roxborough; 215-482-7300. *CH.* Just as Philadelphia is blessed with the largest urban park in the country, Fairmount Park, it also has the largest urban outdoor education center of any city—the Schuylkill Center. Only nine miles from Center City are 360 acres of fields, thickets, ponds, streams, and woodlands, with six miles of winding trails. On clear days, enjoy a spectacular view of Center City from the Upper Fields trail. Indoor facilities include a 5,000-volume library, the Discovery Museum, an auditorium, and a bookstore. Mon-Sat 8:30 am-5 pm, Sun 1-5 pm.

Shoe Museum, Temple University School of Podiatric Medicine, Eighth and Race Sts.; 215-625-5243. *NCH.* Children as well as adults will be amused with the college's display of more than 500 foot coverings dating from early Egyptian times to the present. Included are the skates Bernie Parent wore when the Flyers won their first Stanley Cup, the shoes Joe Frazier wore when he defeated Muhammed Ali, and Sandy Duncan's Peter Pan boots. Included in the "Foolish Foot" case is a pair of 6 1/2-inch high heels from the 1890's. The Museum's Center for the History of Foot Care and Footwear is a major historical resource. By appointment only. Office hours: Wed, Fri, 9 am-1 pm.

Swiss Pines Garden, Charlestown Rd. near Phoenixville; 610-933-6916. *CH.* Covering 11 acres, these private, formal Japanese gardens include waterfalls, stepping stones, steep paths, a beautiful bamboo forest, and a footbridge leading to a Japanese teahouse. Donated by Arnold Bartschi to the Swiss Pines Foundation, these gardens are not for picnicking, but for relaxation and meditation. No buses allowed, and no children under 12 because of the danger of open pools of water. Mon-Fri 10 am-4 pm, Sat 9-11:30 am. Closed from December 15-March 15.

Thomas Massey House, Lawrence Rd. at Springhouse Rd., Broomall; 610-353-3644. *CH.* Dating from 1696, this is one of the oldest English Quaker houses in Pennsylvania. It was the home of Thomas Massey, an indentured servant who arrived in Chester in 1683. The home was about to be torn down in 1964 when a descendant bought it and gave it to Marple Township for restoration. It is now furnished with seventeenth- and eighteenth-century furniture. Tue-Sat 10 am-4:30 pm, Sun 2-4:30 pm. After Labor Day by appointment only. For group tours call in advance.

The Tyler Arboretum, 515 Painter Rd., Media; 610-566-9134. *CH.* Covering 650 acres of woodlands near Ridley Creek State Park, this is an outdoor museum of specialty plants, gardens and trees, with 20 miles of marked hiking trails. It's a superior birding spot too, especially in the autumn, and the historic Lachford Hall is an eighteenth-century building filled with period furnishings. Educational programs for adults and children. Daily 8 am-dusk, Lachford Hall Sun 2-5 pm. Bookstore and Visitors Center open April-October, Mon-Sat 10-4, Sun noon-4, summer noon-3.

University Museum of Archaeology and Anthropology, Thirty-third and Spruce Sts.; 215-898-4000. *CH.* There's a wealth of archaeology and anthropology here, including artifacts from every continent. Hundreds of excavations have brought the museum just about everything from biblical inscriptions to gold of the Incas, and one of its galleries—funded by the Nevil Foundation for the Blind—features more than 30 objects that you're encouraged to touch. Tue-Sat 10 am-4:30 pm, Sun 1-5 pm. Closed summer Sundays, but free Sunday admission until May 23.

Wagner Free Institute of Science, Montgomery Ave. and Seventeenth St.; 215-763-6529. *NCH.* Founded in 1855, housed in its original Victorian building, and using its original display cases, this is one of the best-kept secrets in Philadelphia, featuring dinosaur bones, mounted birds and mammals, and a Children's Discovery Room. Its enormous exhibition hall, which dates back to 1855, has more than 21,000 specimens on display. Free adult science education courses, and museum lessons for school-aged children. Guided tours by appointment. Tue-Fri 9 am-4 pm except holidays.

Welcome Park, Second St. north of Walnut. *NCH.* This attractive park is located on the same site as the Slate Roof House, where William Penn lived with his second wife, Hannah, and where their son, John, was born. It was here in 1701 that Penn granted the famous Charter of Privileges, and the park is now designed in the form of a giant map of Philadelphia—as originally planned by Penn.

HISTORIC GERMANTOWN

Germantown, which celebrated its 300th birthday in 1983, was founded by Francis Daniel Pastorious, a German lawyer and scholar who became interested in the Society of Friends, or Quakers, about the time William Penn founded Pennsylvania. As a close friend of Penn's, Pastorious, with the help of surveyor Thomas Fairman, laid out the 5,700 acres of beautiful land in large lots that eventually were split up as new settlers arrived.

Until the American Revolution, the residents of Germantown, which included Germans, Dutch, Swedes, English, and French Huguenots, enjoyed a rather quiet lifestyle. They were industrious, ethical, private folk. Within five years of the founding of Germantown, the Quakers, including Pastorious, became the first to protest the colonial practice of using blacks as slaves.

When the British army captured and occupied Philadelphia, a major part of Sir William Howe's forces were quartered in some of the old stone houses you see today. On October 4, 1777, Germantown was attacked by George Washington's Continental Army. Although the patriots were repelled, they left the British stunned and shaken. This ultimately influenced France to join the colonial war effort, turning a military defeat into a diplomatic victory.

In 1793, the disastrous outbreak of yellow fever in Philadelphia forced many, including President Washington, to flee to the higher ground of Germantown. Some of the wealthiest stayed, built summer homes, and commuted from the green, airy atmosphere to their jobs in the city, six miles southwest. Before long, Germantown was a bustling industrial city with a road, now Germantown Avenue, that served travelers between Philadelphia and points west. Please note: **Germantown sights are listed in the order of a walking tour:**

Cliveden, 6401 Germantown Ave.; 215-848-1777. CH. This elaborate eighteenth-century, Georgian stone home, built in 1763-67 for then-Pennsylvania attorney general Benjamin Chew, was being used as a fort by the British when they were attacked by the Continental Army. It was the focal point of the fighting during the Battle of Germantown, sustained heavy damage as a result, and some of the cannon ball and bullet marks from October 1777 are still evident today. Thu-Sun noon-4 pm, April-December.

Upsala, 6430 Germantown Ave.; 215-842-1798. CH. Built in 1798-1801, this Federal-style home is highlighted by exquisite detail, authentic furnishings, and a detached, shady setting. It was the site of the American encampment during the Battle of Germantown. Thu, Sat, 1-4 pm, April-October.

Concord Schoolhouse, 6309 Germantown Ave.; 215-843-0943. NCH. This is an excellent example of an eighteenth-century schoolhouse that is now an historical museum. The original bell hangs in the belfry and the schoolmaster's original desk stands in its place. The schoolhouse is adjacent to the Upper Burying Ground, where early settlers and soldiers from the Revolutionary War are buried. By appointment.

Wyck, 6026 Germantown Ave.; 215-848-1690. *CH.* This Greek Revival house, part of which dates back to the 1690s, was owned and occupied for 283 years by nine generations of the Haines family. Revolutionary soldiers were hospitalized here in 1777, and the Marquis de Lafayette was an honored guest in 1825. April-December Tue, Thu, Sat 1-4 pm. Winter tours by appointment.

Ebenezer Maxwell Mansion, Greene and Tulpehocken Sts.; 215-438-1861. *CH.* Built in 1859 for the Philadelphia merchant for which it has been named, this Norman Gothic structure is the city's only mid-nineteenth-century house museum. It highlights Philadelphia-made furniture and household goods. Fri-Sun 1-4 pm. December-March by appointment.

Deshler-Morris House, 5442 Germantown Ave.; 215-596-1748. *CH.* Built in 1772-73 by David Deshler, this house served as Sir William Howe's headquarters following the Battle of Germantown, and later was the residence of George Washington during the 1793 yellow fever epidemic in Philadelphia. Washington returned the following summer with his wife Martha and their two children. It is part of Independence National Historic Park. Tue-Sat 1-4 pm.

Germantown Historical Society, 5501 Germantown Ave.; 215-844-0514. Exhibits about Germantown history, using the society's extensive collections. Mon-Fri 10 am-4 pm, Sun 1-5 pm.

Grumblethorpe, 5267 Germantown Ave.; 215-843-4820. *CH.* This was Germantown's first summer home, built by John Wister in 1744, modernized in 1808, and occupied by Wisters until 1910. John Wister was the brother of Caspar Wistar (they spelled their names differently), founder of the Wistar Museum. Grumblethorpe served as headquarters for British officers during the Battle of Germantown, and Brig. Gen. James Agnew was wounded and died here. He is buried in the Lower Burying Ground. Tue, Thu, Sun, 1-4 pm.

Loudoun, 4650 Germantown Ave.; 215-685-2067. *CH.* Built in 1796-1801 by Thomas Arnat, this is the most imposing of Germantown's Federal-style homes, overlooking Germantown Avenue from the top of Neglee's Hill. It was willed to the city of Philadelphia in 1939. Closed for restoration at the time of this printing. Call for information.

Stenton, Windrim and Eighteenth Sts.; 215-329-7312. *CH.* Built in 1723-30 for James Logan, Penn's secretary, agent, and chief justice of the Supreme Court, Stenton is reminiscent of Penn's manor home at Pennsbury. It served as George Washington's headquarters while en route to Chadds Ford and the Battle of Brandywine. Its eighteenth- and nineteenth-century Philadelphia-style furnishings reflect three generations of the Logan family. Tue-Sat 1-4 pm. Winter months by appointment.

Mennonite Church and Graveyard, 6121 Germantown Ave.; 215-843-0943. In 1708, the German Mennonites built a log cabin for worship here, and almost 60 years later it was replaced by the stone meeting house you see now. The oldest stones in the graveyard date from the 1730s. For tours of the church and graveyard, please contact the Germantown Mennonite Church, 6117 Germantown Ave., Philadelphia 19144; 215-843-0943.

Rittenhouse Town, 206 Lincoln Dr.; 215-438-5711. CH. An eighteenth-century industrial village, surrounding the Rittenhouse Homestead and paper mill. Built in 1707, the house was later added to by William Rittenhouse, the first Mennonite minister and first papermaker in the colonies. It is also the birthplace of the early American scientist and patriot, David Rittenhouse. May-September, Sat-Sun noon-4 pm, or by appointment.

Johnson House, 6306 Germantown Ave.; 215-438-1768. CH. This fine example of Colonial German architecture features a variety of furnishings that reflect Quaker life in the early years of Germantown. The house became part of the pre-Civil War Underground Railroad. Thu-Sat 1-4 pm. At other times for groups by appointment.

HISTORIC PLACES OF WORSHIP

Arch Street Meeting House, Fourth and Arch Sts.; 215-627-2667 (see DOWNTOWN WALKING TOUR).

Arch St. United Methodist Church, 55 N. Broad St.; 215-568-6250. The 1870 white marble, Gothic building was designed by Philadelphia architect Addison Hutton. Today the church is known for its Dixieland All-Saints Sunday, Native American Sunday, and other programs.

Christ Church, 20 N. American St.; 215-922-1695 (see DOWNTOWN WALKING TOUR).

Congregation Mikveh Israel, 44 N. Fourth St.; 215-922-5446. This is the oldest congregation in Philadelphia and the second oldest in America. A Spanish/Portuguese congregation, it was founded in 1740 by Nathan Levy, whose ship the *Myrtilla* carried the Liberty Bell from England to America in 1752. Benjamin Franklin was one of the many contributors to the synagogue building fund, and synagogue artifacts include George Washington's letter to the congregation. Tours.

Congregation Rodeph Shalom, 615 N. Broad St.; 215-627-6747. Today a Reform Jewish congregation, it grew from a minyan (a prayer meeting) to a congregation (an established synagogue) from 1770-

1802. It was the first Ashkenazic (Eastern European) synagogue in the Western Hemisphere. Tours of the Byzantine-Moorish style building and its exhibits.

Gloria Dei Old Swedes Church, Swanson and Christian Sts.; 215-389-1513 (see SIGHTS Queen Village).

Historic Old St. Augustine's Catholic Church, 243 N. Lawrence St.; 215-627-1838. Philadelphia's fourth oldest Catholic Church, Old St. Augustine's was founded in 1796. George Washington was one of the many contributors to this first U.S. foundation of Augustinian Friars. The bell that was purchased to replace the cracked Liberty Bell was acquired by the church in 1830. It now resides at Villanova University.

Historic St. George's United Methodist Church, 235 N. Fourth St.; 215-925-7788. This is the oldest Methodist Church in the United States, and except for the winter of 1777-1778, it has been in constant use since 1769. Tours daily 10-2 pm.

Mennonite Church and Graveyard, 6121 Germantown Ave.; 215-843-0943 (see SIGHTS Historic Germantown).

Mother Bethel A.M.E. Church, 419 S. Sixth St.; 215-925-0616. This National Historic Landmark, founded in 1782 by Richard Allen, stands on the oldest property continuously owned by African-Americans in the United States. Allen was America's first black to be named a bishop, and his tomb is in the basement.

Old First Reformed Church, Fourth and Race Sts.; 215-922-4566. The First Reformed Church was organized in 1727 by refugees seeking religious freedom in Philadelphia. This church, originally built in the mid-1830s, has been authentically restored. Tours.

Old Pine Presbyterian Church, Fourth and Pine Sts.; 215-925-8051. After this lot was donated to the First Presbyterian Church by William Penn's sons in 1764, this structure was built in the latter part of that decade. John Adams was among those who attended services here, and numerous famous colonists are buried in its churchyard, including William Hurry, who rang the Liberty Bell in July 1776.

Old St. Joseph's Church, Willing's Alley, near Fourth and Walnut Sts.; 215-923-1733. Established by the Jesuits in 1733 as the first Roman Catholic Church in Philadelphia, this church was built in 1838. St. Joseph's University had its beginnings here in 1851. The church is part of Independence National Historic Park.

Old St. Mary's Church, 248 S. Fourth St.; 215-923-7930. (see DOWNTOWN WALKING TOUR Society Hill).

Society Hill Synagogue, 418 Spruce St.; 215-922-6590. The Italian revival style building, which is a registered landmark, was completed in 1830, following a design by Thomas U. Walter, one of the architects of the United States Capitol in Washington D.C. Originally the Spruce

St. Baptist Church, it was converted to a synagogue in 1910. In 1967, it was acquired by the Conservative congregation who restored it and currently calls it home. Visitors welcome.

St. Paul's Church, 225 S. Third St.; 215-924-9910 (see DOWN-TOWN WALKING TOUR Society Hill).

St. Peter's Church, Third and Pine Sts.; 215-925-5968 (see DOWNTOWN WALKING TOUR Society Hill).

VISUAL ARTS

A stroll down Benjamin Franklin Parkway is certainly indicative of Philadelphia's reputation as one of the foremost cultural centers in the nation. Four museums—the Philadelphia Museum of Art, the Franklin Institute, the Academy of Natural Sciences, and the Rodin Museum—rank among the finest in the world. More than 100 museums are scattered throughout the Philadelphia area. You'll also find more statues in Philadelphia than in any other city in America, and galleries featuring every art in every medium by national and local artists. Old City, the most exciting gallery district on the East Coast, stays open late every Friday night and has special events and activities.

VISUAL ARTS BY AREA

BUCKS COUNTY
James A. Michener Art Museum

CENTER CITY
AIA Gallery
Art Institute of Philadelphia
    Gallery
I. Brewster and Co. Gallery
Calderwood Gallery
Gilbert Luber Gallery
The GK Collection
Gross McCleaf Gallery
Helen Drutt Gallery
Janet Fleisher Gallery
Locks Gallery
Museum of American Art of the Pennsylvania Academy of Fine Arts
Newman Galleries
Philadelphia Art Alliance

The Print Club
Romanian Folk Art Museum
The Schwarz Gallery
University of the Arts, Rosenwald-
    Wolf Gallery
W. Graham Rader at Charles
    Sessler

CENTER CITY—
PARKWAY AREA
Goldie Paley Gallery of Moore
    College of Art
Levy Gallery of Moore College of
    Art
The Philadelphia Museum of Art
Rodin Museum

CHESTER COUNTY
The Wharton Esherick Museum

143

DELAWARE COUNTY
Brandywine River Museum
Chadds Ford Gallery

MONTGOMERY COUNTY
Barnes Foundation
The Glencairn Museum
Heisman Fine Arts Gallery
Langman Gallery

NORTH PHILADELPHIA
Stephen Girard Collection

NORTHWEST PHILADELPHIA
Artforms Gallery
Hahn Gallery
Jeffrey Fuller Fine Art
LaSalle University Art Museum
Philadelphia Print Shop
Woodmere Art Museum

OLD CITY
Jun Gallery
The Temple Gallery of Tyler
  School of Art
Old City Art Association
Rosenfeld Gallery

SOUTH PHILADELPHIA
Fleisher Art Memorial

SOUTH STREET
de Vecchis Gallery
The Works Gallery

UNIVERSITY CITY
Arthur Ross Gallery
Drexel Museum Collection
Institute of Contemporary Art

MUSEUMS AND INSTITUTIONAL GALLERIES

AIA Bookstore and Design Center, Seventeenth and Sansom Sts.; 215-569-3188. *NCH.* This gallery of the American Institute of Architects features the work of established and promising artists, craftsmen, and designers. Free public lectures on architecture and design. Mon-Sat 10 am-6 pm, Wed 10 am-8 pm, Sun noon-5 pm.

The Art Institute of Philadelphia Gallery, 1622 Chestnut St.; 215-567-7080. *NCH.* Operated by the Art Institute of Philadelphia, this gallery offers changing exhibits by faculty, students, and leading artists and designers. Call for hours.

Arthur Ross Gallery, 220 S. Thirty-fourth St.; 215-898-2083. *NCH.* Housed in the nineteenth-century Furness Building on the University of Pennsylvania campus, the opening of this gallery represented a turning point in the university's history; never before did it have an official gallery to display the 4,000 art treasures it has accumulated in almost two centuries of existence. The gallery showcases a variety of exhibitions of art works, artifacts, and archival materials. Four major exhibitions are presented annually, curated by University faculty, often with their students, and by other scholars. Lectures, symposia, gallery tours, and films are also offered. Tue-Fri 10 am-5 pm, Sat-Sun noon-5 pm.

Barnes Foundation, 300 Latches Lane, Merion; 610-667-0290. *CH.* Housing the late Albert Coombs Barnes collection of some 1,000 paintings, this is the finest private collection of early modern art in the world, including 180 Renoirs, 69 Cezannes, and works by Rousseau, Picasso, Matisse, and others. Also, hundreds of pieces of furniture, medieval ironware, and objets d'art. Fri-Sun 9:30 am-5 pm, Sept-June. Call for summer hours. Reservations recommended.

Brandywine River Museum, Route One, Chadds Ford; 610-388-2700. *CH.* Located on the peaceful Brandywine River, this museum is a century-old grist mill whose charm has been carefully preserved through the years. With its dramatic tower of glass, and brick terraces overlooking the surrounding countryside, it houses the works of Andrew Wyeth, his father N. C. Wyeth, and his son James. Included are the works of Howard Pyle, "the father of American illustration," who began teaching here in 1898 and developed the tradition in American art known as the "Brandywine Heritage." Outdoors, enjoy the wildflower gardens and the mile-long nature trail along the river. Daily 9:30 am-4:30 pm.

Drexel University Museum, Thirty-second and Chestnut Sts.; 215-895-2424. *NCH.* Contains portraits of the Drexel family, as well as nineteenth- and early twentieth-century decorative and fine arts. America's most historic timepiece is here (the David Rittenhouse clock, made in 1773), as well as the Rincliffe Gallery, featuring Philadelphia's largest collection of Edward Marshall Boehm porcelains. Call for hours.

Fleisher Art Memorial, 719 Catharine St.; 215-922-3456. *NCH.* Founded in 1898 as the Graphic Sketch Club, the memorial is still the only art school in the country with free classes for people throughout the city. The building contains the art school and two galleries that stage shows, including four regular exhibits spotlighting the works of area artists, faculty, students, and children. Mon-Fri 9:30 am-5 pm. Sat 9:30 am-3 pm when classes are scheduled.

The Glencairn Museum, 1001 Cathedral Rd., Bryn Athyn; 215-938-2600. *CH (students free).* This sprawling 1928 home built in the Romanesque style houses one of the finest collections of medieval art in the world. The collection of twelfth- and thirteenth-century stained glass and sculpture of the late Raymond Pitcairn is one of the finest still in private hands. The museum also exhibits the Egyptian, Greek, Roman, Eastern, and Native American art of the Academy of the New Church. Beyond the "Great Hall," which houses many items of the collections, is an exquisite retreat, the "Cloister." By appointment Mon-Fri 9 am-5 pm. Open Sun 2-5 pm, the second Sunday of each month, September-June.

Goldie Paley Gallery, Moore College of Art and Design, Twentieth St. and Benjamin Franklin Pkwy.; 215-568-4515. *NCH.*

Begun in the private home of the late artist, Goldie Paley, the museum now exhibits art, architecture, design, photography, and crafts by American and European artists. Tue-Fri 10 am-5 pm, Thu 10 am-7 pm, Sat-Sun noon-4 pm. Summer hours, Mon-Fri 10 am-5 pm.

Institute of Contemporary Art, Thirty-sixth and Sansom Sts.; 215-898-7108. CH. Part of the University of Pennsylvania, the institute features exhibitions of new art via individual shows and timely themes. This is Philadelphia's major institution devoted to contemporary art. Wed-Sun 10 am-5 pm, Thu 10 am-7 pm. Sundays free 10 am-noon. Tours and lectures.

James A. Michener Art Museum, 138 S. Pine St., Doylestown; 215-340-9800. CH. Four galleries of twentieth-century American art and sculpture, with ongoing cultural programs. Included is the permanent exhibition, "James A. Michener: A Living Legacy." Museum shop and tea room. Tue-Fri 10 am-4:30 pm, Sat-Sun 10 am-5 pm.

LaSalle University Art Museum, Twentieth St. and Olney Ave.; 215-951-1221. NCH. This gallery, which opened in 1976, displays Western Tradition paintings, drawings, and sculpture. The Susan Dunleavy collection features ancient illuminated manuscripts from the Judeo-Christian traditions. Sept-April, Tue-Fri 11 am-4 pm, Sun 2-4 pm.

Levy Gallery, Moore College of Art and Design, Twentieth St. and Benjamin Franklin Pkwy.; 215-568-4515. NCH. Founded in 1844, the college is the only art college exclusively for women in the United States. This gallery showcases art by local Philadelphia-area artists. Call for hours.

Museum of American Art of the Pennsylvania Academy of the Fine Arts, Broad and Cherry Sts.; 215-972-7600. CH. The oldest art museum and art school in the United States, the Academy contains more than 4,000 works covering three centuries of American art. It includes the original "Penn's Treaty With The Indians" by Benjamin West, the "Landsdowne Portrait of George Washington" by Charles Wilson Peale, "The Cello Player" and "Walt Whitman" by Thomas Eakins, and "The Fox Hunt" by Winslow Homer. Founded in 1805, the Academy is housed in a magnificent Victorian building designed by the famed Philadelphia architect, Frank Furness. Mon-Sat 10 am-5 pm, Sun 11 am-5 pm. Sundays free 3-5 pm.

Philadelphia Art Alliance, 251 S. Eighteenth St.; 215-545-4302. NCH. Founded in 1915, the Alliance has had a profound creative influence on the artists and cultural life of Philadelphia. Its five galleries display changing exhibitions in various mediums. Lectures are held on a wide range of topics, as well as technical demonstrations in various arts and crafts. The Alliance's Performing Arts committees present internationally known composers, authors, musicians, dancers, and theater personalities. Call for hours.

Pennsylvania Academy of the
Fine Arts on Broad Street, "Avenue of the Arts"

Bob Krist for the Greater
Philadelphia Tourism Marketing
Corporation

The Philadelphia Museum of Art, Twenty-sixth St. and Benjamin Franklin Parkway; 215-763-8100. TDD: 215-684-7600. *CH.* One of Philadelphia's most famous and recognizable landmarks, this massive Greek Revival building occupies ten acres and contains more than 200 galleries. Today the museum, which first opened in 1928, contains more than 300,000 objects spanning 2,000 years of man's creativity, including paintings, carpets, silver porringers, cast-iron stove plates, and every conceivable variety of art object from every corner of the globe. The second floor is devoted to paintings and architectural installations from continental Europe, including French and English period rooms and paintings by such greats as Renoir, Cezanne, Monet, and Van Gogh. There is an Indian temple, a Chinese Palace Hall, and a Japanese Ceremonial Tea House. One of the largest exhibitions is the Kretzchmar von Kienbusch Collection of Armor and Arms. Among the services and programs available are gallery talks, guest lectures, traveling exhibitions, films, concerts, and workshops. Tue-Sun 10 am-5 pm, Wed 10 am-8:45 pm. Admission is free Sun 10 am-1 pm.

The Print Center and Gallery Store, 1614 Latimer St.; 215-735-6090. *NCH.* Founded in 1915 and located in a former carriage house, the nonprofit club's emphasis is on contemporary printmaking and photography. Its three galleries present changing exhibitions which include theme shows, one-person shows, and cooperative exhibitions. There is also a prestigious international competitive exhibition every year, and a gallery store. Tue-Sat 11 am-5:30 pm.

Rodin Museum, Twenty-second St. and Benjamin Franklin Parkway; 215-763-8100. *Donations requested.* Named for the French sculptor Auguste Rodin (1840-1917), this museum contains the largest collection of his work outside France. Among the 200 magnificent bronze, plaster, and marble sculptures are "The Thinker," "The Burghers of Calais," and "Gates of Hell." Tue-Sun 10 am-5 pm.

Romanian Folk Art Museum, 1606 Spruce St.; 215-732-6780. Donations requested. Filled with costumes, rugs, pottery and Transylvanian decorative art, this museum contains the largest collection of folklore artifacts in the country. Thu, Sat, and some Sundays noon-7 pm and by appointment.

Stephen Girard Collection, Founder's Hall, Girard College, 2101 S. College Ave.; 215-787-2680. *NCH.* Accumulated between 1780 and 1830, the Girard collection of furniture, plate, china, and other effects is virtually unique. Among the Philadelphia artists represented in the Greek Revival building are Daniel Trotter, Ephraim Haines, Henry Connelly, William Cox, and J. B. Ackley. Thu only 10 am-noon and 1-3 pm, or by appointment.

The Temple Gallery of Tyler School of Art, Temple University Center City; 45 N. Second St.; 215-925-7379. Monthly exhibitions of

Philadelphia Museum of Art on
Benjamin Franklin Parkway

G. Widman for the Greater Philadelphia
Tourism Marketing Corporation

contemporary art, using all media and disciplines. Wed, Thu, Sat 11 am-6 pm, Fri 11 am-9 pm, or by appointment.

University of the Arts, Rosenwald-Wolf Gallery, Broad and Pine Sts.; 215-717-6480. *NCH.* This gallery offers exhibits of contemporary art, crafts, graphics, sculptures, and mobiles by established artists and designers, faculty, and students. The exhibits change every five weeks. Mon, Tue, Thu, Fri 10 am-5 pm, Wed 10 am-8 pm, Sat-Sun 12-5 pm.

The Wharton Esherick Museum, Paoli; 610-644-5822. *CH.* Included in the artist's studio, which is set high on a wooded hillside overlooking the Great Valley, are more than 200 pieces by Mr. Esherick covering 40 years of work. Featured are paintings, woodcuts, prints, furniture, utensils, and sculpture in wood, stone, and ceramic. Tours, Sat 10 am-5 pm, Sun 1-5 pm. Group tours weekdays 10 am-5 pm. Reservations required.

Woodmere Art Museum, 9201 Germantown Ave., Chestnut Hill; 215-247-0476. *CH.* Woodmere features a permanent collection of paintings, sculpture, tapestry, and objets d'art accumulated by the late Charles Knox Smith. Six exhibitions, focusing on regional art and artists, are hosted throughout the year and art classes are offered for adults and children. Tue-Sat 10 am-5 pm, Sun 1-5 pm.

ART IN PUBLIC PLACES

Philadelphia has more public art than any other city in the United States. This is due to an ordinance stipulating that one percent of the cost of all new buildings, and buildings erected on redevelopment land, must be devoted to the fine arts. All artwork must be approved by the Fine Arts Commission prior to its installment inside or outside a structure.

With such an abundance, we cannot mention all the glorious public art in Philadelphia; just in the last few decades, no less than 400 new pieces have been added. Therefore, we list a blend of new art with some that has blessed the city for many years.

For your convenience, we have arranged Philadelphia's public art by region. We suggest a tour beginning in Fairmount Park on East River Drive. Fairmount Park features more than 200 pieces of sculpture, and a program was launched to conserve the sculpture within its borders. For further reference, please consult *Philadelphia's Treasure in Bronze and Stone*, published by the Fairmount Park Art Association.

East River Drive

Abraham Lincoln, Kelly Drive and Lemon Hill Drive, 1871, a bronze by Randolph Rogers.

Cowboy, Kelly Drive, 1908, a bronze by Frederic Remington, located just northwest of the AMTRAK Railroad Bridge.

The Ellen Phillips Samuel Memorial, Kelly Drive. This series of statues symbolizing the history of America is the work of 16 sculptures working within a span of 20 years.

General Ulysses S. Grant, Kelly Drive and Fountain Green Drive, 1897, a bronze by Daniel Chester French and Edward C. Potter.

The Pilgrim, Kelly Drive, 1904, a bronze by Saint Augustus Gaudens, located near Boat House Row.

Playing Angels, Kelly Drive at Fountain Green Drive, date uncertain (dedicated April 26, 1972), a bronze by Carl Milles (1875-1955).

Washington Monument, in front of the Art Museum, 1897, a bronze and granite by Rudolph Siemering.

The Benjamin Franklin Parkway ————

Atmosphere and Environment, west entrance of the Philadelphia Museum of Art, 1970, is a steel sculpture by Louise Nevelson.

Benjamin Franklin, Franklin Institute, Twentieth Street and the Parkway, 1938, a marble by James Earle Frazer.

Civil War Soldiers and Sailors Memorial, Twentieth Street and the Parkway, 1921, is a marble by Herman Atkins MacNeil.

The Fountain of Three Rivers, Logan Circle, Nineteenth Street and the Parkway, 1924, is a bronze by Alexander Stirling Calder.

Heroic Figure of Man, the Bell Telephone Company, Sixteeenth Street and the Parkway, 1963, is a bronze by Joseph J. Greenberg, Jr.

Jesus Breaking Bread, Saints Peter and Paul Cathedral, Eighteenth Street and the Parkway, 1978, is a bronze by Walter Erlebacher.

Joan of Arc, Kelly Drive at the Philadelphia Museum of Art, 1890, a bronze by Emmanuel Fremiet.

The Lion Fighter, east entrance of the Philadelphia Museum of Art, 1858, is a bronze by Albert Wolfe.

Monument to the Six Million Jewish Martyrs, Sixteenth St. and the Parkway, was the first public Holocaust monument in the United States.

Prometheus Strangling the Vulture, east entrance of the Philadelphia Museum of Art, 1952, a bronze by Jacques Lipschitz.

The Thinker, Rodin Museum, Twenty-second Street and the Parkway, 1880 (enlarged 1902-04), a bronze by Auguste Rodin.

City Hall and Market Street East Area ——

Burst of Joy, The Gallery at Market East, 9th and Market streets, 1977, is of stainless steel by Harold Kimmelman.

Clothespin, Center Square, 1500 Market Street, 1976, is a steel pop sculpture by Claes Oldenburg.

Government of the People, Plaza Municipal Services Building, Broad Street and John F. Kennedy Boulevard, 1976, is a bronze by Jacques Lipschitz.

Leviathan, Penn Center Plaza, 17th Street and John F. Kennedy Boulevard, 1963, is nickel silver on Monel metal by Seymour Lipton.

Love, 15th Street and John F. Kennedy Boulevard, 1976, is the popular painted aluminum work by Robert Indiana.

Three Discs One Lacking, Penn Center Plaza, 17th Street and John F. Kennedy Boulevard, 1964, is a painted steel by Alexander Stirling Calder.

William Penn, top of clocktower, City Hall, Broad and Market Streets, 1894, is a bronze by Alexander Milne Calder.

Independence National Historic Park ——

Commodore John Barry, Independence Square, 1907, is a bronze by Samuel Murray.

Franklin Court, 314-322 Market Street, 1977, is of brick, flagstone, and marble by Venturi and Rauch.

Milkweed Pod, Rohm and Haas Building, Sixth and Market streets, 1966, is a bronze by Clark Fitz-Gerald.

Phaedrus, the Federal Reserve Bank, Sixth Street between Market and Arch streets, 1977, is painted steel by Beverly Pepper.

Voyage of Ulysses, Plaza between 600 Arch Street and 601 Market Street, 1977, is a stainless steel by David Von Schlegell.

White Water, Fifth Street between Market and Arch streets, 1978, is a carbon steel frame by Robinson Fredenthal.

Chinatown ——————————————

Gateway to Chinatown, This gateway into Chinatown, at Tenth and Arch streets, stands 40 feet high, and was created by 12 master artisans from China. They used 142 cases of tiles. It is magnificent.

Benjamin Franklin Bridge ——————

A Bolt of Lightning, Plaza of the Benjamin Franklin Bridge. This ten-story stainless steel structure is a memorial to Benjamin Franklin and was created by Isamu Noguchi. It was installed in 1984, and is still very controversial.

Society Hill

Butterfly, Second and Delancey Streets, 1971, is of stainless steel by Harold Kimmelman.

Floating Figure, Locust Street between Second and Third streets, 1963, is a bronze by Gaston Lachaise.

Kangaroos, Fourth and Fifth streets between Spruce and Pine Streets, 1923, is of welded stainless steel by Harold Kimmelman.

Mustang at Play, Head House Square Corporation, Second and Pine streets, instated in 1969, is a bronze by Margaret Wasserman Levy.

Unity, Fourth Street and Willings Alley, 1970, is a metal piece by Richard Lieberman.

Young Man, Old Man, The Future, Society Hill Towers, Second and Locust streets, 1966, is a bronze by Leonard Baskin.

Rittenhouse Square

Billy, 1914, is a bronze by Albert Laessle.

Lion Crushing a Serpent, 1832, is a bronze by Antoine Louis Barye.

University City

Covenant, Thirty-ninth Street and Locust Walk, 1975, is a painted corten steel by Alexander Liberman.

Dream of Sky, Thirty-seventh Street Walk and Market Street, 1976, is of fiberglass by Timothy Duffield.

Face Fragment, 3500 Market Street, 1975, is of bronze, fiberglass, and polyester by Arlene Love.

Jerusalem Stable, Locust Walk near Thirty-fourth Street, 1979, is a painted steel by Alexander Stirling Calder

Untitled, 3624 Market Street, 1974, is a fiberglass work by James Lloyd.

We Lost, Thirty-sixth Street and Locust Walk, is painted steel by Tony Smith.

GALLERIES

Artforms Gallery, 106 Levering St., Manayunk; 215-483-3030. "The fine arts place." Paintings, works on paper, photography and sculpture by established and emerging contemporary artists. Music, poetry, and lectures are offered in this art-filled setting in historic Manayunk. Wed, Thu, Sun noon- 5 pm, Fri, Sat noon-9 pm.

I. Brewster and Co. Gallery, 1628 Walnut St.; 215-731-9200. With a second location in historic Manayunk, this gallery wholesales modern and contemporary works at discount prices. Warhol, De Kooning, Picasso, Miro, and Chagall are only a few of the names you'll encounter here. Mon-Sat 11 am-6 pm, or by appointment.

Calderwood Gallery, 1427 Walnut St.; 215-568-7475. A vast array of French art nouveau, art deco, modernist, and Forties works are found at this fine Center City location. Tue-Fri 11 am-5:30 pm, Sat noon-5:30 pm.

Chadds Ford Gallery, US 1 and 100, Chadds Ford; 610-459-5510. Located in the quaint Chadds Ford Barn Shops, this gallery presents the largest collection of Wyeth reproductions anywhere. It supports quality artists producing original work in all media and holds three major shows a year, including the popular Christmas miniature exhibit. Mon-Sat 10 am-5 pm, Sun 12-5 pm.

deVecchis Gallery, 404-4 South St.; 215-922-5708. This two-story gallery houses the largest selection of contemporary graphics on the East Coast, everything from original signed and numbered graphics by Picasso, Miro, and Calder to those of the new masters. Expert framing. Tue, Wed, Thu, Sat, 10 am-6 pm, Fri 10 am-8 pm, Sun noon-5 pm. Closed Sundays July and August.

The GK Collection, 226 W. Rittenhouse Square; 215-545-6955. Set in one of Center City's loveliest locations, this art and craft gallery features extraordinary works of glass, jewelry, and sculpture. Mon-Fri 10 am-6 pm, Sat 10 am-5 pm.

W. Graham Rader Gallery at Charles Sessler, 1308 Walnut St.; 215-735-8811. Located within one of Philadelphia's oldest bookstores, this gallery is known for its prints of historical significance. It features botanical and nautical prints, as well as rare books and maps. Restorations, appraisals, and framing are available. Mon-Sat 10 am-5 pm. Appointment advised.

Heisman Fine Arts Gallery, Two E. Lancaster Ave., Ardmore; 610-896-8161. One of the largest galleries on the East Coast, this gallery offers more than 1,000 pieces of work in seven showrooms, each of which represents a different art medium. Well-known artists and new names are both represented. Periodic one-man/woman shows. Mon, Tue, Thu, Fri, Sat 10 am-6 pm, Wed 10 am-8 pm, Sun 11 am-5 pm.

Gilbert Luber Gallery, 1220 Walnut St.; 215-732-2996. A gallery specializing in Asian art, including a fine collection of antique woodblock prints and contemporary prints. Appraisals, custom framing, and print conservation available. Mon-Sat 11:30 am-5:30 pm.

Gross McCleaf Gallery, 127 S. Sixteenth St.; 215-665-8138. The gallery's two floors specialize in the oils, watercolors, and pastels of contemporary, regional artists. Mon-Sat 10 am-5 pm, evenings by appointment.

Hahn Gallery, 8439 Germantown Ave., Chestnut Hill; 215-247-8439. Founded in 1974 by art collectors Maurice and Roslyn Hahn, this gallery concentrates on diverse Philadelphia artists, national and international artists, post World War II School of Paris painters, the estate of Benton Spruance, and antique Japanese woodblock prints. There is also a wide variety of sculpture, photography, crafts, and art glass. The Hahns have helped launch a number of careers, and the shows change every three weeks on both floors. Tue-Sat 10 am-5:30 pm or by appointment.

Helen Drutt Gallery, 1721 Walnut St.; 215-735-1625. Directed by its founder, Helen W. Drutt, a dean of contemporary crafts, this gallery features splendid twentieth-century crafts in fiber, metal, and clay, by internationally known artists. Wed-Fri noon-5 pm, Sat 11 am-2 pm, and by appointment.

Janet Fleisher Gallery, 211 S. Seventeenth St.; 215-545-7562. This gallery specializes in American Indian and American Folk art, and presents ten major shows annually. Mon-Fri 10:30 am-5:30 pm, Sat 11:00 am-5:30 pm.

Jeffrey Fuller Fine Art, Ltd., 730 Carpenter Lane, Mt. Airy; 215-991-1900. Displaying the art of nineteenth- and twentieth-century American and European masters. Jeffrey P. Fuller, ASA, is an accredited senior appraiser of the American Society of Appraisers. Mon-Fri 10 am-5 pm. Saturdays and Summer by appointment.

Jun Gallery, 112 Market St.; 215-413-3555. This gallery offers lithographs, silkscreens, watercolors, woodcut prints, and custom frames made from exotic woods. Mon-Sat 10 am-5 pm.

Langman Galleries, Willow Grove Park, Willow Grove; 215-657-8333. The gallery has the area's largest showroom, featuring quality contemporary paintings, sculpture, and art objects in clay, fiber, glass, and metal. It is craft-oriented, offering sculpture to wear, paintings, prints, and contemporary multimedia objects. Mon-Fri 10 am-9:30 pm, Sat 10 am-9:30 pm, Sun 11 am-6 pm.

Locks Gallery, 600 Washington Square South; 215-629-1000. Known for her exciting shows, Marian Locks is perhaps the area's best discoverer and promoter of local talent. Outstanding examples of contemporary art. Tue-Sat 10 am-6 pm. Closed Sat during July and August.

Newman Galleries, 1625 Walnut St.; 215-563-1779. With a tradition of fine art since 1865, this is Philadelphia's oldest gallery. It specializes in nineteenth- and twentieth-century American and European oil paintings, watercolors, lithographs, silkscreens, and graphics. Mon-Sat 10 am-4:30 pm. In July and August, Mon-Fri 9 am-5:30 pm.

Old City Arts Association; 215-625-9200. An organization of more than 50 showrooms of fine arts, antiques, furniture, and decorative arts in Old City. There are special evening hours during the First Friday event each month.

The Philadelphia Print Shop, 8441 Germantown Ave.; 215-242-4750. This gallery features lovely century-old original prints and watercolors. Also, old Pennsylvania maps and others from throughout the world. Seminars, lectures, and exhibitions are held throughout the year. Mon-Sat 10 am-5 pm.

Rosenfeld Galleries, 113 Arch St.; 215-922-1376. The Rosenfeld Galleries specialize in emerging American artists producing contemporary work in all media. Every July and August the gallery holds a new talent show. Wed-Sat 10 am-5 pm, Sun noon-5 pm.

The Schwarz Gallery, 1806 Chestnut St.; 215-563-4887. This reputable antique shop features an excellent selection of nineteenth-century American and European paintings. Mon-Sat 10 am-5 pm. July and August, Mon-Fri 9 am-5:30 pm.

The Works Gallery, 319 South St.; 215-922-7775. One of the oldest galleries of its kind in the United States, it features 250 artists in all forms of media and crafts. Permanent exhibition area. No shows in July and August. Tue-Sat 10 am-6 pm.

SHOPPING

Philadelphia and its suburban areas can satisfy a shopper's every whim, from small boutiques and specialty shops to the country's largest enclosed urban retail center, The Gallery at Market East; the nation's biggest outlet mall, Franklin Mills Value Mall; as well as the largest suburban retail mall in the U.S., King of Prussia Shopping Complex. Philadelphia is the third-largest clothing manufacturing center in the United States. In addition, bargain hunters from throughout the East come to take advantage of the area's famed factory outlets and antique shops.

SHOPPING DISTRICTS

Center City

Center City is the name for downtown Philadelphia and the headquarters of the retail trade industry in the area. Philadelphia's oldest department stores, John Wanamaker and Strawbridge & Clothier, had been local household words since they were founded in the 1860s. Wanamaker's closed only recently, in the 1990s, but Strawbridge's is still located on its original site, although now it is linked to The Gallery at Market East.

From the 1880s to the early 1900s, when it was redesigned by the famed Chicago architect William H. Burnham, John Wanamaker's was the largest department store in the country. The building is now a registered federal landmark with its open balconies and huge bronze eagle and houses a branch of Lord & Taylor. Free concerts on the world's largest pipe organ in the Grand Court have long been favorite events for Philadelphians (see PERFORMING ARTS).

Strawbridge & Clothier, founded by two Quaker merchants, was until recently a family-operated department store with many national firsts to its credit. Among them, the first promotional sale (Clover Day, which started in 1906), and the first department store to open a branch in the suburbs (1930) and a store in a covered-mall shopping center (1961). Strawbridge's was also the first department store to enter the

157

discount-store field with Clover Stores in 1971, and the first to build in a downtown shopping mall, The Gallery, in 1977.

For several years, Market Street East has been the site of Philadelphia's largest urban development project, and the expanded Gallery complex, The Gallery at Market East, includes 170 shops, restaurants, J.C. Penney, and of course, Strawbridge & Clothier.

The Market Street East shopping area, which includes Market Place East with its own eateries, nightclubs, and shops in a Victorian-style building, is now integrated with the city's transit system, making it one of the most intensive concentrations of retail stores in the nation.

At Independence Mall is The Bourse (French for "place of trade"), which during the early 1900s was the largest and grandest merchant's exchange in America. Now restored to its former grandeur, with international flags and wood-carved upper levels overlooking its main floor, The Bourse is an opulent, cosmopolitan marketplace once again. It is highlighted by a multitude of stores, some of Philadelphia's most elegant shops, and more than a dozen eateries and restaurants, with those on the upper levels serving gourmet fast foods from around the world.

Across the street from the new Convention Center is a special treat, the Reading Terminal Market, founded in 1892. Located underneath the historic Reading Terminal Train Shed at Twelfth and Arch streets, it is a traditional stall market with approximately 80 merchants from a variety of ethnic backgrounds. They operate small restaurants, produce stands, and shops surrounding a beer garden and courtyard, and offer famous Philadelphia products. The Market is particularly renowned for its Pennsylvania Dutch (Amish and Mennonite) farmers and merchants, who bring fresh meats and produce from the surrounding countryside each morning. It is open from eight in the morning to six in the evening; however, the Pennsylvania Dutch merchants are there only from Wednesday through Saturday.

Society Hill

In Society Hill is Head House Square, a delightfully quaint enclave housed in Federal, Georgian, and Victorian architecture. The unique shops, cafés, and restaurants are a genteel treat. And the covered open marketplace in the center of the square is the site of fairs and special events.

Rittenhouse Square Area

Rittenhouse Square has been a popular meeting place and market for more than 200 years. Today, among its stately brownstones and intimate restaurants, you'll find expensive boutiques, salons, and art galleries, as well as flower, jewelry, and gourmet shops. Between the Square and Broad Street, along Walnut Street, you'll encounter the most exclusive establishments in the city. They include The Shops at the Bellevue with Ralph Lauren, Gucci, and Tiffany, and The Shops at Liberty Place, as well as boutiques, bookstores, specialty stores, and an abundance of art galleries.

Chestnut Street

Still more specialty shops and clothing stores are to be found on Chestnut Street, specifically, the "Chestnut Street Transitway" which is closed to automobile traffic between Sixth and Eighteenth streets.

South Street

Then there's South Street, more popularly known as Philadelphia's Greenwich Village, where storefronts have been restored and trees line the cobbled streets. Here you'll find a host of boutiques, and vintage and punk shops that sell the latest styles in fashion.

City Line Avenue

The City Line business and media center is located on Philadelphia's western boundary, a short drive from Center City. Here can be found Lord & Taylor, Saks Fifth Avenue, and many more inviting specialty shops, along with two major hotels, fine restaurants, and exciting night spots. Two TV stations and five radio stations broadcast from this area.

Chestnut Hill

Chestnut Hill, at Philadelphia's extreme northwestern boundary, ten miles from Center City, offers fine shopping along historic Germantown Avenue. More than 100 shops specializing in designer fashions and antiques, and 22 charming restaurants nestle among the tree-shaded, cobblestone streets.

An oasis within the city limits, Chestnut Hill is also a place to gawk at enormous houses, to stop for a snack at some street cafés, to pick up fresh foods at the weekly farmers market—and yes, very much a place to shop. Check out the Little Nook, 8005 Germantown Ave., for some of the most unusual jewelry in town, or Paperia, 8521 Germantown Ave., for funky stationery, greeting cards, and paper goods. Periodic sales are sponsored by the neighborhood vendors association.

Manayunk

Anyone who's made an investment in this Philadelphia area is reaping the benefits now. Formerly a lower-middle class neighborhood nestled along the hills by the Schuylkill River, sections of Manayunk—especially its commercial district along Main Street—have "yuppified" and are infusing an exciting new life here. A variety of restaurants and shops selling wonderfully impractical and decorative goods are attracting new visitors here daily. And if you get tired of all the hoopla, just stroll the hilly, windy streets for a taste of Philadelphia that is reminiscent of Europe.

SUBURBAN MALLS

Philadelphia's surrounding counties offer magnificent shopping malls and unique mini-centers, each with its own distinctive flavor. The King of Prussia Shopping Complex, America's largest suburban retail mall, currently features six major department stores and more than 300 shops and restaurants. The Court has elegant boutiques and Bloomingdale's first store in the Philadelphia area. The Plaza, only 100 yards from The Court, was transformed from an open-air center into an upbeat, contemporary closed mall. Franklin Mills Value Mall is the largest single-story outlet mall in the nation, with more than 250 stores offering discounts of 20-60%. More than 30 restaurants can be found throughout the premises, along with a multiplex movie theater.

Exton Square Mall, Routes 30 and 100, Exton; 610-363-2860.
Franklin Mills Value Mall, 1455 Franklin Mills Circle; 215-632-1500; 800-336-6255.
Granite Run Mall, Routes 1 and 352, Media; 610-565-1650.
King of Prussia Shopping Complex, Routes 363 and 202; (Plaza) 610-265-5727; (Court) 610-337-1210.
Montgomery Mall, Routes 202 and 309, North Wales; 215-362-1600.
Neshaminy Mall, Route 1 North, Cornwells Heights; 215-357-6100.
Oxford Valley Mall, I-95 North, exit at Langhorne; 215-725-0221.
Plymouth Meeting Mall, 1150 Plymouth Meeting Mall, Plymouth Meeting; 610-825-9351.

The Plaza at King of Prussia

G. Widman for the Greater Philadelphia Tourism Marketing Corporation

Franklin Mills Mall

Springfield Mall, Route 320 and Baltimore Pike, Springfield; 610-328-1200.

Willow Grove Park, Easton Rd. and Moreland Rd., Willow Grove; 215-657-6000.

MINI-CENTERS

Smaller shopping centers are prevalent throughout the Philadelphia area. Because it would be impossible to list them all, we have presented some that are intriguing or offer a particular service.

Chadds Ford Barn Shops, Routes 1 and 100, Chadds Ford. This expanded shopping village includes merchandise the malls don't have.

City Line Center, City Ave. and Seventy-seventh St., Overbrook Park. A Main Line area shopping center that emphasizes savings, with T.J. Maxx, Eckerd Drugstore, Radio Shack, and Acme.

Devon Shopping Center, Route 202, Devon. A mini-mall featuring a wide variety of shops.

Fox Croft Square, Route 611, Jenkintown. This shopping center has a host of fine shops.

Haverford Square, Lancaster Avenue, Haverford. A courtyard of popular restaurants and fine shops.

Lawrence Park Shopping Center, Route 320 and Lawrence Rd., Broomall. T.J. Maxx and Today's Man anchor a multitude of other discount and specialty shops.

Marple Crossroads Discount Stores, Routes 1 and 320, Springfield; Linens N Things, Marshall's, Frank's Nursery and Crafts, Ross, to mention only a few of the stores that offer discount savings.

Olde Ridge Village Shoppes, Route 202 one mile south of Route 1, Chadds Ford. Features everything from gourmet food to craft shops, clothing to furniture.

Peddler's Village, Routes 202 and 263, Bucks County. Over 40 shops and several restaurants in a quaint colonial setting.

Pilgrim Gardens, Loehmann's Plaza, Township Line Rd., Drexel Hill. Pilgrim Gardens presents discount fashion shops, including Loehmann's.

Rosemont Village, 1149 W. Lancaster Ave., Rosemont. A small enclosed mall with a skylight, featuring an enticing restaurant and a Borders mega-bookstore.

St. Peter's Village, Route 23 in Chester County, about 15 miles northwest of Valley Forge. A charming village of shops restored to original Victorian style at the Falls of French Creek.

Skippack Village, Route 113 just north of Route 73 in Montgomery County. An eighteenth-century street village with more than 40 shops and boutiques.

Spread Eagle Village, Lancaster Ave., Wayne. The first relay station in colonial times, this center has 27 specialty and boutique shops.

Springfield Park, 420 Baltimore Pike, Springfield. A complex that offers specialty shopping, Strawbridge & Clothier, and Target.

Springfield Shopping Center, Routes 1 and 320, Springfield. Value City, Kidspot/House of Bargains, along with other values and bargains.

Spring House Village Center, Sumneytown and other locations. Built around an old barn, this center offers 40 shops in a country atmosphere.

Suburban Square, Lancaster Ave., Ardmore. The oldest shopping center in the country, it presents specialty shopping on the Main Line with elegant boutiques and the first suburban branch of Strawbridge & Clothier.

Wynnewood Shopping Center, near Lancaster Ave. on Wynnewood Rd. in Wynnewood. Features a series of small specialty shops and branches of Bed, Bath and Beyond and Borders.

SHOPPING BY AREA

BUCKS COUNTY

Booktenders, Books

Bucks County Furniture, Furniture

Crown & Eagle Antiques, Inc., Antiques

David M. Mancuso (At The Church), Antiques

Katy Kane, Antiques

Lahaska Antique Court, Antiques

Lahaska Antique Flea Market, Flea Markets

Oaklawn Metal Craft & Antiques, Antiques

Robertson & Thornton, Antiques

CENTER CITY

Alfred Bullard, Antiques

Alfred of Philadelphia, Florists

American Institute of Architecture Bookstore, Books

American Pants Company, Factory Outlets and Discount Stores

America's Gift Place, Gift Shops and Accessories

Bailey, Banks, & Biddle, Jewelry

Barnes and Noble, Books

Bauman Rare Books, Books

Beige, Shoes

Black Cat Cigar Company, Tobacco

Book Mark, Books

Borders, Books

Born Yesterday, Clothing

Boyd's, Clothing

Braverman's Bakery, Food

The Camera Shop, Photographic Supplies

Center Foods Natural Groceries, Food

Chelsea Silver Plating and Repairing Co., Antiques

Children's Boutique, Clothing

Earl P. L. Apfelbaum, Inc., Coins

Einstein Books and Toys That Matter, Toys

Flower World International, Florist

The Food Hall, Food

Formal Dimensions, Clothing

Freeman Fine Arts, Antiques

The General Store, Gift Shops and Accessories

Grace Book Store, Books

Helen Drutt Gallery, Crafts

Holt's Cigar Company, Tobacco

I. Goldberg, Clothing

Jack's Camera, Photographic Supplies

Jack Kellmer Co., Jewelry

J.E. Caldwell, Jewelry

Jeweler's Row, Jewelry

Joseph Fox Book Store, Books

Kay-Bee Toys and Hobby, Toys

Kitchen Kapers, Gift Shops and Accessories

Knit Wit, Clothing

Louis Vuitton, Leather

The Market, Food

M. Finkel and Daughter, Antiques

Philly Stamp & Coin, Inc. Coins and Stamps

The Photo Cine Shop, Photographic Supplies

Plage Tahiti, Clothing

Polo Ralph Lauren, Clothing

Reading Terminal Market, Food

Reese's, Antiques

Rindelaub's, Food

Robin's Book Store, Books

Robinson Luggage, Leather

Rodier Paris, Clothing

Schaffer's, Antiques

The Schwarz Gallery, Antiques

Sophy Curson, Clothing

Swiss Pastry Shop, Food

Taws Artist's Materials, Art Supplies

Toby Lerner, Clothing

Toppers Spa, Skin Care

Touches, Gift Shops and Accessories

Urban Outfitters, Gift Shops and Accessories

Utrecht, Art Supplies

Waldenbooks, Books

Wayne Edwards, Clothing

WhoDunIt, Books

The Workbench, Furniture

CENTER CITY— FAIRMOUNT PARK AREA

The Museum Shop, Gift Shops and Accessories

Philadelphia Zoo Shop, Gift Shops and Accessories

CHESTER COUNTY

Ball & Ball, Antiques

The Blue Ribbon, Crafts

Chalfont & Chalfont Antiques, Antiques

Chester County Book Company, Books

The Creative Hand, Crafts

Dilworthtown Country Store, Crafts

Elizabeth L. Matlat, Antiques

Entenmann's, Food

Irion Co., Furniture Makers, Furniture

Philip H. Bradley, Antiques

Villanova Cheese Shop, Food

DELAWARE COUNTY

B & S Shoes, Factory Outlets and Discount Stores, Shoes

Calico Corner, Fabrics and Linens

Choice Seating, Furniture

Circuit City, Video Equipment, Tapes, and CD's

Dan Howard Maternity Shop, Clothing

The Eagle's Eye, Factory Outlets and Discount Stores

Franklin Mint Museum and Gallery Store, Gift Shops and Accessories

General Nutrition Center, Food

Hit or Miss, Factory Outlets and Discount Stores

House of Bargains, Factory Outlets and Discount Stores

Hush Puppies, Shoes

Lancaster County Farmer's Market, Food

Larmon's, Photographic Supplies

Linens N Things, Fabrics and Linens

Loehmann's, Factory Outlets and Discount Stores

Pembroke Shop, Antiques

Syms, Factory Outlets and Discount Stores

Today's Man, Factory Outlets and Discount Stores, Clothing

The Wall, Video Equipment, Tapes, and CD's

LANCASTER COUNTY

Carter's Children's Wear Outlet Store, Factory Outlets and Discount Stores

National Brands Outlet Center, Factory Outlets and Discount Stores

The Reading Outlet Center, Factory Outlets and Discount Stores

Reading Station Designer Outlet Center, Factory Outlets and Discount Stores

VF Factory Outlet Complex, Factory Outlets and Discount Stores

MAIN LINE AREA

Albrecht's, Florists

Amaranth, Florists

Ann Taylor, Clothing

Ardmore Farmer's Market, Food

Arrowroot Natural Foods, Food

Bala Judaica, Books, and Gift Shops and Accessories

Bed, Bath and Beyond, Fabrics and Linens

Bestcake, Food

The Boys Connection, Clothing

Bryn Mawr Stereo, Video Equipment, Tapes, and CD's

Buy the Dozen, Food

Children's Book World, Books

Dandelion, Crafts

Eastern Mountain Sports, Sports Equipment

Gladwyne Village Gourmet, Food

Herman's World of Sporting Goods, Sports Equipment

Her Royal Highness, Clothing

Joseph A. Bank & Clothiers, Factory Outlets and Discount Stores

Kidz Shooz, Shoes

Linens By Design, Fabrics and Linens

Mads, Video Equipment, Tapes, and CD's

Main Line Coin & Stamp, Coins

Mapes Toys, Toys

Merion Art and Repro Center, Art Supplies

The Nature Company, Gift Shops and Accessories

NeoJudaica, Gift Shops and Accessories

R&R Produce and Fish, Food

Sam Goody, Video Equipment, Tapes, and CDs

Seidenburg Luggage, Leather

Sharper Image, Gift Shops and Accessories

Sherman Brothers, Shoes

Suky Rosan, Clothing

The Tinder Box, Tobacco

T.J. Maxx, Factory Outlets and Discount Stores

Viking Pastries, Food

Wallach's, Shoes

Women's Exchange, Clothing

Zany Brainy, Toys

Zips Toys To Go, Toys

MONTGOMERY COUNTY

Ashborne Market, Food

The Brookstone Company, Gift Shops and Accessories

Creative Endeavors, Art Supplies
The Eagle's Eye, Factory Outlets and Discount Stores
Edelman's Stamps, Coins and Stamps
Florsheim, Shoes
Ikea, Furniture
Ilona Bio-Aesthetics, Skin Care
Liguorius Bookstore, Books
Marshall's, Factory Outlets and Discount Stores
Modell's, Sporting Equipment

NORTHEAST PHILADELPHIA

Bauer's Pastry Shop, Food
Best Value Kosher Meat Center, Food
Bitar's Middle Eastern Groceries and Pastries, Food
Marlo Book Store, Books
Rosenberg Hebrew Book Store, Books, and Gift Shops and Accessories
Stein Florist, Florists
Toys R Us, Toys
Weiss Family Bakery, Food

NORTHWEST PHILADELPHIA— CHESTNUT HILL—MANAYUNK

Allure, Clothing
The Antique Gallery, Antiques
American Pie, Crafts
Axelrod and Bennett, Florists
Bikes & Books, Books
Bird in Hand, Antiques
Blum's, Antiques
The Brass Boudoir, Furniture
Bredenbeck's Bakery, Food
Chandlee & Bewick, Antiques
The Chestnut Hill Cheese Shop, Food
Chestnut Hill Farmer's Market, Food

The Leather Bucket, Antiques
Propper Brothers, Furniture
Robertson of Chestnut Hill, Florists
The Wooden Train, Toys

OLD CITY—SOCIETY HILL

Ben's Discount Shoes, Factory Outlets and Discount Stores
Betsy's Place, Gift Shops and Accessories
Gargoyle's Ltd., Antiques
National Museum of American History Gift Shop, Gift Shops and Accessories
Thomas David, Factory Outlets and Discount Stores
United American Indians of Delaware Valley Gift Shop, Gift Shops and Accessories
The Works Gallery, Crafts

QUEEN VILLAGE AND SOUTH STREET

Fabric Row, Fabrics and Linens
Garland of Letters, Books
South Street Antiques Market, Antiques
Tower Records, Video Equipment, Tapes, and CDs

SOUTH PHILADELPHIA

Claudio King of Cheese, Food
DiBruno Brothers, Food
Fante's, Gift Shops and Accessories
The Italian Market, Food
Sarcone & Son, Food
The Spice Corner, Food
Torre, Clothing

ANTIQUES

Few areas of the country can match Philadelphia and its surrounding counties for the wide variety and prices of antiques. Antique shops can be found virtually everywhere, from the colonial atmosphere of Pine Street to the rolling hills of the Pennsylvania countryside.

Center City

Alfred Bullard, 1604 Pine St.; 215-735-1879. Late eighteenth- and early nineteenth-century furniture beautifully displayed in an old three-story house.

Chelsea Silver Plating and Repairing Co., 920 Pine St.; 215-925-1132. You can learn the details of the fine art of silverplating. The store features antique lamps and bronze items.

M. Finkel and Daughter, 936 Pine St.; 215-627-7797. Amy and her father are well known for period furniture, fine quilts, and folk art.

Freeman Fine Arts, 1808 Chestnut St.; 215-563-9275. Established in 1805, it holds many sales annually of rare items that have been acquired from Philadelphia estates. Variety of antiques, jewelry, paintings, and Oriental rugs. Auctions on Wednesdays; Gallery Sales three times per year.

Gargoyle's, Ltd., 512 S. Third St.; 215-629-1700. Carries everything from architectural embellishments to decorative items.

Reese's Antiques, 930 Pine St.; 215-922-0796 and 215-561-0781. The oldest store on "Antique Row," this one features seventeenth-, eighteenth-, and nineteenth-century American and Oriental antiques.

Schaffer's, 1032 Pine St.; 215-923-2949. Known for their stained glass and accessories.

The Schwarz Gallery, 1806 Chestnut St.; 215-563-4887. Established in 1930, this well-known family specializes in eighteenth- and nineteenth-century American and European paintings, watercolors, and fine antiques.

South Street Antiques Market, 615 S. Sixth St.; 215-592-0256. The only indoor antiques and collectibles market in Center City.

Chestnut Hill

The Antique Gallery, 8523 Germantown Ave.; 215-248-1700. A shop specializing in art glass, pottery, delft, cloisonné, bronzes, and nineteenth-century furniture. Complete selection of books on antiques.

Bird in Hand Consignment Shop, 8419 Germantown Ave.; 215-248-2473. Great buys here in china, glass, pewter, and silver.

Blum's, 45 E. Chestnut Hill Ave.; 215-242-8877. Carries a general line of antiques, quilts, brass items, and accessories.

Chandlee & Bewick, 7811 Germantown Ave.; 215-242-0375. Features eighteenth- and nineteenth-century furniture and some accessories.

The Leather Bucket, 84 Bethlehem Pike, Chestnut Hill; 215-242-1140. Very fine eighteenth- and nineteenth-century English and American antiques.

New Hope

Crown & Eagle Antiques, Inc., Route 202 three miles south of New Hope, across from Winery; 215-794-7972. Specializes in finest American Indian art, rugs, basketry, beadwork, and pottery. Also china and weapons.

David M. Mancuso Antiques (At The Church), Route 202 and Upper Mountain Rd.; 215-794-5009. Primitive and American furniture displayed in an 1840 Baptist church.

Katy Kane, 34 W. Ferry St.; 215-862-5873. Brides and debs come here for the selection of white lace antique dresses and accessories.

Lahaska Antique Court, Route 202 in Lahaska (across from Peddler's Village); 215-794-7884. Ten antique shops selling everything from country furniture to pottery, blown glass, and paintings.

Oaklawn Metal Craft & Antiques, Route 202 in Lahaska; 215-794-7387. Known for its custom metal work, including lanterns, tools, and hardware. Also reproductions and restorations.

Robertson & Thornton Antiques, Route 202 between Doylestown and Buckingham; 215-794-3109. American antiques sold in a unique 1853 country store.

Other Antique Shops

Ball & Ball, 463 W. Lincoln Highway, Exton; 610-363-7330. Known for its seventeenth- and eighteenth-century brass, iron, and cabinet hardware reproductions.

Chalfont & Chalfont Antiques, 1352 Paoli Pike, West Chester; 610-696-1862. Fine seventeenth-, eighteenth-, and early nineteenth-century American antiques.

Elizabeth L. Matlat, Rt. 202, Brandywine Summit; 610-358-0359. Known for her eighteenth- and nineteenth-century antiques, crafted lighting, and books for the collector.

Pembroke Shop, 167 W. Lancaster Ave., Wayne; 610-688-8185. Carries 1870-90 Centennial furniture, as well as a line of country furniture and accessories.

Phillip H. Bradley, 1101 E. Lancaster Ave., Downingtown; 610-269-0427. The largest collection of American antiques and accessories in the area.

ART SUPPLIES

Any and every art supply needed by the commercial and amateur artist can be found at the centers below.

Creative Endeavors, King of Prussia Plaza; 610-337-3177.
Merion Art and Repro Center, 17 W. Lancaster Ave., Ardmore; 610-896-6161, 800-414-7851.
Taws Artists Materials, 1527 Walnut St.; 215-563-8742.
Utrecht, 2020 Chestnut St.; 215-563-5600.

BOOKS

There are so many excellent bookstores in the Philadelphia area that it is impossible to list them all here. Instead, we have selected those that are unique for one reason or another. Popular bookstores, like **B. Dalton,** can be found throughout Center City and in suburban malls. **Borders** (1727 Walnut St.; 215-568-7400), and **Barnes & Noble** (1804 Walnut St.; 215-972-8275) have opened book mega-stores in the city and suburbs; Borders comes complete with an espresso bar for reading and relaxing. Also, major department stores have extensive book sections with wide selections on varied subjects.

American Institute of Architects' Bookstore, Seventeenth and Sansom Sts.; 215-569-3188. This store has one of the finest selections of architectural writing to be found anywhere, including books on everything from interior design, theory, and history to landscaping and gardening. It also has a wide range of books on Philadelphia travel, a children's section, and an array of cards and stationery.

Bala Judaica Center, 222 Bala Ave., Bala Cynwyd; 610-664-1303. A wide selection of Jewish books for adults and children, from scholarly works to storybooks. Also tapes, videos, toys, games, gift items, fine art, and exquisite jewelry. If you can't find it, they'll order it.

Bauman Rare Books, 1215 Locust St.; 215-546-6466. The New York gallery is in the Waldorf Astoria, and both locations buy and sell rare books, autographs, prints, and maps. They are interested in libraries and single items.

Bikes & Books, 6228 Greene St., Germantown; 215-843-6071. The bikes are gone, but Mr. Gardner has 40,000 books covering almost any topic and subject, including American history, politics, and cooking.

Book Mark, 2049 West Rittenhouse Square; 215-735-5546. A reputable bookstore that carries a large stock of out of print, used, and rare books on almost any subject. It specializes in books on architecture.

Booktenders, 62 W. State St., Doylestown; 215-348-7160. Children up to age 16 love to read the wide range of books on almost any topic or subject. It also carries a large selection of reference books.

Chester County Book and Music Company, West Goshen Shopping Center, Paoli Pike and Route 202, West Chester; 610-696-1661. It offers a wide range of books in many categories, and all are well stocked. There is also an extensive selection of magazines and greeting cards.

Children's Book World, 17 Haverford Station Rd., Haverford; 610-642-6274. Full service bookstore for infants to teenagers. Special orders, too.

Garland of Letters, 527 South St.; 215-923-5946. Feeling tense? This is the store to visit. The specialty here is self-discovery books for relaxation and meditation. Also, music, videos, crystals, incense, jewelry, and crafts.

Grace Book Store, 730 Chestnut St.; 215-922-6868. Religious books are featured here.

Joseph Fox Book Store, 1724 Sansom St.; 215-563-4184. Knowledgeable service is always offered when selecting any of the books. Prominent in art and architectural literature.

Liguorius Book Store, Cheltenham Shopping Center, Cheltenham; 215-886-3675. Two locations. This lovely bookstore features a complete selection of softcover and hardcover books and a large selection of Black literature.

Marlo Book Store, Roosevelt Mall Shopping Center, Cottman and Roosevelt Blvd.; 215-331-4469. If anybody will have it, Marlo will. It sells up-to-date books on almost any subject, including one of the largest selections of computer books. It also has a section on used books and carries the largest selection of magazines in the area.

Robin's Book Store, 1837 Chestnut St.; 215-567-2615. Two locations. More than 30,000 titles on all subjects with a wonderful multicultural section. They also backdate items. Poetry readings are held several times a month.

Rosenberg Hebrew Book Store, 6408 Castor Ave.; 215-744-5205. Two locations. A wide selection of Judaica and Jewish books. Everything a child or adult might be looking for. Also, gifts, toys, tapes, and videos.

Waldenbooks, The Gallery at Market East; 215-922-3647. Two Center City locations for this popular book stop.

Whodunit, 1931 Chestnut St.; 215-567-1478. This shop solves the mysteries of locating your favorite mystery, adventure, and spy books.

CLOTHING

As one of the top clothing centers in America, Philadelphia offers every conceivable style and fashion in its department stores and specialty shops. This section lists some very special shops from which one can choose everything from sportswear to designer labels.

Women's Clothing

The exclusive shops carrying fashions from around the world include Toby Lerner, Sophy Curson, Polo Ralph Lauren, Knit Wit, Rodier Paris, and Plage Tahiti.

In the suburbs are Suky Rosan and Ann Taylor. For maternity clothes, we recommend Dan Howard and A Pea in the Pod, and for the large woman, Lane Bryant and Dress Barn Woman. Fine quality and formal wear for day and night is offered in Center City and malls throughout the area by Casual Corner, Talbot's, Ann Taylor, and Laura Ashley.

For camping and outdoor attire visit Eddie Bauer and I. Goldberg in Center City and suburban malls.

Listed below are the shops mentioned in the text that are not located in designated shopping malls:

Ann Taylor, Suburban Square, Ardmore; 610-642-4293.
Dan Howard Maternity Shop, 1136 Baltimore Pike, Springfield; 610-328-3252; also, 801 Bethlehem Pike, N. Wales; 215-855-6686.
Dress Barn Woman, 67 E. City Line Ave., Bala Cynwyd; 610-664-9720.
I. Goldberg, 902 Chestnut St.; 215-925-9393.
Knit Wit, 1721 Walnut St.; 215-564-4790.
Plage Tahiti, 128 S. Seventeenth St.; 215-569-9139.
Polo Ralph Lauren, The Shops at the Bellevue, Broad and Walnut Sts.; 215-985-2800.
Rodier Paris, 1737 Walnut St.; 215-496-0447.
Sophy Curson, 122 S. Nineteenth St.; 215-567-4662.
Suky Rosan, 102 E. Montgomery Ave., Ardmore; 610-649-3686.
Toby Lerner, 117 S. Seventeenth St.; 215-568-5760. Suburban Square, Ardmore; 610-642-8370.

Men's Clothing

Depending upon the event or occasion, men's dress in Philadelphia can vary from the "preppy" look to the European. You can be sure of finding stores to accommodate these two particular looks, as well as everything in between.

Stores for men in the Center City area include Boyd's, Formal Dimensions, Allure, Morville, Brooks Brothers, and Wayne Edwards.

In the surrounding counties, Bloomingdale's, Macy's, Today's Man, and Strawbridge and Clothier, are always up-to-date in men's fashions.

For the heavy-set man, visit Torre in South Philadelphia and Casual Male; for outdoor wear, see Eddie Bauer and I. Goldberg.

Listed below are the shops mentioned in the text that are not located in shopping malls.

Allure, 4358 Main St., Manayunk; 215-482-5299.
Boyd's, 1818 Chestnut St.; 215-564-9000.
Formal Dimensions, 1105 Walnut St.; 215-925-1174.
I. Goldberg, 902 Chestnut St.; 215-925-9393.
Today's Man, Lawrence Park Shopping Center, Broomall; 610-353-9260.
Torre Men's Fashions, 1217 S. Broad St.; 215-468-7272.
Wayne Edwards, 1517 Walnut St.; 215-563-6801.

Children's Clothing

Philadelphia's oldest department stores, like Strawbridge's, have been popular clothiers for children for more than a century. For further high quality, there is Macy's, Saks Fifth Avenue, and Lord & Taylor. Among the smaller shops featuring fine children's attire are Born Yesterday, The Boys Connection, Children's Boutique, Her Royal Highness, and the Women's Exchange, which carries lovely hand-made items.

Born Yesterday, 1901 Walnut St.; 215-568-6556.
The Boys Connection, 286 Montgomery Ave., Bala Cynwyd; 610-660-9330.
Children's Boutique. 1717 Walnut St.; 215-563-3881.
Her Royal Highness, Suburban Square, Ardmore; 610-642-0456.
Women's Exchange, 185 E. Lancaster Ave., Wayne; 610-688-1431.

COINS AND STAMPS

Trading, gift giving, collecting, investing? Philadelphia is a superb market in which to do all four.

Earl P. L. Apfelbaum, Inc., 2006 Walnut St.; 215-567-5200. Has given area stamp collectors more than 50 years of superb service.

Edelman's Coins and Stamps, 301 Old York Rd., Jenkintown; 215-572-6480. Established in 1926, this store has one of the best stocks of U.S. and foreign stamps to be found anywhere.

Main Line Coin and Stamp, 16 E. Lancaster Ave., Ardmore; 610-649-7900.

Philly Stamp & Coin Co., Inc., 1804 Chestnut St.; 215-563-7341. Rare stamps and coins bought, sold, and appraised. Also deals in scrap gold and silver.

CRAFTS

American Pie. Four locations including 4303 Main St., Manayunk; 215-487-0226. Handcrafted in the U.S.: Art to wear, jewelry, whimsical ceramics, art glass, Judaica, and gifts.

The Blue Ribbon, Ludwig's Corner, Routes 100 and 401, Glenmoore; 610-458-5066. A Victorian home filled with handcrafted items, folk art, pottery, and a variety of Chester County crafts.

The Creative Hand, Exton Square Mall, Routes 30 and 100, Exton; 610-363-1677. A cooperative of local artists and craftsmen selling their wares.

Dandelion, 31 Coulter Ave., Ardmore; 610-649-8303. In three area locations, these unique craft shops feature a large selection of handcrafted silver jewelry, pottery, kaleidoscopes, greeting cards, and novelty items.

Dilworthtown Country Store, 275 Brinton's Bridge Rd., West Chester; 610-399-0560. Built in 1758, this is one of the oldest general stores in Pennsylvania. Features eighteenth-century crafts, folk art, and herbs.

Helen Drutt Gallery, 1721 Walnut St.; 215-735-1625 (see VISUAL ARTS Galleries).

The Works Gallery, 302 Cherry St.; 215-922-7775 (see VISUAL ARTS Galleries).

FACTORY OUTLETS AND DISCOUNT STORES

Pennsylvania is renowned for its factory outlets, and they are abundant in Philadelphia and its nearby counties as well. At the top of the list, of course, is Reading—a scant 56 miles from Philadelphia—which is the capital of outlet shopping in America with hundreds of stores from which to choose. A sampling of the Reading outlets:

National Brands Outlet Center, 601 Hiesters Lane; 610-921-2151.
The Reading Outlet Center, 801 N. Ninth St.; 610-373-5495; 800-5-OUTLET.
Reading Station Designer Outlet Center, 951 N. Sixth St.; 610-478-7000.
VF Outlet Village, 801 Hill Ave.; 610-378-0408; 800-772-8336.

In the Philadelphia area, the Best Buy Company, Circuit City, Target, and Value City discount everything from housewares, gifts, indoor and outdoor furniture, and toys, to electronics, luggage, sports equipment and jewelry. Below is a selection of the Philadelphia area's many apparel discounters.

Women's Clothing Outlets

Hit Or Miss, multiple locations, including 519 E. Baltimore Pike, Media; 610-891-1980. Popular labels at discount prices.
Loehmann's, several locations, including Pilgrim Gardens, Drexel Hill; 610-789-9100. Designer and fine clothing discounted.

Men's Clothing

American Pants Company, five locations including 12-22 S. Eleventh St.; 215-751-2706. One block from the Convention Center, here are Levi's at discount prices and contemporary men's clothing.
Thomas David, several locations, including 401 Race St.; 215-922-4659.
Today's Man, several locations, including Lawrence Park Shopping Center, Broomall; 610-353-9260.

Children's Outlets

Carter's Children's Wear Outlet Store, 35 S. Willowdale Dr., Lancaster; 717-299-5685. Children's clothing from toddler to age 14 at 20%- 60% off. Clothing for men and women, also.
Kidspot/House of Bargains, multiple locations, including Springfield Shopping Center, Routes 1 and 320, Springfield; 610-543-8034.

Women's, Men's, and Children's Clothing

The Eagle's Eye, three locations, including Spread Eagle Village, 503 W. Lancaster Ave., Suite 900, Strafford; 610-989-0440. Other area locations are in Lancaster and Tannersville. Classic sportswear for women and children at healthy savings.

Joseph A. Bank Clothiers, Inc., two locations, including 379 Lancaster Ave., Haverford Square; 610-896-8500. Traditional clothing at excellent savings.

Marshall's, many locations, including Valley Forge Shopping Center; 610-337-2346. A fine selection of discounted clothes for men, women, and children.

Syms, two locations, including 100 Swedesford Rd., Berwyn; 610-644-2000. A wonderland of discounted clothing with Syms Bashes dropping prices even lower.

T.J. Maxx, several locations, including City Line Shopping Center, Overbrook; 215-879-2602. Clothing, housewares, and gifts at discounted prices.

Shoes

Ben's Discount Shoes, 231 Market St.; 215-925-2675. Fine fashions for men.

B & S Shoes Inc., Drexeline Shopping Center, Drexel Hill; 610-284-1070. Discount shoes for the family, including Rockport, SAS, and Easy Spirit.

FABRICS AND LINENS

Bed Bath & Beyond, a chain of inviting stores that lives up to its name, including 70 E. Wynnewood Rd., Wynnewood; 610-642-9296.

Calico Corner, a chain of stores, including 653 W. Lancaster Ave., Strafford; 610-688-1505. Choice seconds on the finest imported and domestic decorative fabrics for drapery, slipcovers, and upholstery. Also, savings of up to 50% on bolt material and remnants.

Fabric Row, South Fourth St., Queen Village. A row of shops dealing with every kind of fabric imaginable at extraordinary prices.

Linens By Design, 18 Haverford Station Rd., Haverford; 610-896-9290. Custom imported linens.

Linens N Things, multiple locations, including 400 S. State Rd., Springfield; 610-541-0120. Everything for the kitchen, bedroom, bath, and more.

FLEA MARKETS

Lahaska Antique Flea Market, Route 202 in Lahaska; 215-794-0300. Almost 50 indoor shops featuring a host of antiques and collectibles. Tue-Sun.

Quaker City Flea Market, State Rd. and Comly Sts.; 215-744-2022.

FLORISTS

Whether it's flowers for a friend, a wedding, or your own pleasure, try one of these noted shops.

Albrecht's, Flowers & Greenhouses, Montgomery Ave. and Meeting House Lane, Narberth; 610-664-4300. Since 1882, three generations of the Albrecht family have supplied the Philadelphia area with beautifully designed floral arrangements. They carry everything from exotic flowers to cut orchids and imported tulips.

Alfred of Philadelphia, 259 S. Twenty-first St.; 215-985-1198. These florists carry flowers, plants, dried material, and gifts. They specialize in gourmet fruit baskets. Plant rental is available.

Amaranth, 1400 Mill Creek Rd., Gladwyne; 610-649-9107. Fresh flowers and rentals. Friendly service.

Axelrod and Bennett, 921 E. Chelten Ave.; 215-843-3904; 800-468-3530. More than 80 years of excellence and floral decorations. Fruit baskets, balloons, and sweet trays, too.

Flower World International, 230 S. Broad St.; 215-567-7100, 800-257-7880. Send flowers worldwide. Never closes.

Robertson of Chestnut Hill, 8501 Germantown Ave.; 215-242-6000. Creative florists, known for imported tulips and unusual novelty and gift items.

Stein Florist, 7059 Frankford Ave.; 215-338-7100. Mr. Stein has the largest volume of flowers of any retail store in the city.

FOOD

Philadelphia's ethnic mix has produced a rich variety of international foods and American "firsts," such as ice cream, the Philadelphia cheese steak sandwich, and the Hoagie. Shopping for food is fun in this special city.

Bakeries

Bauer's Pastry Shop, 9825 Bustleton Ave.; 215-673-6560. Sixty years old now, this bakery continues to serve up delightful renditions of butter cake, forest cake, and cinnamon buns. But these are only a sampling of the many German specialties that also include super wedding and birthday delicacies.

Bestcake, 7594 Haverford Ave., Overbrook Park; 215-878-1127. Wedding and Bar/Bat Mitzvah cakes. "Kosher for All Occasions." Challah, rye bread, hamantashen, and sufganiot, too.

Braverman's Bakery, Reading Terminal Market, 215-592-0855. "Outrageously delicious baking." Large selection of European pastries, tortes, cannoli, and much more.

Bredenbeck's Bakery, 8126 Germantown Ave., Chestnut Hill; 215-247-7374. Its English tea scones are considered the best in Philadelphia.

Buy the Dozen, 219 Haverford Ave. (second floor), Narberth; 610-667-9440. "Strictly Kosher, Strictly the Best." Croissants, cookies, challah, kamish bread.

Entenmann's, 690 E. Lincoln Highway, Exton; 610-363-2290. Cakes, cookies, and doughnuts at discount prices.

The Pink Rose Pastry Shop, 630 S. Fourth St.; 215-592-0565. This small, intimate café serves espresso coffee, tea from China, and a wide variety of French, Italian, German, and American pastries—including spectacular homemade tarts, cookies, and cakes.

Rindelaub's. Two locations including 128 S. Eighteenth St.; 215-563-3993. For approximately 50 years, the upstairs bakery has continued to turn out famous German chocolate cake, peerless cinnamon buns, decorated gold cakes, and all-butter sponge cake. The breads and rolls are outstanding, too.

Sarcone & Son, 758 S. Ninth St.; 215-922-0445. Since 1918, has specialized in traditional Italian breads, rolls, bread sticks, pizza shells, and pepperoni bread (its center is a piece of thinly sliced pepperoni in tomato sauce).

Swiss Pastry Shop, 35 S. Nineteenth St.; 215-563-0759. Since 1925, delightful Swiss cakes including dobash, a seven-layered vanilla cake with chocolate buttercream filling. Also, Viennese crescent rolls and unique salt sticks.

Viking Pastries, 39 Cricket Ave.; 610-642-9227. This established Scandinavian bakery specializes in breads, croissants, Viking onion rolls, Swedish fruit tarts, rum balls, and cookies.

Weiss Family Bakery, 6635 Castor Ave.; 215-722-4506. "New York's Famous Kosher Bakery." Try the doughnuts, then try everything else.

International & Gourmet Foods

Ashbourne Market, 7909 High School Rd., Elkins Park; 215-224-1288. Hard-to-find items include a large selection of imported and domestic cheeses, coffees and teas from around the world, caviar, fresh baked goods, and much more.

Bitar's Middle Eastern Groceries & Pastries, 947 Federal St., Kensington; 215-755-1121. Lebanese specialties. Great pita bread, spinach pies, cheese pies, and a unique strudel-like pastry made with heavy cream.

Best Value Kosher Meat Center, 8564 Bustleton Ave.; 215-342-1902. Three shopping areas of fine meats and poultry, deli, homemade foods, baked goods, dairy products, and a grocery stocked with Kosher, Middle Eastern, and Israeli specialties.

The Chestnut Hill Cheese Shop, 8509 Germantown Ave., Chestnut Hill; 215-242-2211. This little shop brims with all kinds of cheeses and gourmet foods.

Claudio King of Cheese, on Ninth St. between Carpenter and Christian; 215-627-1873. A nineteenth-century shop featuring imported and domestic cheeses, 40 different oils, and Italian, French, and Greek groceries.

DiBruno Brothers, 930 S. Ninth St.; 215-922-2876. For approximately 70 years, the DiBrunos have operated this popular deli and gourmet food shop in South Philly. Not only are they well known for their cheeses from around the world, but also for their own homemade cheese spreads and popular wine vinegars. Customers still come in every day for their delicious gourmet salads and large selection of Italian cold cuts.

The Food Hall, Strawbridge & Clothier, The Gallery at Market East; 215-629-6000. An English kitchen offering fresh breads and pastas, deli meats, a selection of gourmet foods, Godiva chocolates, and a fine line of cookware.

Gladwyne Village Gourmet, 358 Righters Mill Rd., Gladwyne; 610-642-6022. Two locations. Shelves stocked with gourmet goodies; cheese sculptured into whatever shape you desire.

The Market, The Gallery at Market East; 215-925-7162. A collection of fresh-food specialty grocers in a lively market atmosphere.

R&R Produce and Fish, 7551 Haverford Ave., Overbrook Park; 215-878-6264. Besides the fresh produce and fish, and the unusual packaged and frozen goods, this delightful small shop is filled with an array of kosher cheeses and Israeli foods, many of them homemade. Rob and Ruth will try to meet your every need.

The Spice Corner, Ninth and Christian; 215-925-1660. Carries a large selection of spices, teas, fresh-ground coffee, and dried and glazed fruits.

Villanova Cheese Inc., The Shops at Great Valley, Malvern; 610-647-6160. There are so many items to choose from that many customers like to view this as their food hardware store. Carries everything from imported truffles and pâtés to a large selection of teas, coffees, jams, and mustards.

Markets

Ardmore Farmer's Market, Suburban Square, Ardmore; 610-896-7560. Open 6 am-10 pm Thu, noon-10 pm Sat, 11 am-6 pm Sunday. On the Main Line, this market features merchants selling everything from fresh produce and meat to Dutch delicacies.

Chestnut Hill Farmer's Market, 8229 Germantown Ave., Chestnut Hill; 215-242-5905. Located behind the Chestnut Hill Hotel, this group of individual stalls features fresh produce and a large assortment of cheeses, pastas, salads, pastries, candies, and cut flowers. Thu-Fri 9 am-6 pm, Sat 8 am-5 pm.

Italian Market, Ninth St., from Wharton to Christian Sts., South Philadelphia. This vibrant, bustling marketplace, the nation's largest outdoor food market, is a magnificent and energetic place to shop. With neighborhood merchants' stores filled to overflowing, and even more to be found on the sidewalk tables and pushcarts, you'll find everything from fresh fruits and vegetables to a full range of meats, poultry, seafood, pastas, cheeses, and baked goods. Not only is it all fresh, but it's reasonably priced, too.

Lancaster County Farmer's Market, Lancaster Ave. and Eagle Rd., Wayne; 610-688-9856. Open Wed, Fri, and Sat, 6 am- 4 pm. Popular Main Line spot that offers fine produce, a large selection of meat and fish, herbs, and Pennsylvania Dutch cooking. Some merchants sell craft items and antiques.

Reading Terminal Market, Twelfth and Arch Sts.; 215-922-2317. Open Mon through Sat, 8 am-6 pm. Directly across the street from the new Convention Center, the Market in the historic Reading Train Shed is a fun place to shop and eat around a beer garden and courtyard. Approximately 80 merchants sell produce, meat, fish, groceries, prepared foods, books and other merchandise. Amish and Mennonite farmers sell poultry, produce, and baked goods from Wednesday through Saturday.

Natural Foods

Arrowroot Natural Foods, 834 W. Lancaster Ave., Bryn Mawr;

610-527-3393. More than 100 bins of natural bulk items, and a large selection of discounted vitamins.

Center Foods Natural Groceries, 1525 Locust St., 215-732-9000. One of the largest selections of organic and natural foods; now carries a full line of macrobiotic items.

General Nutrition Center. Several locations including Springfield Mall; 610-543-9524. A full range of vitamin supplements, natural diet aids, body care products, and physical fitness equipment.

FURNITURE

If you are furniture shopping, take advantage of the varied offerings below.

The Brass Boudoir, 8000 Germantown Ave., Chestnut Hill; 215-247-3815. Handcrafted, custom-made beds and accessories by local craftsmen.

Bucks County Furniture, Inc., 174 Keystone Dr., Telford; 215-257-1135. Manufactures antique furniture reproductions. Each piece is signed, dated, and numbered, and an authenticated certificate accompanies each when purchased. Call for dealer locations.

Choice Seating Galleries, four locations including 32 E. Baltimore Ave., Lansdowne; 610-626-3199. "500 Furniture Styles, 2,000 Fabrics, 3-5-day Delivery."

Ikea, Plymouth Commons, Plymouth Meeting; 610-834-1520. Swedish furnishings, deeply discounted, with a supervised playroom for the children of shoppers.

Irion Co. Furniture Makers. Call the workshop in Christiana, 610-593-2153, to find out where these fine eighteenth-century American reproductions can be seen.

Propper Brothers, Cresson and Levering Sts., near Green Lane Bridge, Manayunk; 215-483-0544. Since 1888, fine quality furniture at everyday discount prices.

The Workbench, 30 S. Seventeenth St.; 215-665-9221. With its main furniture store based in New York, this spot offers European Bauhaus furniture with a simple look and contemporary lines.

GIFT SHOPS AND ACCESSORIES

There are many unique gift shops throughout the Philadelphia area. These are among the best.

America's Gift Place, Sixteenth and JFK Blvd.; 215-636-1665. This shop, located inside the Philadelphia Visitors Center, carries a wide array of commemorative souvenirs and gifts. Open seven days a week.

Bala Judaica Center. (See BOOKS.)

Betsy's Place, 323 Arch St.; 215-922-3536. Among the large selection of souvenirs at the historic Betsy Ross House are brass and pewter reproductions, handcrafted wooden banks, and replicas of historic row houses. The miniatures and annual Christmas ornaments are popular collectibles.

The Brookstone Company, The Court at King of Prussia; 610-337-0774. Everything you need but can't find, featuring all kinds of tools and household and personal items.

Fante's Gourmet Cookware Shop, Italian Market, 1006 S. Ninth St.; 215-922-5557; 800-878-5557. Since 1906, one of the finest gourmet cookware shops, including fine coffees, spices, and a complete line of cake decorating equipment.

Franklin Mint, Route I, Franklin Center; 610-459-6884. Also, Willow Grove Park, Jenkintown. A fine line of collectible items, including pewter, bronze, crystal, sculptures, lithographs, and jewelry.

The General Store, 260 S. Twentieth St., Philadelphia; 215-732-6858. Everything you can imagine, from penny candy to Tiffany lampshades and lots in between.

Kitchen Kapers, 213 S. Seventeenth St.; 215-546-8059. This cutlery and specialty tea and coffee shop features handpainted trivets and a line of high-quality kitchen utensils.

National Museum of American Jewish History Gift Shop, 55 N. Fifth St.; 215-923-3811. Judaica gifts and ceremonial art. Unusual menorah and spice box collection. Magnificent display of ketubot.

The Museum Shop, Philadelphia Museum of Art, Twenty-sixth St. and Benjamin Franklin Parkway; 215-684-7960. The finest collection of art books to be found anywhere, including educational books for children and illustrated storybooks. Also, a fabulous collection of contemporary jewelry, giftware reflecting the Museum's collection, wonderful pottery, and posters representing Museum works.

The Nature Company, several locations including Suburban Square, Ardmore; 610-649-7121. Everything from ponds and fountains, sundials, and bird feeders, to books, games, kits.

NeoJudaica, Wynnewood; 610-649-7018. A private, eclectic Judaica shop. Flexible hours, by appointment. Specializing in comprehensive collections of Judaica jewelry—many one-of-a-kind, and reproductions. Custom design available. Yemenite, sterling ceremonial objects a specialty. Artwork, ketubot, and Judaica books.

Philadelphia Zoo Shop, Thirty-fourth St. and Girard Ave.; 215-243-1100. This shop is housed in a replica of an old carriage house built in 1876. Caters to children as well as adults with its fine line of zoo-related gift items, games, books, stuffed animals, mugs, figurines, ceramics, and jewelry.

Rosenberg Hebrew Book Store. (See BOOKS.)

The Sharper Image, several locations including 61 Anderson Ave., Ardmore; 610-896-9030. A toy store for adults. Chairs that relax you, office basketball hoops, electronic everythings.

Touches, 225 S. Fifteenth St.; 215-546-1221. This shop helps accessorize your outfits with beautiful handbags, shawls, and belts. It helps accessorize your home, too. Also carries an unusual collection of handmade jewelry and children's items.

United American Indians of Delaware Valley Gift Shop, 225 Chestnut St.; 215-574-9020. Wide-ranging display of Native American ceremonial and folk art. Books, greeting cards, pottery, clothing, artwork.

Urban Outfitters, 1627 Walnut St.; 215-569-3131. A contemporary department store with an urban attitude that carries trendy high-style clothing and home furnishings. Also a variety of housewares and toys. Sportswear is a specialty.

JEWELRY

Bailey, Banks & Biddle, Sixteenth and Chestnut Sts.; 215-564-6200. Outstanding since 1832. Diamonds and gold, famous brand watches, fine china, and crystal. Also, international gift department.

Jack Kellmer Co., two locations including 717 Chestnut St.; 215-627-8350. Diamond importers and gemologists specializing in precious stones and estate jewelry, plus objets d'art.

J.E. Caldwell, several locations including Chestnut and Juniper Sts.; 215-864-7800. With its fine jewelry and gifts, this has been a Philadelphia landmark for more than 150 years.

Jeweler's Row, Sansom St., between Seventh and Ninth, and Eighth St. between Chestnut and Walnut. More than 300 wholesale and retail jewelers make this the largest jewelers' district in the nation, except for New York.

LEATHER

Louis Vuitton, 1413 Walnut St.; 215-557-0225. Elegant selection of luggage and handbags.

Robinson Luggage, five locations including Broad and Walnut Sts.; 215-735-9859. Among the widest arrays of luggage in the area.

Seidenburg Luggage, two locations including Suburban Square, Ardmore; 610-642-7800. Large selection of fine luggage and leather goods.

PHOTOGRAPHIC SUPPLIES

The following retail stores provide full customer service, including equipment sales, repairs, and developing for both amateur and professional photographers.

The Camera Shop, Inc., numerous locations throughout the area including The Gallery at Market East; 215-925-9500 and 572-0300.
Jack's Camera, twenty-six locations throughout the area including 2135 Walnut St.; 215-751-1195.
Photo Cine Shop, 129 S. Eighteenth St.; 215-567-7410.

For quick, guaranteed, one-day film developing, see the following:

The Camera Shop, Inc. (see above).
Jack's Camera (see above).
Larmon's, Granite Run Mall, Media; 610-565-1920. Promises to develop and print your 35mm color negative film in one hour.

SHOES

Beige, 1715 Walnut St.; 215-564-2395. Catering to the woman's needs in fine shoes in a wide range of colors and styles.
B & S Shoes, Drexeline Shopping Center, Drexel Hill; 610-284-1070. Family discount shoe store. Tap, ballet and parochial school shoes. Wide and narrow widths. Handicapped ramp.
Florsheim, eleven locations throughout the area including Plymouth Meeting Mall, Plymouth Meeting; 215-753-1827. High-quality shoes for men and women.
Hush Puppies Shoes, several locations including Granite Run Mall, Media; 610-891-0912. Specializing in wide widths for men and women.
Kidz Shooz, Three W. Lancaster Ave., Ardmore; 610-645-9445. American and European designer shoes for children.
Sherman Brothers, Lancaster Ave., Rosemont; 610-527-2323. Fine men's shoes for 50 years. Famous brands, hard to fit sizes.
Wallachs, 21 Haverford Station Rd., Haverford; 610-642-6070. Master Shoe Fitters since 1939. Specializing in good-looking comfortable shoes and the hard-to-fit.

SKIN CARE

Ilona Bio-Aesthetics, 411 E. Lancaster Ave., Wayne; 610-687-4444. Face and skin care offered in a relaxing, nurturing environment.

Toppers Spa, Rittenhouse Square, 117 S. Nineteenth St.; 215-496-9966. Full service body care—pamper yourself.

SPORTS EQUIPMENT

Eastern Mountain Sports, Suburban Square, Ardmore; 610-896-0627. Features cross-country and downhill skiing equipment, plus backpacking and climbing supplies.

Herman's World of Sporting Goods, several locations including City Line and Belmont Aves., Bala Cynwyd; 610-617-0340. A chain of sporting goods shops that carries a large selection of name-brand sports clothing and equipment.

Modell's, multiple locations including King of Prussia Plaza; 610-337-3030. A large selection of all types of sporting goods.

TOBACCO

Black Cat Cigar Company, 1518 Sansom St.; 215-563-9850. Prices here may well be the lowest in Philadelphia.

Holt's Cigar Company, 1522 Walnut St.; 215-732-8500. Philadelphia's oldest and largest tobacco and cigar importer.

The Tinder Box International, Three Bala Plaza, Bala Cynwyd; 610-668-4220. Carries a large line of tobaccos and gifts.

TOYS

Einstein Books and Toys That Matter, Seven Walnut St.; 215-665-EMC2 (665-3622). "Books, Toys, Gifts, Memorabilia and Ephemera." Only in Philadelphia, and perhaps the best toy store in the country.

Kay-Bee Toy and Hobby Shop, several locations including The Gallery at Market East; 215-238-1248. Wide selection of favorite toys and games for children.

Mapes Toys, several locations including 210 W. Lancaster Ave., Ardmore; 610-658-9505. Broad selection of all the toys, games, crafts, and sporting goods you're probably looking for.

Toys R Us, many locations in the Philadelphia area including 201 Franklin Mills Center; 215-281-0222. Best discounts and selection.

The Wooden Train, 8433 Germantown Ave., Chestnut Hill; 215-242-5660. This old-fashioned toy store features original and hard-to-find toys.

Zany Brainy. Several locations including 270 E. Lancaster Ave., Wynnewood; 610-645-7987. Intelligent selection of educational and fun toys and books. Frequent special events for children.

Zips Toys to Go, 16 W. Lancaster Ave., Ardmore.; 610-649-2555. Classic toys, dolls, and imports like Playmobil.

VIDEO EQUIPMENT, TAPES, AND CD'S

Bryn Mawr Stereo. Two locations including 1016 W. Lancaster Ave., Bryn Mawr; 610-525-6300. Large selection of quality CD's and equipment.

Circuit City. Multiple locations including the Marple-Springfield Shopping Center, Routes 1 and 320, Springfield; 610-544-7598. Electronic heaven.

Mads, Nine W. Lancaster Ave., Ardmore; 610-642-0764. Hard to find folk, bluegrass, and blues.

Sam Goody. Several locations including 133 W. Lancaster Ave., Ardmore; 610-649-3830. Wide selection of tapes, CD's, videos, and equipment.

Tower Records. Several locations including 537-39 South St.; 215-925-0422, and 608-10 South St.; 215-574-9888. One store is devoted to classical music, while the other caters to the contemporary sound—right across the street from one another. Together, they should be able to meet any of your musical needs, and with an enormous sign, you can't miss Tower.

The Wall, the Granite Run Mall, Media; 610-566-5553. Numerous locations throughout the area. These stores carry one of the largest selections of home entertainment equipment. Prices are competitive.

SPORTS

SPORTS TO SEE

Philadelphia can certainly lay legitimate claim to being "The City of Winners." In fact, in 1993, *The Sporting News* ranked it second among America's Most Livable Sports Cities. It all began in May of 1974, when the Philadelphia Flyers of the National Hockey League won their first of two consecutive Stanley Cup championships, bringing two million people into the streets of the city for the largest parade in its history. Two years later, the Philadelphia Phillies won their first of three straight National League East baseball titles, which they crowned with their first World Series championship in 97 years in October of 1980. In 1993, a scrappy, lovable, come-from-behind team took the National League Championship.

Not to be outdone, the Philadelphia Eagles of the National Football League soared to the top of their division and, in January of 1981, flew to the Super Bowl in New Orleans, Louisiana. Since then they have secured a berth in the playoffs two more times. The Philadelphia 76ers won the NBA world championship in 1983, and have reached the finals of the National Basketball Association playoffs year after year.

These professional teams attract sellout throngs, and now they have been joined by the Philadelphia Phantoms (American Hockey League), Philadelphia Wings (lacrosse), the Philadelphia Kixx (soccer), and the Philadelphia Bulldogs (roller hockey). The city is also the site of major professional golf, tennis, and cycling competitions, as well as a host of amateur sports events—among them rowing, track, cricket, and rugby. Horse racing at Philadelphia Park, as well as auto racing in the Pocono Mountains, also flourish.

Auto Racing

Every summer, the world's finest stock-car drivers come to the Pocono International Raceway in nearby Long Pond, Pennsylvania, for

500-mile superspeedway cup events. Throughout the summer the raceway hosts various exciting racing competitions.

Boxing

Philadelphia has produced some of the best prizefighters in the world, including former heavyweight champion Joe ("Smokin' Joe") Frazier. Today the major bouts are held in nearby Atlantic City, New Jersey, a pleasant ride from Center City on the Atlantic City Expressway, AMTRAK, or Greyhound.

College Basketball

Eighty-eight area colleges and universities have a 200-year history of spirited athletic competition. Today there is the Big Five, the Big East, and the Atlantic 10.

The Big Five Conference presents some of the most competitive collegiate basketball to be found anywhere. Conference members Temple, University of Pennsylvania, LaSalle, Villanova, and St. Joseph's square off against each other and the nation's top basketball powers on their home courts, as well as at the new, state-of-the-art Apollo at Temple, and in the festive Palestra at Penn. The annual Big Five Tournament is an event in itself. For tickets and information, call 215-898-4747.

Cycling

Philadelphia hosts the First Union USPRO Cycling Championship Bike Race in June. The race, with starting and finish lines on Benjamin Franklin Parkway near the Philadelphia Art Museum, has become a two-week event in the city. Much of the action centers in Manayunk around the fabled and grueling "Manayunk Wall."

Cricket

This forerunner of what we know as baseball is played on two fields in West Fairmount Park and various other locations, including the Merion Cricket Club. The C.C. Morris Cricket Library at Haverford College is a major authority on the sport. For information and a schedule of upcoming events, call the Library at 610-896-1162.

Golf

The Philadelphia area has some of the most beautiful and challenging golf courses in the world that on occasion are the sites of major Professional Golf Association tournaments. For information contact the clubs in the "Sports To Do" section below.

Horse Racing

Thoroughbred racing is held at Philadelphia Park, Street Road, Bensalem: 215-639-9000. Admission includes parking. Call for schedules and post times. Thoroughbred racing is also offered at Delaware Park near Wilmington, Delaware (302-994-2521), while standard bred racing takes place at the Garden State Race Track in Cherry Hill, New Jersey (856-488-8400).

The Turf Club Restaurants in Center City and Upper Darby are Off Track Betting locations, broadcasting races from Philadelphia Park, Penn National, The Meadows, and Pocono Downs. (See DINING.)

Horse Shows

Among the nation's most prestigious equestrian events is the Devon Horse Show and Country Fair, which is staged in suburban Devon in late May and early June. In September comes the annual American Gold Cup Horse Show, also in Devon. (See SPECIAL EVENTS.)

Major Leagues

The Philadelphia Eagles, National Football League. Exhibition games in August, regular-season games from September through December at Veterans Stadium. For tickets and information, call 215-463-2500.

The Philadelphia Flyers, National Hockey League. Exhibition games in September and early October, regular-season games from October through April at the First Union Spectrum. For tickets and information, call 215-465-4500.

The Philadelphia Phillies, National Baseball League. Games from April through October at Veterans Stadium. For tickets and information, call 215-463-1000.

The Philadelphia 76ers, National Basketball Association. Exhibition games in September and early October, regular-season games from October through April at the First Union Spectrum. For tickets and information, call 215-339-7676.

Rowing

This is a sport whose roots run deep in Philadelphia's history, offering a perfect excuse for a family outing complete with a picnic on the banks of the beautiful Schuylkill River. Among the top events are the annual Dad Vail Regatta in May (the largest intercollegiate regatta in the world) and the Independence Day Regatta on July 4. Admission is free; depending upon the event, however, plan to arrive early for a choice spot on the riverbank. Check local newspapers for details, or call the Schuylkill Navy, the oldest amateur sporting organization in the U.S., founded in 1858: 215-232-7689, or 215-978-6919.

Tennis

One of the major stops on the professional tour is the annual Advanta U.S. Indoor Tennis Championships, held at the Spectrum in February and featuring the world's top male players. For information, call: 800-995-BALL.

In the fall, the top female players are featured in the Advanta Women's Tennis Championships. In the summer, the Women's Grass Nationals take place at the Merion Cricket Club: 610-642-5800.

Track and Field

Some of the world's finest athletes compete each September in the Philadelphia Distance Run. The month of April features the Penn Relays, the oldest amateur track and field meet in the nation. (See SPECIAL EVENTS.)

Wrestling

Among Philadelphia's most raucous crowds are those attending the World Wrestling Federation matches at the First Union Center. For tickets and information, call 215-336-3600. Website: www.comcast-spectacor.com.

SPORTS TO DO

Many Philadelphians lead sporting lives, and visitors and new residents are encouraged to join in the fun. Whether it's rowing on the Schuylkill River, hiking through the Wissahickon Valley, rollerblading on Kelly Drive or West River Drive, hunting in French Creek State Park, rafting on Brandywine Creek, or playing a snappy match of tennis or round of golf, the Philadelphia area offers a myriad of sports to do.

Faimount Park, the nation's largest urban park, presents 8,900 landscaped acres to enjoy. Its offerings include 73 baseball diamonds, 115 tennis courts, 13 football fields, 14 soccer fields, 2 cricket fields, 2 field hockey fields, a rugby field, a bowling green, an archery range, 3 bocce courts, five 18-hole golf courses, 6 indoor recreation centers, 3 outdoor swimming pools, 75 miles of bridle paths and hiking trails, 25 miles of bikeways, the finest rowing course in the nation, a trout-stocked fishing stream, Pennsylvania's only fish ladder, countless picnic areas, and magnificent views.

Bicycling

Municipally sponsored events start in the early spring and continue through mid-fall, and include the popular Philadelphia-to-Atlantic City Bike Ride. For information, call the Department of Recreation (215-683-3600) or the Fairmount Park Commission (215-685-0000).

The Brandywine Bicycle Club organizes rides at all levels throughout the year, primarily in scenic Chester County; 610-983-9127. Website: www.hometown.aol.com/brandybike.

In the city, Fairmount Park has 23 miles of bike paths, including Kelly Drive and West River Drive, in the Wissahickon Valley from Ridge Avenue to Rittenhouse Street, and Forbidden Drive. The Philadelphia-Valley Forge Bikeway runs from Independence Hall to Valley Forge National Park. For bike rentals and tours of the Philadelphia area contact Trophy Bike Tours, 311 Market St.; 215-625-7999.

Ridley Creek State Park has trails winding among old buildings and plantations, picnic areas, and even a stocked stream. Telephone: 610-892-3900. (No rentals available).

Tyler State Park features more than ten miles of paved bike trails. However, the trails on the west side of Neshaminy Creek are very hilly, so be sure to dismount and walk when weary. Telephone: 215-968-2021 (no rentals available).

Valley Forge National Historical Park offers 2,500 historic acres, including miles of bicycle paths. Motorized vehicles and skateboards are prohibited from the bike trails. Call 610-783-1077.

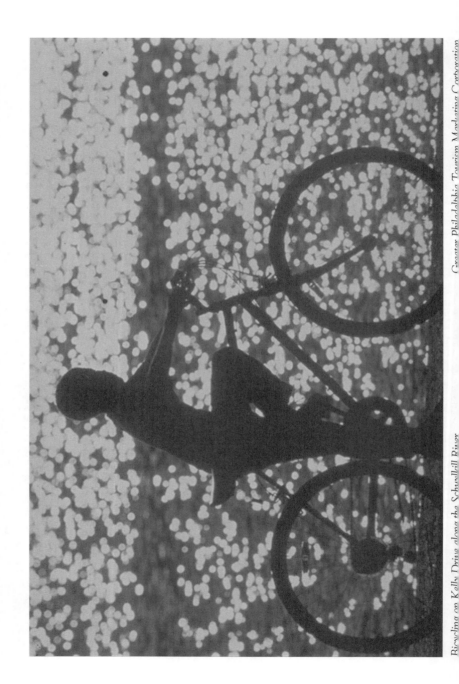

Bicycling on Kelly Drive along the Schuylkill River

Bocce

This traditional European staple of the Philadelphia sports scene combines elements of bowling, horseshoes, and croquet. The Fairmount Commission offers Bocce courts at Broad and Oregon streets, and Sixty-third and Daggett streets.

Bowling

Though universally known as bowling, this sport was called "ten-pins" by many in Philadelphia, where bowling alleys (once called "pin palaces") abound. Two of the many area bowling alleys are:

Boulevard Lanes offers 48 lanes, a pro shop and restaurant, at 8011 Roosevelt Blvd.; 215-332-9200.

Wynnewood Lanes presents 24 lanes and a cocktail lounge at Haverford Rd. and Karakung Dr. in Delaware County; 610-642-7512.

Golf

Philadelphia and its surrounding counties have more than 100 golf courses, including private, semi-private, and public facilities. Six are located in Fairmount Park.

Cobbs Creek, Seventy-second St. and Lansdowne Ave.; 215-877-8707.
Franklin Roosevelt, Twentieth St. below Pattison Ave.; 215-462-8997.
J.F. Byrne, 9500 Leon; 215-632-8666.
Juniata, M and Cayuga Sts.; 215-743-4060.
Walnut Lane, Walnut Lane and Henry Ave.; 215-482-3370.

Among the better county-operated courses outside the city are:

Paxon Hollow Golf Club, Paxon Hollow Rd. in Marple Township: 610-353-0220.
Pine Crest Golf Club, Route 202 in Montgomeryville; 215-855-4113.
Valley Forge Golf Club, on Rt. 23 in King of Prussia; 610-337-1776.

Health Clubs

Health clubs are popular in the Philadelphia area. We list our recommendations.

Bally Total Fitness Centers, multiple locations where you can "Shape Your Body and Your Life." Telephone: 800-695-8111.

The Fitness Company presents a full range of health equipment and instruction. Included are a pool, saunas, and a whirlpool. In the Wyndham Franklin Plaza Hotel, Seventeenth and Vine Sts.; 215-569-4404.

JCC, the Jewish Community Centers in the city and the suburbs offer state-of-the-art fitness centers, jogging tracks, sports facilities, saunas, and Olympic-size pools. Main branch: 401 S. Broad St.; 215-545-4400.

Lucille Roberts Health Club has several salons in the Philadelphia area including 121 City Ave., Bala Cynwyd; 610-617-7350.

Paoli Health & Fitness offers professional, individual instruction. Located at 1564 Lancaster Ave., off Route 30 in Paoli, near the train station; 610-296-0433.

Riverside Aquatic and Fitness Center, 600 Righters Ferry Rd., Bala Cynwyd; 610-664-6464. Features state-of-the-art exercise machines, fitness evaluation and classes, aerobics, sauna, swimming, tennis, and raquetball.

Sporting Club at the Bellevue, an upscale, full-service club. Pool, whirlpool, steam room, sauna, Cybex, free weights, hammer, spinning, and sports. 224 S. Broad St.; 215-985-9876.

YMCA, with 17 branches throughout Philadelphia and its surrounding counties, offers a wide variety of recreation programs and facilities for men and women. Located at 1421 Arch St.; 215-557-0082.

Hiking

With the abundance of parks and open, rolling hills in the Philadelphia area, hiking is both popular and historically stimulating. The Wanderlust Hiking Club (215-725-2011) sponsors year-round hikes (215-580-4847). The Sierra Club (215-592-4073) sponsors hikes and outdoor environmental activities. The Batona Hiking Club (215-482-4397) and the Chester County Trail Club (610-431-7509) are other groups to contact.

Fort Washington State Park gives one a chance to hike and step back into history at the same time. Located on Militia Rd. off Bethlehem Pike, Whitemarsh; 215-591-5250.

Great Valley Nature Center winds through 10 1/2 acres of ponds and fields. There's even a springhouse. Afterward, be sure to check out the exhibits, bookstore, and gift shop. On Route 29 at Hollow Rd. in Phoenixville; 610-935-9777.

Horseshoe Trail is for the professional hiker. It features a 120-mile trail that starts at Routes 23 and 252 in Valley Forge State Park and, marked by yellow horseshoes along the way, courses west until it meets the Appalachian Trail, which covers 2,000 miles from Maine to Georgia. If you're up to it, call the Horseshoe Trail Club at 610-469-1916 for further information.

Peace Valley Nature Center is not only a hiking trail but also a nature center of 1,500 acres. There's also Lake Galena, field trips, bird and butterfly walks, a butterfly garden, and a children's area. In Doylestown; 215-345-7860.

Ralph Stover State Park in Bucks County offers wonderful hiking trails, fishing, and sheltered picnic areas. The High Rocks section with its spectacular views was donated by James Michener. There is rock climbing in the park, too, but it is high-risk, only for properly trained climbers. For information call the Bucks County Visitors Bureau, 215-345-4552; 800-836-2825.

The Tyler Arboretum has acres of plants, blossoms in season, and rare trees. Located at 515 Painter Rd., Media; 610-566-9134.

Schuylkill Center for Environmental Education offers trails, including one for the handicapped. It offers educational and nature-hike programs. Also, this is the only facility in the area that tends to injured wildlife. Located at 8480 Haggy's Mill Rd., Roxborough; 215-482-7300.

Wissahickon Valley is a magnificent part of Fairmount Park, and has trails that were traveled by the Lenni Lenape Indians. Telephone: 215-685-0000.

Horseback Riding

The Philadelphia municipal area has 80 paths of riding trails in Fairmount Park, the Wissahickon, and Pennypack Park. In the surrounding counties, horseback riding ranks high on the popularity list because of the miles of hills, dales, and trails that meander through thick stands of trees. Much of the best areas are, of course, also historical.

In Philadelphia, rentals are available at **Pelzer's Stables,** 4800 Parkside Ave., 215-473-6700. Guided trail rides and carriage rides through Fairmount Park.

Valley Forge National Historical Park has miles of trails, including the famed 120-mile Horseshoe Trail. 610-783-1077.

More horseback riding in Chester County is available at the following stables:

Gateway Stables, Merrybell Lane, Kennett Sq.; 610-444-1255. Guided trail rides, lessons, and camps. Tours are $35 per hour. English and western riding. Reservations must be made.

Sheeder Mill Farm, Pughtown Rd., Spring City; 610-469-9382. Guided trail rides, $25 for one hour. Instruction. Reservations required.

Thorncroft Equestrian Center, Malvern; 610-644-1963. They offer riding instruction at all levels, specializing in riding for the handi-capped.

In Bucks County, there is riding in **Tyler State Park,** one of the largest state parks in Pennsylvania. Horses can be rented privately from nearby Covered Bridge Farms, 215-860-1791.

In Montgomery County, horseback riding is available at **Ashford Farms,** River Rd., Miquon; 610-825-9838. Trail riding Tue-Sun 9 am-5 pm.

Hunting

Hunting is a major sport in Pennsylvania. So major, in fact, that hunters annually spend millions pursuing this sport throughout the state. No less than six state game lands are located near Philadelphia—four in Bucks County, one in Chester, and one in Berks.

French Creek State Park has 5,000 acres available for hunting and trapping from the fall archery season through March 31 of the follow-ing year. Located seven miles northeast of the Pennsylvania Turnpike Interchange (Exit 22) on Route 345; 610-582-9680.

Nockamixon State Park offers 3,000 acres for hunting and trapping from the fall archery season through March 31 of the following year. Located five miles east of Quakertown on Route 313; 215-529-7300.

For further information about game lands, licenses, and the exact dates of the various hunting seasons, call the Pennsylvania Game Commission at 610-926-3136. Website: www.pgc.state.pa.us. Licenses required if over 17. They are available at local sporting goods stores throughout the five counties.

Ice Skating

When it's cold enough in the winter, ice skaters flock to the creeks and ponds of the Philadelphia area. Otherwise, they're skating on the ice of numerous artificial rinks in and around the city. Five of them are operated during the winter months by the Department of Recreation; 215-683-3600.

Cobbs Creek Center, Cobbs Creek Parkway and Walnut St.; 215-685-1995.

Rizzo Recreation Center, Washington Ave. at Interstate 95; 215-685-1593.

Scanlon Recreation Center, "J" and Tioga Sts; 215-685-9893.

Simons Recreation Center, Walnut Lane and Woolston St.; 215-685-2888.

Tarken Recreation Center, Frontenac and Levick Sts.; 215-685-1226.

Other popular rinks in the city include:

Blue Cross River Rink (an outdoor rink), Penn's Landing; 215-925-RINK (7465).

University of Pennsylvania Class of '23 Rink, 3130 Walnut St.; 215-898-1923.

Among those outside the city are:

Ardmore Ice Skating Rink, Holland Ave. and County Line Rd., Ardmore; 610-642-8700.

Ice Line, 700 Lawrence Dr.; West Chester; 610-436-9670.

Old York Road Skating Club, Church and York Rds., Elkins Park; 215-635-0331.

Skatium, Darby and Manoa rds., Havertown; 610-853-2225.

Wintersport Ice Sports Arena, 551 York Rd., Willow Grove; 215-659-4253.

Wissahickon Ice Skating Club, 550 W. Willow Grove Ave.; 215-247-1907.

Roller Skating

Carman Roller Skating Rink, 3226 Germantown Ave.; 215-223-2200.

Palace Roller Skating Center, 11600 Roosevelt Blvd.; 215-698-8000.

Villanova Skating Center, 789 Lancaster Ave., Villanova; 610-527-7243.

WOW Family Fun Center, 7017 Roosevelt Blvd.; 215-335-3400.

Running

Among other jogging activities, Philadelphia is the annual site of three formidable events: The Broad Street Run every May (see SPECIAL EVENTS); the Philadelphia Distance Run in September (see SPECIAL EVENTS); the Philadelphia Marathon in November (see

SPECIAL EVENTS). For further information, call the Dept. of Recreation at 215-683-3600, or the Fairmount Park Commission at 215-685-0000.

If you want to practice for these events or just get in shape, **Fairmount Park** has a half-dozen trails complete with distance markers. There's also a Perrier Parcourse Fitness Circuit along Forbidden Drive in Fairmount Park, with 18 exercise stations along the course.

Valley Forge National Historical Park is also a superior area (2,500 historical acres) to jog. Telephone: 610-783-1077.

Tennis and Raquetball

As is true throughout the country, Philadelphians have found tennis and racquetball to be excellent ways to get fit and stay that way.

Fairmount Park operates more than 100 all-weather tennis courts, as well as offering free instruction for children. The park also sponsors the Fairmount Fall Festival Championship, an annual amateur event. Another 150 courts, operated by the Department of Recreation, are scattered throughout the city. Telephones: 215-683-3600 and 215-685-0000.

Among the popular courts in Philadelphia are:

The Fitness Company, in the Wyndham Franklin Plaza Hotel; Seventeenth and Vine Sts.; 215-569-4404. Outdoor tennis, raquetball, outdoor track.

Northeast Raquet Club and Fitness Center, Krewstown Rd. and Grant Ave.; 215-671-9969.

Riverside Aquatic and Fitness Center, 600 Righters Ferry Rd., Bala Cynwyd; 610-664-6464.

Robert P. Levy Tennis Pavilion at the University of Pennsylvania, 3130 Walnut St.; 215-898-4741. Indoor courts.

Among the popular courts in surrounding counties are:

Club la Maison, 215 Sugartown Rd., Strafford; 610-964-8800.

Narberth Raquet Club, 630 Montgomery Ave., Narberth; 610-664-2696.

Philadelphia Sports Club at High Point, Upper State and County Line Rds., Chalfont; 215-822-1951. Tennis and racquetball along with a full fitness center.

Radnor Racquet Club, 175 King of Prussia Rd., Radnor; 610-293-1407.

Tennis Addictions, Pickering Creek Industrial Park, off Route 100, Lionville; 610-363-1052.

Water Sports ————————————————

Fishing

Rivers, streams, creeks, and lakes in the Philadelphia area are fished primarily for trout, though many other species can be hooked, too. Licenses are required if over 16. These are available at bait and tackle shops throughout the five counties. For specific information about fishing in Pennsylvania, consult the summary book that accompanies your license, or call the Pennsylvania Fish and Boat Commission, 717-626-0228.

Fort Washington State Park. Fish surrounded by history, on Militia Rd. off Bethlehem Pike, Fort Washington; 215-591-5250.

French Creek State Park (610-582-9680), with Scott Lake and Hopewell Lake, features warm-water species, including pike, chain pickerel, tiger muskie, perch, bass, blue gill, catfish, and of course, trout.

Hibernia County Park in Chester (610-384-0290) features Brandywine Creek, which is stocked with three kinds of trout, and also has a small pond where children can fish for its stocked trout.

Marsh Creek, west of the town of Eagle on Route 100 in Downingtown; 610-458-5119.

Newlin Mill Park, in Glen Mills (610-459-2359), is bordered on the west by Chester Creek, which also has the three species of trout, a few palominos, small- and large-mouth bass, and carp.

Nockamixon State Park (215-529-7300) is fed by three creeks (Tohickon, Maycock, and Three-Mile Run), which are filled with muskie, walleye, small- and large-mouth bass, yellow perch, and channel cat fish. Some say this is absolutely the best fishing in the area.

Ridley Creek State Park (610-892-3900) and its namesake, Ridley Creek, are also known for trout.

The Schuylkill River, which features rainbow, brook, and brown trout, as well as muskie, can be fished from Manayunk to Fairmount Park. Also available are five miles of the **Wissahickon** from Germantown Pike to the Walnut Lane Bridge, and **Pennypack Creek** from State to Pine Rd. **F. D. Roosevelt Lake** is located at Twentieth St. and Pattison Ave.

Tyler State Park (215-968-2021) in Newtown.

Valley Forge National Park (610-783-1077) is bordered on the west by Valley Creek and on the north by the Schuylkill, both of which have rainbow, brook, brown trout and muskie.

Wissahickon Creek can be fished for free in many places in the northwestern part of the city, including Valley Green. For information call 215-685-0000 or 215-683-3600.

Rafting, Boating, Canoeing, and Tubing

The Philadelphia area is replete with water sports, and with the Schuylkill River winding through the heart of the city, rowing is at the top of its list. (Those stately boathouses of Boat House Row are sufficient testimony to that.) If you're broad of back and would like further information about participating, call **The Schuylkill Navy** at 215-232-7689, or 215-978-6919.

If you'd rather canoe or sail the placid Schuylkill, the **Philadelphia Canoe Club**, at 4900 Ridge Ave. (between Duron Paints and the entrance to Kelly Drive), offers lessons and conducts outings for experienced oarspeople. 215-487-9674.

At times, the Park Canoe House has rowboats, canoes, and sailboats available for rent. It's located on Kelly Drive, south of the Strawberry Mansion Bridge. Call for details: 215-685-3936.

Among the popular rafting, canoeing, sailing, and tubing sites outside the city where rentals are available, are:

Brandywine Creek, where tubing, rafting, and canoeing are offered by the Northbrook Canoe Co., 1810 Beagle Rd., West Chester; 800-898-2279. These people are *very* popular, however, and reservations are a must.

French Creek State Park, about seven miles northeast of the Pennsylvania Turnpike's Morgantown interchange (Exit 22); 610-582-9680.

Hidden River Adventures, Route 724, Monocacy; 610-582-5800 and 800-FLOAT-PA. Website: www.floatpa.com.

Marsh Creek, west of the town of Eagle on Route 100 in Downingtown; 610-458-5119.

Nockamixon State Park, five miles east of Quakertown on route 313; 215-529-7300.

Point Pleasant, Byron Rd., Point Pleasant. (Route 32, eight miles north of New Hope/Yardley exit on Interstate 95). This is one of the finest river recreation facilities in the East with five locations offering canoeing, tubing, and whitewater and quiet rafting on the scenic Delaware River. Rentals, changing facilities, picnic area, food concession. Call Bucks County River Country for reservations: 215-297-TUBE (8823), or 215-297-5000.

Tyler State Park in Newtown; 215-968-2021. Canoe rentals. Canoes, tubes, kayaks, and rafts.

Or call the Bucks County Department of Parks and Recreation, 215-757-0571.

Swimming

Philadelphia has more municipal swimming pools than any other city in the country. **Fairmount Park** offers four outdoor pools, all fully staffed with lifeguards. Admission is free, and the pools are open through Labor Day. 215-683-3600 and 215-685-0000.

Many hotels, motels, and private clubs in and around the city have swimming facilities, and the four counties surrounding Philadelphia offer them as well. Among the most popular outdoor sites outside the city are:

French Creek State Park, about seven miles northeast of the Pennsylvania Turnpike's Morgantown interchange (Exit 22); 610-582-9680.

Marsh Creek State Park, west of the town of Eagle on Route 100 in Downingtown; 610-458-5119. Swimming pool, 610-458-8390.

Nockamixon State Park, five miles east of Quakertown on Route 313; 215-529-7300.

Tohickon Valley, one mile north of Point Pleasant on Cafferty Rd.; 215-297-0754 and 215-757-0571.

Skiing

The Philadelphia area offers a number of slopes from which to choose, all within easy driving. For really superb skiing, try going a little farther to the Pocono Mountains. (See ONE-DAY EXCURSIONS.)

Spring Mountain, off Routes 19 and 73 near Schwenksville; 610-287-7900. Website: www.springmountain-fun.com.

Among the better skiing areas within 75 miles are:

Blue Marsh, one-half mile south of Bernville on Route 183; 610-488-6396.

Blue Mountain, five miles east of Palmerton, 30 miles north of Allentown; 610-826-7700.

Bear Creek Ski and Recreation Area, 15 miles southwest of Allentown off Routes 29 and 100; 610-682-7109. Website: www.skibearcreek.com.

Cross-Country Skiing

Fort Washington State Park, Militia Rd. off Bethlehem Pike, Fort Washington; 215-591-5250.

French Creek State Park, seven miles northeast of the Pennsylvania Turnpike's Exit 22 on Route 345; 610-582-9680.

Ridley Creek State Park, two and one-half miles west of Newton Square on Route 3; 610-892-3900.

Tyler State Park, Newtown; 215-968-2021.

Valley Forge National Historical Park, Valley Forge; 610-783-1077.

SPECIAL EVENTS

Through the years, Philadelphia has developed a host of events to satisfy every whim. Indeed, there is so much going on in and around Philadelphia that something—be it a fair, tour, festival, concert, or sporting event—is unfolding every day of the year.

Nevertheless, there are some annual events that have become synonymous with the seasons in which they occur; unique experiences that, in view of the crowds they attract year after year, clearly have a hold on Philadelphians and their friends.

This is the nature of the events we have listed below. Some are traditional, some are cultural; some are inspirational, while others are educational and informative; still others are held strictly for the sheer fun and joy that they produce. Regardless of their purpose, however, these are the kinds of events that are sure to appeal to visitors as much as they do to Philadelphians themselves.

Please be aware that although these events are held in the same season of every year, the month in which they take place may vary slightly. For further information about locations and a current calendar of events, contact the Philadelphia Convention and Visitors Bureau at 215-636-1666. Website: www.libertynet.org/phila-visitor.

January

Chinese New Year, Chinese Cultural Center, 126 N. Tenth St.; 215-928-1616 or 413-0668. The celebration begins in January or February with a ten-course banquet at the Cultural Center, and continues for two months. CH. Reservations required.

Martin Luther King Day Observance; 215-574-0380 or 751-9300 Special events and ceremonies are held at various sites throughout the city, including a musical tribute at the African-American Historical and Cultural Museum, and a bell-ringing ceremony at Independence Hall. On Dr. King's birthday, a luncheon honoring national and international civil rights leaders is held. Events are free.

Mummers Parade. This world-famous New Year's Day parade, known as Philadelphia's Mardi Gras, features 30,000 costumed

203

Mummers, including string bands, fancies, and comics performing the traditional "Mummers Strut" before adoring crowds of hundreds of thousands of people. Fancy Brigade finale at the Pennsylvania Convention Center, Twelfth and Arch Sts. Information: 215-336-3050.

Philadelphia Auto Show, the largest in the area. PA Convention Center, Twelfth and Arch Sts.; 215-636-1666.

Philadelphia Boat Show, PA Convention Center, Twelfth and Arch Sts.; 215-418-4989 and 418-4700. An annual display that features more than 500 yachts, sailboats, and power boats. Also sophisticated marine gear and even boat homes.

February

Advanta U.S. Indoor Tennis Championship, the First Union Spectrum, Broad St. and Pattison Ave.; 215-389-9543. This event brings the best players from the men's professional tour to the Spectrum for the largest indoor men's tournament in the world. Top players compete for more than $400,000 in prize money. *CH.*

Black History Month, African-American Historical and Cultural Museum, Seventh and Arch Sts.; 215-574-0380. In commemoration of African-American contributions to the nation's history, the museum hosts numerous free lectures, exhibitions, and musical presentations. Philadelphia churches, museums, colleges, schools, community centers, libraries, and theaters also offer unusual and entertaining opportunities to learn about black culture.

Ice Capades, the First Union Spectrum, Broad St. and Pattison Ave.; 215-336-3600. Spectators of all ages are thrilled by these lavish shows on ice. Call for exact dates and prices. *CH.*

Junior Jazz Weekend for children at the Please Touch Museum; 215-963-0667.

Mummers Show of Shows. Extravagantly costumed Mummers "strut" in an indoor performance at the First Union Spectrum. 215-336-3600.

PECO Energy Jazz Festival, at various sites. For information, call the Convention and Visitors Bureau: 215-636-1666. A jazz-packed weekend of more than 90 events with Philadelphia jazz legends and emerging artists. Jazz workshops, films, vespers, brunches, and nightcaps.

Philadelphia Home Show, PA Convention Center, Twelfth and Arch Sts.; 215-418-4989 and 800-756-5692. Decorating and remodeling ideas and products are showcased at this exhibition. *CH.*

Thaddeus Kosciuszko National Memorial, 215-739-3408. Ceremonies honoring the Polish patriot include a commemorative wreath-laying ceremony.

Washington's Birthday Weekend, Valley Forge National Park, Route 202, King of Prussia; 610-783-1077. Special events include an actual reenactment of the Continental Army's hard winter here more than two centuries ago.

March

Atlantic 10 Men's Basketball Tournament, at the First Union Complex; 215-336-3600. March madness at its best.

The Food Network's Book and the Cook Festival, various Philadelphia-area locations; 215-636-1666. A restaurant and cookbook event; you have the opportunity to wine and dine at fine restaurants in the company of major food and wine book authors. *CH varies.*

The Food Network's Book and The Cook Fair, Pennsylvania Convention Center, Twelfth and Arch Sts.; 215-418-4989 and 636-1666. An annual festival of food including gourmet food exhibits, demonstrations, and book signings.

Philadelphia Flower Show, PA Convention Center, Twelfth and Arch Sts.; 215-418-4989 and 988-8899. This, the largest and most prestigious flower show in the nation, covers more than ten acres of the Convention Center with flowers, landscapes, nurseries, garden clubs, and competitive exhibits. It includes more than 170 major exhibits and at least as many minor ones. *CH.*

St. Patrick's Day Parade, along the Benjamin Franklin Parkway and on to Independence Mall; 215-945-0563. The city and its environs celebrate this traditionally festive day with bands, banners, and lots of green beer.

April

Battle of Manila Bay Commemoration on the battleship Olympia at the Independence Seaport Museum, Penn's Landing; 215-925-5439. Celebrate this monumental historic event with re-enactors depicting life during the Spanish-American War. Free with Olympia admission or membership.

Cambodian New Year Celebration, marked with a parade and outdoor festival. 215-324-4070.

Easter Promenade. This stroll on the waterfront features music, entertainment, and celebrity guests. Call for information: 215-636-1666.

Memorial Ceremony for the Six Million Jewish Martyrs. A gathering at the Holocaust Memorial, Sixteenth St. and Benjamin Franklin Pkwy., or at Rodeph Shalom Synagogue in case of rain. 215-922-7222.

Mummers String Band Show of Shows, First Union Spectrum; 215-336-3600. Extravagantly costumed bands perform, drill, and strut before large crowds.

Passover Prep Time. Try your hand at baking matzos—unleavened bread—for the Jewish holiday of Passover that commemorates Moses leading the Jews out of Egypt. Holiday crafts and music, too. Passyunk Ave. and South St.; 215-725-2030.

Penn Relays, University of Pennsylvania's Franklin Field, Thirty-third St. near South St; 215-898-6145. World's oldest and largest track meet. Bill Cosby used a scene from the relays in one of his shows. CH.

Philadelphia Antiques Show, 103rd Engineers Armory, Thirty-third and Market Sts.; 215-387-3500. Reputed to be the finest antique show in the nation, this event features guided tours, lectures, and gourmet luncheons—all for the benefit of the Hospital of the University of Pennsylvania. CH.

Philadelphia Festival of World Cinema, various locations; 215-895-6542. A two-week celebration of more than 100 premieres and film classics from 30 countries, representing the best new world cinema.

Philadelphia Furniture Show. Furniture dealers from around the country show samples of some of the best styles of furniture. Pennsylvania Convention Center, Twelfth and Arch Sts.; 215-440-0718.

Philadelphia Phillies Baseball Home Opener, opening day at Veteran's Stadium, Broad St. and Pattison Ave.; 215-463-6000 or 685-1500. CH.

Philadelphia Open House, various sites; 215-928-1188. During April and May, the Friends of Independence National Historical Park coordinate this series of walking and bus tours giving people a chance to enjoy private homes, gardens, and historic buildings usually closed to the public. Homes included are in Society Hill, Rittenhouse Square, Independence National Historic Park, Chestnut Hill, Germantown, and on the Main Line. CH.

Valborgsmassoafton, American Swedish Historical Museum, 1900 Pattison Ave.; 215-389-1776. The Swedish tradition of welcoming the arrival of spring features food, fun, dancing, and a bonfire at night. CH *nominal.*

May

Africamericas Festival, various sites; 215-636-1666. A celebration of African-American culture with entertainment, a parade, a film festival, and talent contests.

The Blue Cross Broad Street Run; 215-563-6184. Philadelphia's premier 10-mile racing event down Philadelphia's longest street, from Somerville Ave. to FDR Park.

Bonfires and Barbeques. Join in the fun on the Jewish holiday of Lag B'Omer, traditionally celebrated with hiking, picnicking, and of course, bonfires. Sites vary so call for details. 215-725-2030. NCH.

Canal Day, in historic Manayunk; 215-482-9565. The canal made the Schuylkill River passable and provided waterpower for the industries that built this town, but on this day, Main Street is closed to traffic. Come enjoy the shops, the ambience, and the entertainment, and take some refreshment at an outdoor table overlooking the canal that made it all happen.

Devon Horse Show, Devon Fairgrounds, Route 30, Devon; 610-964-0550. The nation's finest riders compete for prize money in America's largest, and one of the most prestigious, outdoor horse shows. Up to 150,000 turn out to enjoy the country fair atmosphere of this week-long event, begun in 1896. CH.

First Union Jam on the River, The Great Plaza at Penn's Landing; 215-636-1666. A Memorial Day Weekend event packed with all the excitement of New Orleans, including Creole and Cajun cooking, and Dixieland, Zydeco and jazz. Check newspapers for specific events. Junior Jam presents children's activities. CH *varies.*

International Black Doll Convention. Hosted by the first Black Doll Museum in the country, the show brings together collectors and craftspeople from around the country to present the African-American image in doll-making through history. Pennsylvania Convention Center, Twelfth and Arch Sts.; 215-787-0220.

Israel Independence Day Celebration, Penn's Landing; 215-636-1666. Annual celebration of Israel's independence with a Center City parade and a sprawling day-long bazaar including music and entertainment.

Italian Market Festival, at the Italian Market, Ninth St. between Catherine and Dickinson Sts.; 215-922-5557. A feast of Italian foods, music, and special events at the largest outdoor food market in the nation.

Penn's Landing Summer Season; 215-922-2FUN. May to September are filled with free concerts and celebrations on the waterfront. And Sundays are free "fun-days" for kids from 2-4 pm.

Pennsylvania Fair. Rides, food and entertainment for the whole family. Philadelphia Park. 215-639-9000.

Philadelphia International Theater Festival for Children, various locations including the Annenberg Center, 3680 Walnut St.; 215-898-6791. More than 100 performances of theater, folklore, dance, music, and puppets from around the world, with participatory events for children.

Radnor Hunt Races. The nation's top steeplechase horses, riders, trainers, and owners vie for purse money totaling $130,000. The event benefits the Brandywine Conservancy. Radnor Hunt Club. 610-647-4233.

Stotesbury Cup Regatta, on the Schuylkill River; 215-923-5352 or 978-6919. One hundred high schools across the country participate in this event sponsored by the Schuylkill Navy. The Navy, founded in 1858, is the oldest amateur sporting organization in the United States.

Strawberry Festival, at Peddler's Village, Lahaska; 215-794-4000. Welcome spring in April and May with craft demonstrations, puppet shows, music, and fresh strawberries, preserves, and fritters.

Sunoco Dad Vail Regatta, on the Schuylkill River starting at Boathouse Row; 215-248-2600. The largest college regatta in the world, with approximately 3,000 scullers from 60 colleges and universities competing.

Vassar Show House. The Philadelphia Vassar Club's annual scholarship benefit. The area's top designers and landscape architects meet the challenge of decorating and landscaping beautiful homes in the area. 610-527-9717.

Vietnam Veteran's Memorial Annual Run. A 10-kilometer run in remembrance of those who served in the Vietnam War, beginning and ending at the Memorial. Christopher Columbus Blvd; 215-333-5032.

June

Elfreth's Alley Fete Days, Elfreth's Alley; 215-574-0560 or 636-1666. Private homes on this, the oldest continuously occupied street in America, are opened to the public on the first weekend in June. Also, a craft show, featuring 25 Colonial craftspeople, troop re-enactments, music, a children's garden with clowns, candle dipping and papermaking, food and baked goods. CH.

First Union USPro Cycling Championships, start/finish line on Benjamin Franklin Parkway, near the Philadelphia Museum of Art; 877-5SERIES (73-7437) or 215-636-1666. Top cyclists compete for prize money in the nation's largest one-day professional cycling race. The course is 156 miles long and includes the legendary and grueling "Manayunk Wall." A two-week celebration, with many events in Manayunk, leads up to the race, which is the longest and richest single-day cycling event in North America.

Flag Day, Betsy Ross House, 239 Arch St.; 215-627-5343. Special activities in honor of the red, white, and blue at the house where it is all reputed to have begun.

Head House Square Crafts Fair, Head House Square, Second and Pine Sts; 215-636-1666 or 215-790-0782. Craftspeople demonstrate their skills and display their wares on this Colonial square every weekend from Memorial Day to September. Free children's workshops every Sunday from 1-3 pm.

Islamic Heritage Festival, Penn's Landing; 610-352-0424. A cele-bration of Islamic culture with music, foods, crafts, and educational programs.

Manayunk Arts Festival; 215-482-9565. The largest outdoor two-day juried arts and crafts show and sale in the Delaware Valley, with more than 250 artists from all over the country.

Mann Music Center, Fifty-second St. and Parkside Ave.; 215-546-7900. The Philadelphia Orchestra and guest stars perform in the pas-toral setting of Fairmount Park in June and July. Free tickets available for a $2 handling fee by calling 215-893-1999. *CH/NCH.*

Mellon Jazz Festival (see PERFORMING ARTS Summer Concerts).

Midsommarfest, at the American Swedish Historical Museum, 1900 Pattison Ave.; 215-389-1776. This summer festival includes folk music, food, children's games, and dancing around the maypole. *CH nominal.*

Odunde, Twenty-first and South Sts.; 215-732-8508 or 732-8595. African-American Festival celebrating the beginning of the traditional Yoruba New Year. Ten blocks of vendors and performances.

Philadelphia County Fair at Memorial Hall in Fairmount Park, 215-878-0110. Go back in time to a fair with food, rides, and fun.

Philly Dock Party at Independence Seaport Museum, Penn's Landing; 215-925-5439. Celebrate the museum's birthday with kids' arts and crafts, games, prizes, music, and other surprises. Also, in honor of the birthday, tour the museum's galleries and ships for a special, one day only, all ages price of $3.

Ringling Brothers Barnum & Bailey Circus, the First Union Spectrum, Broad and Pattison sts.; 215-336-3600. The "Greatest Show on Earth" wows young and old alike. *CH.*

Rittenhouse Square Fine Arts Annual, Rittenhouse Square; 215-634-5060. This is the oldest outdoor exhibit of fine art in the country, and it is strung up on clotheslines every June with more than 20,000 works in oil, watercolor, and acrylic. Prints, graphics, silk-screens, etch-ings, and sculpture also are on display—and for sale.

July

African-American Heritage Festival; 215-684-1008. A showcase of the African Diaspora. Live entertainment, education, and an African marketplace.

Fort Mifflin Freedom Blast. A costumed reenactment at Fort Mifflin on the Delaware presented by ARAMARK. 215-492-1881.

Greek Picnic. All of the "black Greek" fraternities and sororities congregate in Fairmount Park and other locations to enjoy concerts, shows, workshops, and displays, to benefit the United Negro College Fund. Website: www.phillygreek.com.

Hispanic Fiesta. Two fun-filled days featuring music, dance, entertainment, ethnic food, and artisans from Puerto Rico and other parts of Latin America. Penn's Landing; 215-627-3100.

Independence Day Regatta, on the Schuylkill in Fairmount Park; 215-923-5352 or 978-6919. In an area in which rowing is among the most traditional sports, this is one of the highlights of the season. Thousands line the banks of the river with picnic blankets, tents, tables of food, and coolers while enjoying the races.

Kutztown Pennsylvania German Festival. A celebration of Pennsylvania Dutch culture with taste-tempting foods, pageantry, quilting, folklore seminars, children's activities, authentic folk art and evening dinner theater performances. Kutztown. 888-674-6136.

Philadelphia International Film Festival (PhilaFilm); 215-849-2716. A four-to-five day event hosted by the International Association of Motion Picture Producers showcasing independent film and video artists, motion pictures, and TV productions.

Robin Hood Dell, East Fairmount Park; 215-685-9560. Top stars from the popular entertainment world of music and dance featured in a series of low-cost summertime concerts. Through August. CH.

Sunoco Welcome America!, various locations; 215-636-1666 and 800-770-5883. The city's July Fourth celebration is one of the biggest, brightest, and noisiest to be found anywhere—and understandably so. Special events leading up to and including Independence Day include The Great American Liberty Parade, spectacular fireworks set to music, Native American ceremonies and dances, a Mummers' strut, festivals, concerts, and the Liberty Medal Award Ceremony at Independence Hall. Website: www.americasbirthday.com.

Vitetta Group Sand Sculpture. Beginning in June and into July, watch the art of sand sculpturing as artists create their masterpieces. Each year features a different theme. The Shops at Liberty Place, Sixteenth and Chestnut Sts.

August

Beat the Heat Weekend. As the temperature rises in the third week of August, let the Franklin Institute cool you down with cool fun for the entire family. Twentieth St. and Benjamin Franklin Pkwy.; 215-448-1200.

Caribbean Festival. A celebration of Caribbean culture with live stage entertainment and traditional foods and crafts. Great Plaza at Penn's Landing; 215-879-9352.

Pennsylvania Dutch Festival, Reading Terminal Market, Twelfth and Arch Sts.; 215-922-2317. Quilting demonstrations and sales, hex sign painting, folk music, scrapple and sausage making, farm animals, ice cream making, produce, preserves, crafts.

Philadelphia Folk Festival (see PERFORMING ARTS Summer Concerts).

Pow Wow in the Park. A celebration of Native American heritage. Memorial Grove, Fairmount Park; 215-574-9020.

September

American Gold Cup, Devon Fairgrounds, Route 30, Devon; 610-964-0550. Outstanding horse-jumping for prize money at the Fairgrounds. CH.

Brandywine Battlefield, Route 1, Chadds Ford; 610-459-3342. An authentic reenactment of the historic eighteenth-century battle is staged annually.

Chadds Ford Days, Chadds Ford Historical Society, Route 100 (1/4 mile north of Rt. 1), Chadds Ford; 610-388-7376. The weekend following Labor Day, country rides and knee-slapping music are just part of the fun. There's also an art show, and artisans in Colonial garb at workbenches and selling their wares. CH.

Feria del Barrio. The Latino community's biggest summer festival, which features live music from nationally acclaimed Latino artists, plus arts and crafts, book sales, games and native foods. Fifth St. and Lehigh Ave.; 215-426-3311.

Irish Traditional Music and Dance Festival. A day of Irish culture, with entertainment, food and dancing. Doylestown; 215-849-8899.

Philadelphia Distance Run; 610-293-0900. A half marathon (13.1 miles), one of the nation's premier running races, through Center City and Fairmount Park, ending at JFK Plaza, Sixteenth St. and JFK Blvd.

Philadelphia Harvest Show, Horticulture Center in Fairmount Park, off North Belmont Ave. on N. Horticultural Drive; 215-988-8800. Homegrown vegetables and fruit compete for ribbons at a fall flower and garden show. Entertainment, children's games, tree climbing, cooking demonstrations. CH.

Philadelphia Orchestra's Opening Night Gala, Academy of Music; 215-893-1935. The Philadelphia Orchestra launches its season with Maestro Wolfgang Sawallisch.

Puerto Rican Day Parade. Annual parade and festival celebrating the best of Puerto Rican heritage. Benjamin Franklin Parkway to Independence Hall; 215-627-3100.

Scarecrow Festival Weekend, Peddler's Village, Lahaska; 215-794-4000.

A celebration of fall and scarecrows with pumpkin painting, entertainment, American Folk Art, and $4,900 in prizes for the best scarecrows.

South Street Seven Arts Festival; 215-636-1666. Craft booths, live performances, and art work on this happening street.

Taste of the Harvest. Fifty regional growers and producers provide samples of their products, plus demonstrations by top area chefs, children's events and more. Reading Terminal Market; 215-635-4463.

Von Steuben Day Gala and Parade, Benjamin Franklin Pkwy. from Twenty-ninth St. to Independence Hall; 215-742-3587. A celebration of German heritage and culture, and a colorful tribute to the German general who trained the soldiers of the Continental Army at Valley Forge.

YO! Philadelphia; 215-636-1666. A two-day celebration of Philadelphia's neighborhoods, with local performers, foods, traditions, and "firsts." Penn's Landing.

October

African-American Rodeo. This event is presented by the Minority Arts Resource Council and features performances by the Thyrl Latting Rodeo Spectacular. The Apollo, Temple University; 215-236-2688.

Avenue of the Arts Festival. A celebration of the arts on South Broad Street; 215-731-9668.

Battle of Germantown, 6401 Germantown Ave., Cliveden; 215-848-1777. A reenactment of the battle in which the Continental Army suffered its devastating defeat. *NCH*.

Candlelight Tours of the Edgar Allen Poe National Historic Site, 532 N. Seventh St.; 215-597-8780. Candlelight tours of the house where Poe wrote the horror tales, "The Black Cat," "Gold Bug," and "The Tell-Tale Heart." Free, but reservations are required.

Civil War Days. Civil War and navy living history program, with children's games, reenactors and military tacticals. Fort Mifflin; 215-432-1881.

Columbus Day Parade, on Broad St.; 215-686-3412. Ethnic cuisine and entertainment to celebrate the historic voyage.

Greater Philadelphia Blues Fest. Three fun-filled days of blues beginning with the "TGIF Blues Party," followed by a Black Tie Blues Dinner-Dance and an all-day Sunday Blues brunch. Various venues; 215-662-1612.

Halloween Ghost Tours. The Eastern State Penitentiary is the setting for this ghoulish event. 215-763-6483.

Haunted Ferry Ride. Independence Seaport Museum, Penn's Landing; 215-413-8621 and 215-925-5439. Come in costume and join the ghosts and goblins of Independence Seaport Museum for a cruise aboard the RiverLink Ferry, offering pirate stories, activities, treats, and more. Call for admission price and details.

Philadelphia AIDS Walk. Annual walk in Fairmount Park to raise money for various AIDS organizations. 215-731-9255.

Pulaski Day Parade, Benjamin Franklin Pkwy. to Independence Mall; 215-739-3408. Presented each year by the Polish American Congress, this parade is highlighted by ethnic bands and costumes and commemorates the contributions of Gen. Casimir Pulaski during the Revolutionary War.

Radnor Hunt Three-Day Event, Radnor Hunt Club, Providence Rd., Malvern; 610-648-1440. This annual event for the benefit of Paoli Memorial Hospital presents competition in a wide range of equestrian divisions that include dressage, cross country, road and track, and steeplechase. The country fair features specialty foods, crafts, antiques, jewelry, and clothing. *CH.*

Russian Festival. A celebration at St. Michael's Orthodox Church with live music, food and crafts honoring Russian heritage. Fourth St. and Fairmount Ave.; 215-627-6148.

Schuylkill Regatta. A two and three-quarter mile course on the Schuylkill River that attracts rowers from all over North America. It is considered one of the premier fall regattas in the nation. Strawberry Mansion Bridge to Boathouse Row; 609-654-7963.

Super Sunday, Benjamin Franklin Parkway; 215-636-1666. This huge block party, started in 1970, provides a great opportunity for friends and families to enjoy exhibits, games, rides, and a variety of foods, while celebrating Philadelphia's cultural and educational institutions.

USArtists Exposition of American Art at the Thirty-third St. Armory; 215-972-0550. A "walking tour" of American Art, with 50 galleries and dealers represented. Works are for sale and benefit the Pennsylvania Academy of Fine Arts.

November

Advanta Tennis Championships. The top names in tennis compete at the First Union Center; 215-336-3600.

Apple Festival. Craftspeople gather to show their wares and demonstrate their skills. Sample country apple butter cooked over an open fire. Live music, marionettes, medicine shows, and pie-eating contests add to the festivities of this traditional fall celebration. Peddler's Village, Lahaska; 215-794-4000.

Books, Toys and Giant Tinkertoys, Franklin Institute, Twentieth

St. and Benjamin Franklin Parkway; 215-448-1175. Kids and the young-at-heart let their imaginations run wild, creating the most extraordinary configurations from giant Tinkertoys.

October Gallery African American Art Expo. The largest African-American art show and sale in the country that attracts more than 20,000 art lovers to view the work of the nation's leading artists and emerging stars. The Apollo, Temple University; 215-629-3939.

Philadelphia Museum of Art Craft Show, Pennsylvania Convention Center; 215-684-7931. Some of the finest artists and artisans in the country present outstanding works in glass, ceramics, fiber, wood, jewelry, quilts, clothing, weaving, and mixed media. CH.

Philadelphia Marathon; 215-685-0051. This 26.2-mile race, Philadelphia's reply to those in Boston and New York, starts and ends at the Art Museum on Benjamin Franklin Parkway. By the time it concludes, participants, including some of the finest runners in the world, have covered a course that truly captures the breadth and character of Philadelphia.

Thanksgiving Day Parade; 215-581-4529. Started in 1919, this is the oldest parade of its kind in the nation. You'll enjoy floats, bands, clowns, the Philly Phanatic, even Santa Claus, and the largest number of helium balloons in any parade in the country.

Yuletide Tour, at Winterthur Museum, Wilmington, Delaware; 800-448-3883. Featuring more than 20 rooms highlighting America's winter holiday celebrations of the eighteenth and nineteenth centuries.

December

Army-Navy Football Classic, Veterans Stadium, Broad St. and Pattison Ave; 215-685-1500. The most colorful gridiron game of all.

Blue Cross RiverRink Party. Bring family and friends to the biggest non-alcoholic party in the region with non-stop skating, food, music, and party favors. Penn's Landing; 215-925-7465.

Chanukah Menorah Lighting Ceremony, Judge Lewis Quadrangle, across from Independence Mall; 215-725-2030 or 222-3130. Witness the lighting of one of the world's tallest menorahs, a 40-foot-high monolith, usually on the first night of the eight-day celebration of Chanukah. Sponsored by Lubavitch House, the ceremony is accompanied by a celebration complete with music and refreshments. NCH.

A Chanukah Wonderland. Family fun in a Dreidel House, trying out an olive press to produce oil for the Menorah, visiting Chanukah websites on computers, doing crafts, and of course, lighting a giant Menorah. Sites vary so call for information; 215-725-2030. NCH.

Charles Dickens' A Christmas Carol. The tradition continues of this holiday display based on Charles Dickens' classic tale. The 6,000-square foot animated version of the story will delight young and old alike. Strawbridge's, Gallery at Market East; 215-629-6000.

Christmas at Brandywine Museum, Brandywine River Museum, Route 1, Chadds Ford; 610-388-2700. Lavish Christmas exhibits include model trains, antique porcelain dolls, and courtyard shops in winter dress. Area crafts at the museum's Christmas Shops. *CH.*

Christmas Light Show. Lord and Taylor celebrates in the grand tradition with this annual light show in the Grand Court of its Center City store at Thirteenth and Market Sts. The show features 100,000 lights, a 60-foot Christmas tree, dancing waters, and computerized figures that create a fairyland of color to accompany the narration of Christmas classics. The store's Grand Organ, the largest pipe organ in the world, is played twice daily, at 11:30 am and 5:30 pm, featuring favorite sounds of the season. 215-241-9000. *NCH.*

City Hall Christmas Tree Lighting. Join celebrities and choral groups in City Hall Courtyard, Market and Broad Sts., for this annual event. 215-636-1666. *NCH.*

A Colonial Holiday on Elfreth's Alley. Daytime and candlelight house tours, an array of one-of-a-kind handcrafted treasures from local artisans and area museums, a wine and wassail party, and afternoon tea will be offered to visitors; 215-574-0560.

Disney World on Ice, the First Union Spectrum, Broad St. and Pattison Ave.; 215-336-3600. The world-famous characters of Walt Disney make their annual appearance at the Spectrum. *CH.*

Fairmount Park House Tours; 215-684-7926. The historic houses of Fairmount Park come alive with lights and authentic eighteenth-century Christmas decorations. Candlelight tours in the evenings. *CH.*

First Union Musical Tree. Thirty-piece orchestra staged in a 30-foot high spectacularly lit tree-shaped structure, playing traditional holiday favorites with a jazzy flair. The Gallery at Market Street, lower level, center court; 215-925-7162.

Franklin Institute Holiday Celebration of Lights—Friday after Thanksgiving through New Year's Eve. This spectacular display of lights and sounds is presented annually by PECO Energy in the Benjamin Franklin National Memorial, featuring festive holiday music and dazzling visuals and sound effects. Don't miss this exciting holiday celebration. Twentieth St. and Benjamin Franklin Pkwy.; 215-448-1200.

Gingerbread House Competition and Display. Gingerbread house competition for more than $5,700 in cash prizes. The winning entries are displayed throughout the holiday season in the Village Gazebo at Peddler's Village, Lahaska; 215-794-4000.

Kwanzaa Celebration; 215-769-7324. A seven-day celebration throughout the city. Named for the Swahili word for "the first fruits of the harvest." Performances, storytelling, and enrichment.

Longwood Gardens, Route 1, Kennett Square; 215-388-1000. This spectacular display of poinsettias (four acres of them in heated indoor gardens) and Christmas trees is a must. So, too, is the sparkling Christmas Tree Lane. There are also more than 100 organ and choral concerts in the conservatory. CH.

Lucia Fest & Julmarkand, American Swedish Historical Museum, 1900 Pattison Ave.; 215-389-1776. Swedish Christmas traditions come alive in music, pageantry, and foods of the season. CH.

Neighbors in the New Year Celebration, Penn's Landing. 215-636-1666. Greet the New Year with fireworks and a music spectacular featuring the lights of the Benjamin Franklin Bridge. NCH.

New Year's Hip-Hop Bash. A New Year's celebration for the little ones. Ring in the New Year with a huge party filled with dancing, music and confetti. Children can make costumes, play instruments, learn to do the Mummer's strut, and parade around the gallery. Please Touch Museum, 210 N. Twenty-first St.; 215-963-0667.

"The Nutcracker," Academy of Music, Broad and Locust Sts.; 215-551-7000. The Pennsylvania Ballet delights young and old alike with this traditional presentation every Christmas season. CH.

Philadelphia Music Conference. A conference for artists and bands trying to get into the music industry. Selected musicians and groups will showcase their talents at various venues throughout the city with styles ranging from rap to hip-hop and rock to folk. Adams Mark Hotel, City Line Ave. and Monument Rd.; 215-587-9550.

Washington Crosses the Delaware, Washington Crossing Historic Park; 215-493-4076. An authentic reenactment of Washington leading his troops across the Delaware River on Christmas Day, 1776, before surprising the British at Trenton.

SELF-GUIDED CITY TOURS

Included in this chapter are three tours that will enable you to discover Philadelphia on your own. The first tour covers the downtown area of the city from Independence National Historic Park through many exciting areas, concluding at the Powel House. It is a walking tour, the best way to explore this section of Philadelphia. The remaining two tours are driving tours. One travels a scenic route through Valley Forge and the Brandywine Valley. The other is a Metro tour beginning at Fairmount Park and following an exciting course that ends at Philadelphia's famous waterfront area.

For all tours, a companion to read directions or to walk with will almost certainly increase your enjoyment and fun. We recommend that you take your time and set your own pace. Philadelphia has too much to see and do to rush through its marvelous attractions!

DOWNTOWN WALKING TOUR

Philadelphia has an unmistakable reverence for the old, the traditional, and the historic. To fully grasp this appreciation, certain areas of Philadelphia must be explored on foot, and you'll find that to do so is a joy.

Our downtown walking tour is keyed to Independence National Historic Park—"America's most historic square mile"—and the bordering areas of Old City and Society Hill. Since there is so much to see, we suggest you tailor this tour to the time you can afford. At a brisk pace, stopping at only a few sites along the way, you can make it in one day. But should you wish to spend time at the points of interest and pause for lunch, we strongly recommend you divide the tour into two days. In the first section, explore Independence National Historic Park and Old City, which will require between four and five hours, depending upon the lines outside Independence Hall. In the second section, enjoy Society Hill, for a three-to-four-hour tour.

Sights along the route and where they are listed:

217

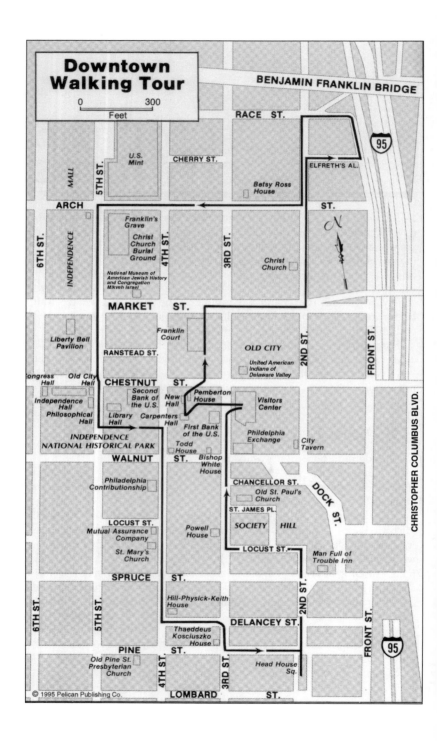

Arch Street Friend's Meeting House, Arch Street
Aurora Print Shop, Franklin Court
Betsy Ross House, Arch Street
Bishop White House, Visitor's Center and Chestnut Street
Carpenter's Hall, Carpenter's Hall
Christ Church, Franklin Court
Christ Church Burial Ground, Arch Street
City Tavern, Powel House
Congregation Mikveh Israel, Liberty Bell
Congress Hall, Liberty Bell
Elfreth's Alley, Elfreth's Alley
Fire Museum, Elfreth's Alley
First Bank of the United States, Visitor's Center
Franklin Court, Franklin Court
Franklin Statue, Arch Street
Franklin Tenant House, Franklin Court
Free Quaker Meeting House, Arch Street
Head House, Headhouse Square
Hill-Physick-Keith House, St. Mary's Churchyard
Independence Hall, Independence Hall
Liberty Bell Pavilion, Liberty Bell
Liberty Hall, Chestnut Street
Loxley Court, Arch Street
Man Full of Trouble Tavern, Man Full of Trouble
Mantua Maker's House, Elfreth's Alley
Mutual Assurance Company, Society Hill

National Museum of American Jewish History, Liberty Bell
New Hall, Carpenter's Hall
Old City Hall, Liberty Bell
Pemberton House, Carpenter's Hall
Penn's Landing, Man Full of Trouble and Metro Driving Tour
Pennsylvania Horticultural Society, Chestnut Street
Philadelphia Contributionship, Society Hill
Philadelphia Exchange, Powel House
Philosophical Hall, Independence Hall
Postal Museum, Franklin Court
Powel House, Powel House
Second Bank of the United States, Chestnut Street
Society Hill, Society Hill
Society Hill Towers, Man Full of Trouble
St. Mary's Church, St. Mary's Churchyard
St. Paul's Episcopal Church, Powel House
St. Peter's Church, Kosciuszko House
Thaddeus Kosciuszko House, Kosciuszko House
Three Bears Statue, St. Mary's Churchyard
Todd House, Visitor's Center and Chestnut Street
United States Mint, Arch Street
U.S.S. Olympia, Man Full of Trouble and Metro Driving Tour
Visitor's Center, Visitor's Center

Independence National Historic Park——

Begin at the Visitors Center, Independence National Historic Park, Third and Chestnut streets. If you have driven into the area, you'll find convenient parking in the garage at Second and Sansom streets. The brick walkway between the garage and the Visitors Center is a nice convenience.

At the Visitors Center

In the center, you'll find exhibits and information about regular events and special activities of the day. Pick up a copy of the Philadelphia Gazette to help you plan your visit, and to find out about the programs of Historic Philadelphia, Inc. At the Center, sign up for the free guided tours of the *Bishop White House* and the *Todd House*, which are open by guided tour only. Sign up for *Independence Hall* tours at that site.

Most park buildings are open daily from 9 am-5 pm, and the hours of some are extended during the summer. The hours are subject to change, so check at the Visitors Center for the latest information.

At the Center, we strongly recommend the interactive kiosk computer exhibit, "Touch and See Philadelphia." To properly set the mood for the tour, take in the 20-minute film, "Independence," directed by the famed John Huston.

From the front entrance of the Visitors Center, cross Third Street. To your left is the *First Bank of the United States*, which is probably the nation's oldest bank (built between 1795 and 1797). The building, though not open to the public, is an outstanding example of neoclassical architecture.

Carpenters' Hall

Also on your left, facing the First Bank is *Carpenters' Hall*, where delegates gathered to air their grievances against King George III during the First Continental Congress in September of 1774. The following spring, the Second Continental Congress met in the State House, now Independence Hall. Carpenters' Hall later served as a hospital and an arsenal for American forces during the Revolutionary War.

To the right of Carpenters' Hall is *New Hall*, which served as the Office of the War Department in 1791 and 1792. It is now a museum of United States Marine Corps history.

Upon leaving New Hall, you will see *Pemberton House*, a replica of the eighteenth-century home of Joseph Pemberton, a wealthy Quaker merchant. It is now a museum depicting the development of the United States Army and Navy from 1775 to 1800.

On to Franklin Court ─────────────

Cross Chestnut Street and follow the sign to Franklin Court, which is located on Market Street between Third and Fourth streets. If you're lucky, you'll be greeted by Philadelphia's own Ben Franklin look-alike, who will regale you with stories about "his" life. He might have some Colonial musicians with him for added entertainment. The ramp will take you to the underground museum, a tribute to the genius and inventiveness of one of Philadelphia's most famous citizens, Benjamin Franklin. In addition to an original music stand and stove, which were among his many inventions, enjoy the multimedia salute to Franklin's wit and diplomatic accomplishments. A bank of telephones will "connect" you with many of his contemporaries, providing a verbal portrait of Franklin the man. There is a delightful marionette theater extolling his success and a film, "The Real Ben Franklin," depicting the life of Franklin and his family.

Leave the movie theater and enter the Franklin courtyard, where the only house he ever owned once stood. Built between 1763 and 1765, it was 34 feet square and three stories high, with the kitchen in the cellar. It was, he once said, "a good House contrived to my Mind."

Also in the courtyard are three of the five Market Street buildings Franklin designed. They are the *Franklin Tenant House*, which contains artifacts from the site of his home; the *Aurora Print Shop*, which was once operated by his grandson; and the *Postal Museum*, now an eighteenth-century United States Post Office where every piece of mail is cancelled with the signature, "B. Free Franklin." As postmaster of the new nation, Franklin used "Free" as his middle name because the country had freed itself of English rule.

Now turn right on Market Street, then left on Second Street to *Christ Church*. Built in 1727, the church was attended by 15 signers of the Declaration of Independence, including Benjamin Franklin and George Washington.

Elfreth's Alley ─────────────────

Continue north on Second Street, cross Arch Street to Elfreth's Alley. Turn right into the Alley. Dating back to 1690, this is the oldest continuously occupied street in the nation. Thirty homes which line the alley were built in the 1720s and 1730s. Numbers 120 and 122 are the oldest, built between 1724 and 1728; they are private homes and open to the public only on the first Saturday in June.

You may tour Number 126, however. Built around 1750, it is named "The Mantua Maker's House" because it was the home for two mantua makers, or dressmakers, between 1762 and 1794. The period furnishings and original woodwork of the interior are more than two centuries old. The best time to visit Elfreth's Alley is the first weekend in June, when "Fete Days," a tradition since 1935, bring a host of colonial demonstrations to the street.

The Alley ends at Front Street. Turn left (north) on Front Street and walk one block to Quarry Street, turn left, and, on your right, you'll see an authentic 1876 fire house that now houses the *Fire Museum*.

Return to Arch Street

From there, turn left (south) on Second Street, return to Arch Street, and turn right (west) on Arch Street. Mid-block on your right at 234 Arch Street is the *Betsy Ross House*, where legend has it the seamstress stitched the first American flag at the personal request of George Washington. This is an outstanding example of the eighteenth-century Philadelphia home.

Continue on Arch Street across Third Street to *Loxley Court*, which was owned by the Loxley family from the 1740s to 1901. This is a quaint courtyard that's worth a peek through the iron fence; some of these row houses were built between 1775 and 1827.

Continue on Arch Street to Franklin Statue, a bust 16 feet high and covered with 80,000 pennies symbolizing his slogan, "A penny saved is a penny earned." Across the street is the *Arch Street Friends Meeting House*, built on land that William Penn gave to the Quakers in 1693.

In the next block, on the north side of the street, at Fifth Street and Arch, is the largest of the nation's three *United States Mints*. An audiovisual tour explaining the manufacture of coins takes about 45 minutes. You'll see real coins being minted and overflowing in carts.

Also the *Christ Church* burial ground is at **the corner of Arch and Fifth streets.** Through an opening in the brick wall, view the plain gravestones of Deborah and Benjamin Franklin. It's an old custom to toss a penny on the gravestones for good luck.

On the southwest side of Arch and Fifth is the *Free Quaker Meeting House*, built in 1783 by the Quakers who supported the Revolution.

The Liberty Bell ——————————

Turn left on Fifth Street, and on your way toward Market Street, you will see, on your left, the National Museum of American Jewish History, and Congregation Mikveh Israel. The second oldest congregation in the United States, one of its founding members was Nathan Levy, whose ship, the *Myrtilla,* brought the Liberty Bell to America.

Cross Market Street, and continue to the Liberty Bell Pavilion which is on your right. The *Liberty Bell,* the symbol of American freedom, was ordered in 1751 to commemorate the anniversary of William Penn's Charter of Privileges for the State of Pennsylvania. The bell, which was cast in London, cracked while being tested. It was subsequently recast and in 1776 fulfilled the Old Testament prophecy with which it is inscribed, "Proclaim liberty throughout the land, unto all the inhabitants thereof."

Although nobody is certain when the bell cracked next, it occurred according to legend during the funeral of Chief Justice William Marshall in 1835. The last time the bell rang formally was on Washington's birthday in 1846.

When you leave the *Liberty Bell Pavilion,* **take the tree-lined sidewalk to the left, cross Chestnut Street, and go directly to the East Wing of Independence Hall,** where free guided tours of the Hall originate. The Hall is open by tour only, and sign-up is on a first-come, first-served basis.

While you're waiting for your tour, you may want to visit the old *City Hall* to the left at Fifth and Chestnut Streets. This structure was built in 1790 as the home of Philadelphia's government, but used by the United States Supreme Court until 1800. On the right side of Independence Hall is *Congress Hall,* site of the inaugurations of Washington (his second) and John Adams.

Consider returning here after dark and participating in the sensational Lights of Liberty interactive tour that originates at the PECO Energy Liberty Center at Sixth and Chestnut Sts. (See SIGHTS.)

Independence Hall ——————————

Independence Hall was constructed between 1732 and 1756 as the State House of the Province of Pennsylvania, and from 1775 to 1783 (except for the time of the British occupation) was the meeting place for the Second Continental Congress. The Assembly Room was the site of five major events—the appointment of Washington as Commander in Chief of the Continental Army in 1775; the adoption of the Declaration of Independence on July 4, 1776; agreement on the design of the American flag in 1777; the adoption of the Articles of Confederation in 1781; and the writing of the Constitution in 1787.

Since most of the original furniture was destroyed during the British occupation, most of what you see are period pieces. However, the silver inkstand on the President's desk in the Assembly Room is the one used during the signing of both the Declaration and the Constitution, and the "rising sun" chair is the original used by Washington during the Constitutional Convention.

Upon leaving Independence Hall, *Philosophical Hall* will be to your left. This is the only privately owned building on Independence Square, the home of the American Philosophical Society, which was founded by Franklin in 1743. The building is not open to the public.

Pause for a Rest

It might be a good idea here to pause for a rest on one of the benches in Independence Square, where the first public reading of the Declaration of Independence took place on July 8, 1776. Notice the reproductions of eighteenth-century street lamps; there are 56 of them, one for each signer of the Declaration of Independence.

On to Chestnut Street

Cross Fifth Street from the square at Philosophical Hall. Facing this building is *Liberty Hall,* built in 1789-90, the oldest subscription library in the United States.

Behind the Hall is the *Second Bank of the United States,* built between 1819 and 1824 and one of the finest examples of Greek Revival architecture in America. Today it contains an extensive collection of paintings of colonial and federal leaders (most by Charles Wilson Peale) called "Faces of Independence." **Enter by Chestnut Street.**

Continue down Chestnut Street to Fourth Street. Turn right on Fourth Street. On the corner of Fourth and Walnut Street on the left is *Todd House,* which was occupied from 1791 to 1793 by lawyer John Todd, Jr., and his wife, Dolley Payne. After her husband died during the 1793 epidemic of yellow fever, Dolley married James Madison, who later became the nation's fourth president. They subsequently moved to the Madison estate in Virginia, but the home still reflects the lifestyle of the eighteenth-century middle class in Philadelphia.

After leaving the Todd House, take a peek at the garden next door. Many of the plants, trees, shrubs, and flowers found here grew in the same spot before the eighteenth century. Next door you will come to the *Pennsylvania Horticultural Society*. The lobby features ever-changing exhibits, and in its library you will find 13,000 volumes and 200 periodicals with a full collection of seed catalogues. The Society, the oldest of its kind, sponsors the world's largest and most elaborate flower show every year at the Pennsylvania Convention Center.

Continue walking east on Walnut Street to The Bishop White House. This lovely row house was built by the Reverend William White in 1787. He was the first Episcopal Bishop of Philadelphia and chose this location because it was midway between Christ Church and St. Peter's Church, for both of which he served as rector. The home has been magnificently restored to the way he and his family lived in the eighteenth century. Many of the items you see throughout the house actually belonged to the Reverend.

Walk to Walnut and Third Street and our tour of Society Hill begins.

At this point you may wish to conclude the tour and reserve the following Walking Tour of Society Hill for another day.

Society Hill ———————————————————

Though it could have been so named because the wealthy lived here in colonial times, Society Hill actually traces back to the Free Society of Traders, a group of businessmen and investors persuaded by William Penn to settle here in 1683.

Continue on Fourth Street, crossing Walnut Street until you come to the Philadelphia Contributionship on your right. By now you might have noticed a hand-in-hand firemark on various historical properties on your tour; this is the symbol of America's oldest fire insurance company, the Contributionship, which was founded by Franklin in 1752. The Greek Revival style headquarters were built in 1836. The charming museum inside features a wealth of fire-fighting and insurance memorabilia.

Next, on your right, are the two buildings that house the offices of the *Mutual Assurance Company*. One was occupied by Dr. William Shippen, a Pennsylvania delegate to the Continental Congress, and a man who wrote the first American treatise on anatomy. Later, this was the home of the president of the American Philosophical Society, Dr. Caspar Wistar, after whom the wisteria vine was named. A genial, scholarly man, Wistar started what became known as "Wistar Parties," inviting scientists and statesmen to his home every Saturday night; these parties are still held by the society.

The Mutual Assurance Company is also known as The Green Tree, because prior to its founding in 1784, no company would sell fire insurance to those who owned buildings and homes with trees in front of them. The Green Tree did, however, and you can see its symbol on a number of homes and buildings in the area.

See St. Mary's Churchyard

Next door at 244 S. Fourth Street is *St. Mary's Church*, founded in 1763 and the principal Roman Catholic Church during the Revolution. Walk back to the churchyard and view the gravestones of some of the famous people buried here. Among them are Thomas Fitzsimmons, a signer of the Constitution, and Commodore John Barry, the "Father of the American Navy."

Proceed farther south on Fourth Street across Spruce Street. The *Hill-Physick-Keith House* is at 321 S. Fourth Street. Built by Henry Hill five years after the Revolution, it was later occupied by Dr. Philip Syng Physick, "the father of American surgery." The house is bordered on three sides by a nineteenth-century garden. For tours of ten or more, call ahead.

From the house, turn left (east) on Delancey Street between Third and Fourth streets. If you wish to pause and rest, there are benches in a lovely, small park. Here you'll see Sherl Joseph Winter's statue of the "Three Bears." The homes around the park are splendid examples of eighteenth- and nineteenth-century federal row houses.

The Kosciuszko House

At the corner of Delancey and Third streets, turn right on Third Street and, on the corner at Pine Street, you'll see the *Thaddeus Kosciuszko House*. It was here that Kosciuszko, the Polish engineer who designed America's impregnable defensive fortresses at Saratoga and West Point during the Revolution, lived during his second visit in 1797-98. In the words of Thomas Jefferson, Kosciuszko was "as pure a son of liberty as I have ever known, and of that liberty which is to go to all, and not to the few or the rich alone."

On the southwest corner of Third and Pine streets is *St. Peter's Church*, whose tall white spire dominates the area. Built in 1760, the church still has the original white pew (Number 41) where George and Martha Washington worshipped with their good friends, the Samuel Powels. Buried in the churchyard are naval hero Stephen Decatur, artist Charles Wilson Peale, and John Nixon, who first read the Declaration to the people.

Headhouse Square

Turn left on Pine Street, continuing east to Headhouse Square, built in 1745 and the last of Philadelphia's original street-wide markets. At Pine and Second streets is the *Head House*, built in 1805 as a fire house and community center, and so named because it is located at the head of the square. Now completely restored, with numerous shops, restaurants, and cafés surrounding it, Headhouse Square is a delightful place to visit, especially in the summertime, when local entertainers, craftsmen, and artists add to the bustle.

On the east side of the square, at the hub of Society Hill, Head House Square and South Street, is the 350-seat *New Market Theater*, that offers off-Broadway hits, concerts, bands, and dancing.

The Man Full of Trouble

Now walk north on Second to Spruce Street. To your right is *Man Full of Trouble Tavern*. This is the only remaining eighteenth-century tavern in Philadelphia, handsomely restored by the Knauer Foundation to look just as it did in 1759, and now a museum. Beyond the tavern, Spruce Street ends at *Penn's Landing* and the *Independence Seaport Museum* that encompasses the *U.S.S. Olympia,* Commodore George Dewey's flagship and the only survivor of the Spanish-American War fleets, and the World War II submarine, *Becuna.* Both vessels are open for tours.

Continue on Second Street and turn left (west) on Locust Street. To the right are the 30-story apartment buildings of *Society Hill Towers,* which were completed in 1964 during the major thrust of restoration in the area.

The Powel House

Proceed on Locust. At Third Street, turn right (north). On your left is *Powel House.* Built in 1765 by Samuel Powel, a wealthy property owner and the city's mayor in 1776, this was one of colonial Philadelphia's most fashionable houses. The Powels often entertained the Washingtons here and, in turn, visited the President and First Lady at Mount Vernon.

Continue farther north on Third Street to the former St. Paul's Episcopal Church on your right. Built in 1765, it was once the headquarters of the Episcopal Diocese of Pennsylvania. Buried in the churchyard is Edwin Forrest, the great eighteenth-century actor for whom the Forrest Theater was named.

On the corner of Third and Walnut Streets is the *Philadelphia Exchange,* which was built in 1832 through 1834 and was the commercial hub of the city for half a century.

Turn right on Walnut Street. The restored and fully functioning *City Tavern* is on your left, an ideal place to conclude your walking tour. John Adams called it the "most genteel" tavern in America and it may well have been. Adams, Franklin, and members of the Continental Congress and Constitutional Convention often gathered here for discussion over mugs of ale.

MAIN LINE—VALLEY FORGE— BRANDYWINE VALLEY DRIVING TOUR

This tour begins a few blocks southwest of the Adams Mark Hotel on City (Line) Avenue. **At Route 23—Conshohocken State Road— turn right (northwest)** and you soon will be in the hills and dales and streams and brooks of Philadelphia's prestigious Main Line. The homes, you will discover, are magnificent.

Route 23 is our primary course to Valley Forge. If you wish to stay aboard, you will not be disappointed—especially in the fall, when the foliage is spectacular. However, for those who would rather gain a greater appreciation of the Main Line, we offer a scenic alternative.

Sights along the route and where they are listed:

Brandywine Battlefield Park, Brandywine Battlefield Park
Brandywine River Museum, Brandywine Battlefield Park
Longwood Gardens, Longwood Gardens
Phillips Mushroom Place, Longwood Gardens
Valley Forge National Historical Park, Valley Forge Visitors' Center
Winterthur Museum and Gardens, Winterthur Museum

The Scenic Route

Follow these directions: **After the intersection with Rock Hill Road, on the right, stay on Route 23 as it bears gradually to the left and watch carefully for Manayunk Road on the left. Turn left on Manayunk Road, and, very soon, right on Bryn Mawr Avenue.** Follow that to Old Gulph Road. Turn right and at the fork with Hagy's Ford Road bearing right, stay to the left on Old Gulph Road. Next, turn left on McClenaghan Rd. and then bear right onto Gypsy Lane. Follow that to Montgomery Avenue and turn right, but quickly you will turn right on Cherry Lane. Follow that until the dead end at Mill Creek Road, and turn right. Soon this will dead end with Old Gulph Road, where you turn left. When it joins Youngs Ford Road, Old Gulph Road winds to the left.

Proceed straight ahead, on Youngs Ford to Williamson Road, which intersects from the left. Turn left, and follow that to the dead end with Morris Avenue where you will turn right. Follow that to Spring Mill Road, and turn left. After that crosses Old Gulph Road, turn right on Montgomery Avenue—Route 320—and follow the signs to U.S. 76. Take U.S 76 west to the Valley Forge exit.

Those taking the Route 23 tour will pick up U.S. 76 at Conshohocken. **Just follow the signs to U.S. 76 west and, once you're on the expressway, follow it to the Valley Forge exit.**

Valley Forge Visitors' Center

At the junction of Routes 23 and 363 is the Visitors' Center for *Valley Forge National Historical Park.*

Here, an audio-visual program and various exhibits await you. Should you choose to linger in the area where George Washington and his Continental Army of 11,000 troops spent the bitter winter of 1777-78, the park's staff will help you plan your visit.

Enjoy the Park

There is much to be seen here. From the tower on Mount Joy, for example, there is a panoramic view of the 2,000-acre park, which is a gripping sight any time of the year. Colonial atmosphere abounds in three furnished headquarters, and reconstructed huts, memorials, and monuments seem to be everywhere. Markers throughout the park help tell the story of one of the most important chapters in American history.

When you decide to move on, **follow Route 23 through the park.** Eventually it will intersect with North Gulph Road, and, as you turn right, will continue west as Route 23. **At the intersection of Route 252, on the left, you should turn left and follow Route 252 to Route 202. There, turn right and follow Route 202 south to U.S. 1.** This will take you about half an hour.

Brandywine Battlefield Park

At U.S. 1, turn right, and soon, on the right, will be *Brandywine Battlefield Park.* Here, audio-visual presentations in the Visitors' Center

Valley Forge National Historical Park   R. Kennedy for the Greater Philadelphia Tourism Marketing Corporation

tell the story of Washington's defeat by the British in the Battle of Brandywine on September 11, 1777. There are two historic houses in the park, the headquarters of Washington and the Marquis de LaFayette, which depict life as it was during the Revolution.

Farther on U.S. 1, on the left, is the *Brandywine River Museum,* which houses three generations of Wyeth paintings (see VISUAL ARTS).

Longwood Gardens

Nearby are the magnificent *Longwood Gardens,* one of the nation's most vital horticultural showplaces. Established by the late Pierre S. du Pont, its water gardens, conservatories, arboretum, fountain displays, and open-air theater are famous for their beauty. December is a splendid month to visit. There is nothing quite like Longwood at Christmas time.

Farther on U.S. 1 in Kennett Square is *Phillips Mushroom Place* (610-388-6082), which houses a museum explaining the history and lore of mushrooms through various audio-visuals. You will also see mushrooms in various stages of development, and there are plenty to buy.

Should you wish to proceed directly back to Philadelphia at this point, **backtrack east on U.S. 1, cross Route 202, and continue east to Route 322, turn right, and this will take you to Interstate 95.** Here, you simply head north to Philadelphia.

Winterthur Museum

However, if you're still in a sightseeing mood **turn right off U.S. 1 soon after you leave Phillips Mushroom Place on Route 52 going south.** This, too, will lead you to I-95, but along the way you can visit *Winterthur Museum and Gardens,* 800-448-3883.

Just across the Delaware border, the museum is in Henry Francis du Pont's 200-room mansion, and features the world's finest collection of decorative arts made or used in America between 1640 and 1840.

From here, **continue on to I-95, and take it north to Philadelphia.**

METRO DRIVING TOUR

Plan a full day to take in this sweeping look at Philadelphia. This will allow time to explore some of the many fascinating sites along the way. Without stops, the drive will take about two hours. You will see Fairmount Park, drive down the magnificent Benjamin Franklin Parkway, past City Hall, and through Penn's Landing.

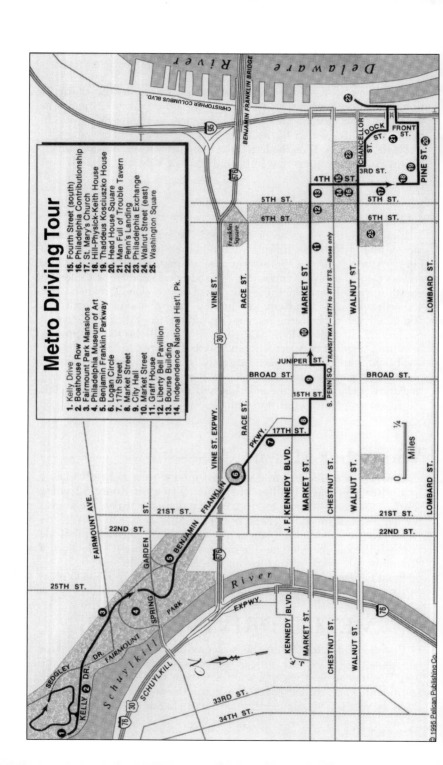

Metro Driving Tour

1. Kelly Drive
2. Boathouse Row
3. Fairmount Park Mansions
4. Philadelphia Museum of Art
5. Benjamin Franklin Parkway
6. Logan Circle
7. 17th Street
8. Market Street
9. City Hall
10. Market Street
11. Graff House
12. Liberty Bell Pavillion
13. Bourse Building
14. Independence National Hist'l. Pk.
15. Fourth Street (south)
16. Philadelphia Contributionship
17. St. Mary's Church
18. Hill-Physick-Keith House
19. Thaddeus Kosciuszko House
20. Head House Square
21. Man Full of Trouble Tavern
22. Penn's Landing
23. Philadelphia Exchange
24. Walnut Street (east)
25. Washington Square

© 1995 Pelican Publishing Co.

The tour begins in Fairmount Park, but it can easily be joined anywhere along the way.

Sights along the route and where they are listed:

Academy of Natural Sciences, Benjamin Franklin Parkway
Azalea Garden, Waterworks
Belmont Mansion, Belmont Mansion Drive
Belmont Plateau, Belmont Mansion Drive
Boathouse Row, Boathouse Row
Cathedral of Saints Peter and Paul, Benjamin Franklin Parkway
Cedar Grove, Japanese House
City Hall, City Hall
East Laurel Hill Cemetery, Strawberry Mansion
Fairmount Park, Fairmount Park
Fels Planetarium, Benjamin Franklin Parkway
The Franklin Institute Science Museum, Benjamin Franklin Parkway
Free Library of Philadelphia, Benjamin Franklin Parkway
The Gallery, Market Street East
Graaf House, Market Street East
Grant Monument, Mount Pleasant
Headhouse Square, Independence Square
Horticultural Center, Horticultural Center
Independence Hall, Independence Square
Independence Seaport Museum, Independence Seaport Museum
Independence Square, Independence Square
International Sculpture Garden, Independence Seaport Museum
Japanese House, Japanese House
Laurel Hill Mansion, Laurel Hill Mansion

Lemon Hill, Zoological Garden
Liberty Bell Pavilion, Independence Square
Lincoln Monument, Boathouse Row
Lord and Taylor, Market Street East
Mann Music Center, Belmont Mansion Drive
Market Place East, Market Street East
Memorial Hall, Japanese House
Mount Pleasant, Mount Pleasant
New Jersey State Aquarium, Independence Seaport Museum
Ohio House, Belmont Mansion Drive
Ormiston, Mount Pleasant
Penn's Landing, Penn's Landing
Pennsylvania Convention Center, Market Street East
Philadelphia Museum of Art, Waterworks
Philadelphia Zoological Garden, Zoological Garden
Reading Train Shed, Market Street East
Riverbus, Independence Seaport Museum
Robin Hood Dell, Strawberry Mansion
Rockland, Mount Pleasant
Solitude, Zoological Garden
Spirit of Philadelphia, Independence Seaport Museum
Strawberry Mansion, Strawberry Mansion
Sweetbriar, Japanese House
U.S.S. Olympia, U.S.S. Olympia
Waterworks, Waterworks
Washington Square, Washington Square
Woodford, Laurel Hill Mansion

Begin at Fairmount Park ───────────

William Penn's vision of Philadelphia as a "greene Countrie Towne" is enhanced by *Fairmount Park*, the largest city park in the world, whose 8,900 acres are replete with forests, parks, gardens, and wide-open spaces. It also embraces more than 400 acres of waterways and 100 miles of trails, bridle paths, and bikeways. Stretching northwest from the heart of the city, along the Ben Franklin Parkway and the Schuylkill River, the park also has some of Philadelphia's most notable historical attractions—including the *Art Museum*, the *Philadelphia Zoo*, and perhaps the finest array of original Early American homes to be found anywhere.

In 1812, the city purchased five acres along the river to build a reservoir and public gardens; eventually, even the park's magnificent mansions were brought under the city's official umbrella. In 1876, the park was the site of the Centennial Exposition honoring the nation's 100th birthday. And the area of the park along the river and Wissahickon Creek has long been listed in the National Register of Historic Places.

Certainly a delightful way to explore the park is by riding one of the replicas of trolley cars that weave through it, pausing at many locations along the way. Pay a single fare, and you will have on-and-off privileges all day, as well as discount admissions to the historic houses and museums on the route. Call Philadelphia Trolley Works for routes, schedules, and fares. 215-925-TOUR (8687).

Mount Pleasant ─────────────────

Begin in Fairmount Park at the Grant Monument on Kelly Drive. Take Fountain Drive to the first left. This is Mount Pleasant Drive. Soon you will come upon the Georgian mansion of *Mount Pleasant*. John MacPherson, a Scottish sea captain, built this mansion in 1761 with the fortune he had made by privateering. In 1775, John Adams dined here and called it "the most elegant seat in Pennsylvania." Later, Benedict Arnold bought Mount Pleasant for his bride, Peggy Shippen, but he was convicted of treason before they could move in.

Nearby is *Rockland*, one of Philadelphia's most handsome federal homes, and *Ormiston*, restored by the city in 1976. Rockland is not open to the public.

Laurel Hill Mansion ───────────

Now bear left onto Randolph Drive, and soon on your left will be *Laurel Hill Mansion*, a classic brick summer house overlooking the

Schuylkill. It was built by Francis and Rebecca Rawle in 1760, but the octagonal dining room was not added until after the Revolutionary War. Laurel Hill was later owned by "the father of American surgery," Dr. Philip Syng Physick, who left it to his daughter, Sally Randolph. The city paid the Randolphs $68,000 for the mansion in 1869.

At Strawberry Mansion Drive, turn left, and on your left is *Woodford,* whose ground floor was built in 1756 by Quaker judge William Coleman, a close friend of Benjamin Franklin. Later the home was owned by David Franks, who lavishly entertained Tory officers during the British occupation of Philadelphia.

Strawberry Mansion

Now turn left to Strawberry Mansion, so named in the mid-1800s because it was a dairy farm that served strawberries and cream. The mansion had been purchased in the 1820s by Judge Joseph Hamphill, who entertained the renowned John C. Calhoun, the French Marquis de Lafayette, and Daniel Webster. While building a racetrack on the property, Hamphill's son, Coleman, started growing strawberries imported from Chile.

As you leave Strawberry Mansion, again turn left on Strawberry Mansion Drive; on your right is *Robin Hood Dell East,* in June, July, and August a favorite site of thousands for its music, big bands, and ethnic programs. Beyond the Dell is *East Laurel Hill Cemetery;* the mausoleums and monuments there are of sufficient architectural interest to be named in the National Register of Historic Places.

Belmont Mansion Drive

Cross Strawberry Mansion Bridge, and as you begin to bear left, turn right on Greenland Drive, then left on Chamounix Drive. Follow this past Ford Road to Belmont Mansion Drive, turn left, and next, on your left, is *Belmont Plateau,* which offers a sweeping view of the river and the city. On your right is *Belmont Mansion.* During the Revolution, Judge William Peters, its owner, returned to England, leaving his patriot son here to entertain the likes of George Washington, James Madison, and Benjamin Franklin.

Now turn right, continue across Belmont Avenue, and follow South Georges Drive past Ohio House to the Mann Music Center. This is the summer home of the Philadelphia Orchestra, which presents open-air concerts Monday, Tuesday, and Thursday nights in June and July.

Horticultural Center

Continue on South Georges Drive around Catholic Fountain, then bear left onto States Drive, cross Belmont Avenue again, and follow North Horticultural Drive to the Horticultural Center. Opened in 1979, the center has numerous examples of the more than 2,000 species of plants that have been identified in Fairmount Park. Many are descendants of seeds that arrived in the ballasts of ships from around the world.

Japanese House

Next on Horticultural Drive is *Japanese House*, an authentic reconstruction of a Seventeenth-century Japanese house, tea house, and garden. Built in 1957, it is graced in the springtime by blooming azaleas. In 1976, Japanese craftsmen refurbished Japanese House as a gift to the United States on its 200th birthday. Nearby is *Memorial Hall*; it and Ohio House are the only buildings remaining from the Centennial Exposition. A scale model of the centennial grounds is displayed in the basement.

Directly to the east of Memorial Hall is *Cedar Grove*, a Quaker farmhouse that was built in the 1740s and contains a fine collection of Jacobean, Queen Anne, Chippendale, and Federal furniture. Just down the road is *Sweetbriar*, built in 1795 by Samuel Breck so that he and his bride could escape the yellow fever epidemic that killed thousands of Philadelphians. The Brecks lived here for 40 years—until their daughter died of "river fever."

Zoological Garden

Now backtrack out of Sweetbriar, turn left on Lansdowne Drive, and follow it across Girard Avenue to Thirty-fourth St. and the *Philadelphia Zoological Garden*. Opened in 1874, this was America's first zoo, and its 42 acres are now home for more than 1,800 animals, including rare and endangered species. The zoo includes Bear Country, African Plains, the Reptile House, the Carnivore Kingdom, rare white lions, and America's only giant river otters. It celebrated its 125th anniversary in 1999 with the opening of the new Primate Reserve. Among its Victorian buildings there is also a Children's Zoo, a monorail, a delightful tree house exhibit, and special programs throughout the year. For information, hours, and rates call: 215-243-1100.

Actually, a botanical garden preceded the arrival of the animals; in

1785, *Solitude*—the manor of Penn's grandson—was a home surrounded by an "English garden" where Washington and Franklin were guests.

Return to Girard Avenue, turn right, and cross the Girard Avenue Bridge to Poplar Drive. Turn right, follow it across Sedgely Drive, and on your right will be *Lemon Hill*. This is another mansion that was built by Robert Morris, a signer of the Declaration of Independence and a close friend of Washington. Originally named "The Hills," it later was sold to Henry Pratt, who built the current house in 1800. When the lemon trees flourished, it was renamed Lemon Hill.

Boathouse Row

Continue on Poplar Drive until you turn left to Kelly Drive. On your left will be one of Philadelphia's most famous series of landmarks—*Boathouse Row*. Originally named to designate the row of fishermen's houseboats that used to anchor between the dam and the boathouses, these houses were later built by private groups. They are now occupied by rowing clubs, and serve as racing and social headquarters for numerous rowing events in the spring, summer, and fall.

At the end of Boathouse Row, in the middle of an intersection, you will see the Lincoln Monument, with the President holding the Emancipation Proclamation.

See the Waterworks

Bear right at the intersection and see the *Waterworks*; this is a National Historic Engineering Landmark of Greek Revival buildings restored to their original grandeur. Its machines pumped water from the river to the reservoir in the nineteenth century. In the mid-1920s, however, the reservoir was replaced by the Art Museum.

As you backtrack, bear right on Kelly Drive and you will pass the Azalea Garden, where more than 2,000 bushes explode in color every spring. Soon, on your right, looms the awesome *Philadelphia Museum of Art* (see VISUAL ARTS).

Benjamin Franklin Parkway

Now continue down Benjamin Franklin Parkway, the broad, grand boulevard that stretches all the way from *Fairmount Park* to *City Hall*. Calling this "Philadelphia's Champs-Elysees" is no exaggeration—it was the idea of architect Jacques Greber, who was born in Paris

Boathouse Row on the Schuylkill River

Bob Krist for the Greater Philadelphia Tourism Marketing Corporation

and completed it in 1918 at a cost of $22 million. Not surprisingly, most of Philadelphia's parades pass this way.

As you approach Logan Circle, to the left is the *Free Library of Philadelphia* (see SIGHTS), which is a replica of the Ministry of Marine on the Place de la Concorde in Paris. To the right is *The Franklin Institute Science Museum*, IMAX theater, and the *Fels Planetarium* (see SIGHTS), the magnificent museum that also contains the national memorial to Benjamin Franklin. Next on your right is the *Academy of Natural Sciences* (see SIGHTS), which is the oldest natural history museum in the country. Logan Circle is circular now, but it was one of the five squares that Penn originally designed in the city. Today it is an absolute delight, and its fountain figures are the work of the famed sculptor Alexander Calder.

Head out of Logan Circle and then farther down the Parkway, and catch a glimpse of the *Cathedral of Saints Peter and Paul* on your left. This impressive Roman-style church is the head church of the Philadelphia archdiocese. It was completed in 1864 and six of Philadelphia's last nine bishops and archbishops are buried beneath its altar.

City Hall

As you approach the end of the Parkway, turn right on Seventeenth Street, drive to Market Street and turn left, and *City Hall* will reappear before you.

At the laying of its cornerstone in 1874, the orator closed with these words: "Do we not say, `Dear, dear Philadelphia,' when we leave behind us this noble building to say it for us?"

Larger than the U.S. Capitol, City Hall required 30 years to build, and is the tallest building in the world without a steel support system. The statue of Penn on top of it (37 feet high, 26 tons) is the world's largest on the top of a building. It may have cost $24 million to construct City Hall, which was a lot of money then, but $1 billion would be needed to duplicate it today. Bearing the richest array of sculpture of any public building in the nation, its architecture is French Renaissance or "Second Empire," patterned after the New Louvre in Paris. It contains more than 600 rooms, and below the statue is a breezy observation gallery with a sweeping view of Philadelphia in all directions.

If you do not choose to visit City Hall, you will still get a good idea of its imposing nature by turning right off Market, left on South Penn Square, and following that to the left. This will have taken you halfway around City Hall, and bring you again to *Market Street*; **turn right and continue east.**

Market Street East Area

For several years, this area—known as Market Street East—has been the city's largest urban development project, and ranks among the most intensive concentrations of retail stores in the nation. **On your right, at the corner of Thirteenth and Market,** looms a reminder of when it all started: *Lord and Taylor* in the former *John Wanamaker* building, the latter being the first department store in America. On Twelfth Street, two blocks to the north at Arch Street, is the new Pennsylvania Convention Center which, along with its spectacular Grand Hall and Ballroom in the 100-year-old *Reading Train Shed*, has speeded up the momentum.

The Gallery comes next, at Ninth and Market Streets. Spanning four city blocks and four levels high, it is the nation's largest enclosed shopping center and includes *Strawbridge and Clothier*, the second of Philadelphia's historic department stores.

Farther east, **at Seventh and Market Streets,** is *Market Place East*, a Victorian-style building filled with restaurants, nightclubs, and shops. **Across Market Street, on the right,** is *Graaf House*, where Thomas Jefferson lived when he wrote the Declaration of Independence. Now reconstructed, Graaf House has a film that deals with Jefferson's contributions to American history, and displays regarding the Declaration of Independence. You can also see the actual room where it was written.

Independence Square

After driving one block farther, you are facing an area that is known as "America's most historic square mile." Turn right, and on the left you will pass the *Liberty Bell Pavillion*, *Independence Hall*, and *Independence Square*. It was in 1948 that the federal government designated Independence Square and the blocks surrounding it as "Independence National Historic Park," pouring millions of dollars into its reconstruction, and today it is Philadelphia's greatest tourist attraction.

At Pine Street, turn left and continue east to Front. Along the way you will see quaint cobbled streets lined with Colonial homes and fenced-in gardens. You will also pass some historic churches, as well as Head House Square. (For more on the Independence Square area, see DOWNTOWN WALKING TOUR.)

Penn's Landing

At Front Street, turn left and drive north to Chestnut Street, turn right, and follow Chestnut Street across Interstate 95 to Christopher

Columbus Blvd. Turn left and follow the signs into Penn's Landing.
It was here on the banks of the Delaware River that William Penn's ship, *Welcome*, docked more than 300 years ago; and he certainly would not recognize it now. More than $35 million has been spent on the 37 acres here, turning it into another pride and joy for Philadelphia, and one of its most popular tourist spots. Now a waterfront designed for people, its half-mile esplanade is the site of many festivals, much music, and nighttime fun.

The *U.S.S. Olympia*

Here you will also find some old ships, the most noteworthy being the *U.S.S. Olympia* and the World War II submarine, *Becuna*. The *Olympia* is the only survivor of the Spanish-American War fleets, and as Commodore Dewey's flagship, it was from her bridge that he gave the command, "You may fire when you are ready, Gridley," that signaled the start of the Battle of Manila Bay on May 1, 1898. It was victory in that battle that informed the world that America had arrived as a world power.

The *Olympia's* last mission was in October of 1921, when she brought the body of the Unknown Soldier from Le Havre, France, to its resting place of honor in Arlington Cemetery.

Independence Seaport Museum

The *Maritime Museum*, renamed the *Independence Seaport Museum*, moved to Penn's Landing in 1995. It spearheaded Philadelphia's waterfront renaissance and provides a direct interpretive link to other attractions on the water—the historic ships at Penn's Landing that are part of the museum, the New Jersey State Aquarium, Camden Children's Garden on the opposite shore, and the connecting RiverLink ferry, which travels between Camden and Philadelphia and docks at the Museum door.

In its new, expanded quarters, the Museum launches its central, interpretive exhibition, "Home Port Philadelphia." Supplemented by a series of changing exhibitions and media programs developed for the Museum's auditorium and 360-degree theater, "Home Port" uses artifacts, audiovisual materials, computerized databases, and mechanical interactives to provide an entertaining, yet educational experience.

Farther down the waterfront is the *International Sculpture Garden*, whose permanent outdoor exhibit of historic sculpture was developed by the Fairmount Park Art Association.

For further appreciation of the Port of Philadelphia—the world's largest freshwater port—Penn's Landing is also the departure point for the *Spirit of Philadelphia* which offers sightseeing cruises on the Delaware, buffet meals, dancing, and live entertainment, including the "Salute to Broadway" revue performed by the waiters and waitresses. For information call 215-923-1419. (See DINING.)

Washington Square

To finish off your tour, **leave the Port and take Dock Street to Chancellor Street. Turn left onto Chancellor, right at Third Street, left at Walnut, and follow Walnut** to *Washington Square* between Walnut and Locust Streets. In 1704, this square was designated as a Potter's Field, and later, hundreds of soldiers of the Revolutionary War and many victims of the great yellow fever epidemic of 1793 were buried here. The Tomb of the Unknown Soldier in the square is alone in the United States in honoring unknown Revolutionary War soldiers.

ONE-DAY
EXCURSIONS

Within an hour and a half of Philadelphia you can find yourself among rolling hills and some of the most gorgeous countryside to be found anywhere. To the west is Lancaster County, land of Mennonite and Amish folk for generations, and which served as a setting for the film *Witness*; to the northeast is New Hope, the "Patchwork of Americana" and site of some of the most original and creative arts and crafts shops in the nation; for a change of pace, there is Atlantic City to the southeast with its casinos, boardwalk, and beaches; and the Pocono Mountains to the north, a place of beauty and non-stop fun. While we have listed a visit to the Poconos in this chapter, the trip could easily be extended.

Lancaster County and New Hope are both accented by Pennsylvania's seasons, which furnish not only dramatic changes in the countryside, but also bring a unique atmosphere to the individual times of the year. Compared to metropolitan Philadelphia, the pace is so slow that you'll find yourself tempted to meander down the numerous obscure roads that invariably wind through quaint towns and past pert antique shops and out-of-the-way historic sites. And the food. . . well, come with an appetite.

Because of the wealth of things to do, see, and appreciate in the Lancaster County and New Hope areas, we strongly suggest at least one overnight stay to relax in an inn, experience bed-and-breakfast with a local family, and simply enjoy yourself far from the hustle and bustle of the big city. If you are just out for a drive with no stops, however, you can do the entirety of either tour in one day. But if you are a Philadelphia area resident, you might wish to divide the trips into several days.

243

NORTHWEST TO LANCASTER COUNTY

Leave the City via the Schuylkill Expressway

Follow the Schuylkill Expressway (Route 76) west to Route 202 and, following the signs to Paoli, continue on Route 202 south past Paoli to the Exton bypass exit (Route 30 Lincoln Highway). Turn right (west) and follow the Route 30 bypass, as it will speed the rest of your trip to Lancaster.

At Route 10 turn right. This road is stunning, especially in the fall when the foliage is bursting with color. At the intersection with Route 340 you may want to visit *The Knittery* on the right; some great deals on sweaters are available in this quaint red barn.

First Stop—Intercourse

Continue west on Route 340, which will take you into Intercourse, PA. Turn right on 772, and on your right is the entrance to the *Kitchen Kettle*, a neat little village where you can indulge in homemade fudge, jams, and baked goods while watching local craftsmen at work. Having parked in the Kitchen Kettle lot, you can also stroll back to Main Street (Route 340) and visit the *Old Candle Barn*, the *Old Country Store*, and *Trudy's Doll Village*. It's fun to browse through these and other nearby places, if only to admire the lovely homemade crafts.

Amish Country

The best way to familiarize yourself with the Mennonite and Amish people and their traditions is to drop by *People's Place*. Here you'll find an *Amish Story Museum*, films, and a craft and book shop; and on the second floor, a tribute to a self-taught Amish craftsman named Aaron Zook.

Proceed west on Route 340 toward the tiny town of *Bird-In-Hand*, passing the *Amish Experience and Plain & Fancy Farm and Dining Room* complex. Here you'll find the Amish Experience FX Theater, The Country Homestead available for guided tours, another group of shops, a Gay Nineties Museum, an antique doll house, buggy rides, and an animal barn. There is also the *Plain & Fancy Farm and Dining Room,* where giant portions of homemade cooking are served family-style. Near Bird-In-Hand is the *Weavertown One Room School* where hundreds of children from first to eighth grade were taught "The Three R's" by a single teacher. Children especially enjoy this site.

Backtrack to Route 772 and proceed north. You'll come to a fork in the road. To the right is the *Phillips Lancaster County Swiss Cheese Company.* If you're there between 9 am and noon, you'll be able to watch them make the kind of cheeses you're sure to buy before leaving.

Ephrata Cloister

Now continue north on Route 772 (left at the fork in the road). This will take you through a vintage stretch of Amish and Mennonite fields and farms. **At Route 222, turn right and continue to the Ephrata exit. After exiting right, turn left on Route 322** and, after driving through the middle of town, you'll soon come to the *Ephrata Cloister* on your left.

This retreat was founded in 1732 by Conrad Beissel, who led a German Protestant sect, the Seventh-Day Baptists, which decided to withdraw from the world. Pious and celibate, they led a harsh, self-sustaining existence, eating one meal per day and sleeping on wooden benches with hard blocks for pillows. Tours of some of the buildings are available and you may explore others on your own. Members of the original settlers are buried in the graveyard.

There are daytime tours all year, Mon-Sat 9 am-5 pm, Sun noon-5 pm. CH. For schedule and information call 717-733-6600.

Moravians Settlements

As you leave the Cloister, turn left on Route 322 and, as you approach the overpass, follow the sign which will put you on Route 272 south. Follow Route 272 south to Route 772, turn right, and follow it through Rothsville to Lititz. This magnificently quaint little town was settled by the Moravians in the mid-1700s and still has original buildings from that time.

Don't miss the *Sturgis Pretzel House,* 219 E. Main Street, which was America's first pretzel bakery and which still has the original ovens, now more than 200 years old. After you've watched the pretzels being made, you'll learn how to twist them yourself before you leave.

Continue west on Main Street to the fountain in Moravian Square, turn right on Broad Street, and on your left you'll find the

Candy Americana Museum & Wilbur Chocolate's Factory Candy Outlet. Here you'll see a wide variety of chocolate candies in the making, and will no doubt buy some upon your departure.

To Donegal Mills Plantation

Now, return to Route 772 west and proceed to the square in Mannheim, PA. There, take the Mannheim-Mount Joy Road (still Route 772) to Mount Joy, cross Main Street (Route 230), and continue on New Haven Street to the dead end. Turn right and continue south on Route 772 exactly three miles. At the sign of Donegal Mills Plantation, turn right at Musser Road and follow the signs to the plantation. This is a nineteenth-century Georgian mansion and restoration of a community that was settled in the 1700s by a Scotch-Irish adventurer who found the area irresistible.

Guided tours include the mansion itself, where the antiques date back to the Empire and Victorian periods. Excellent dining is to be found in the mill. Another superior choice for dining is nearby, on Pinkerton Road, in Mount Joy.

Now take Route 772 south to Marietta, PA, turn left on Route 23, and, about two miles after crossing Route 30, you'll come to Wheatland on your right. This was the home of Pennsylvania's only president, James Buchanan, and the tour is well worth the 45 minutes it requires.

Lancaster

Continue on Route 23 into Lancaster, PA, and, at 15 West King Street, join the Historic Lancaster Walking Tour. Call ahead for schedules at 717-392-1776. This outstanding tour, which lasts 90 minutes and starts at 10 am and 1:30 pm, takes you to more than 50 points of interest in a historic city that was the capital of the United States for a day. *CH.*

Afterward, consider visiting the *Rock Ford Plantation* at 881 Rock Ford Road. This magnificently preserved mansion on the banks of the Conestoga River was once the home of Gen. Edward Hand, an Irish doctor whom George Washington named as his Adjutant General.

There's also the *Heritage Center Museum of Lancaster County.* Located on the corner of Center Square and Queen Street, the museum features works spanning generations of the country's renowned craftspeople and artists.

Since a trip to Pennsylvania's Dutch country isn't really complete without a visit to a farmer's market, stop by the *Central Market* on Penn's Square. In a huge market typical of many in the area, your mouth will water at baked goods only minutes from the oven, tantalizing meats in the butcher shop, and fruits and vegetables straight off the farm. The least you can do is pick up some shoo-fly pie for the short trip to the *Amish Homestead,* **a few miles east on Route 30 (Lincoln Highway).**

The Amish Homestead is a 71-acre farm dating back to 1744 that is occupied and operated by an Amish family. It includes acres of crops, a tobacco shed, and animals everywhere. You can bring a picnic lunch and enjoy it on the farm.

Next is *Dutch Wonderland,* an amusement park for children, with a Pennsylvania Dutch flavor. It is accented by covered bridges, an Amish farmhouse, and scenes from an Amish quilting bee. There's also an abundance of rides, including one by monorail that provides a sweeping view of the 44-acre park.

Next door at the *National Wax Museum* are reproductions of such historical figures as William Penn, Ben Franklin, and Daniel Boone.

At the *Amish Farm and House,* at 2395 Lincoln Highway East, you'll see a working Pennsylvania Dutch farm and farmhouse and learn in detail of Amish history, religion, and customs during guided and self-guided tours.

Now turn south on Route 896. Soon you'll come to the *Amish Village,* featuring a schoolhouse, a blacksmith shop and springhouse, an operating smokehouse, and more animals.

A few miles farther south on Route 896, turn left on Route 741 to visit the *Choo Choo Barn,* where an elaborate collection of model trains courses through scale-model reproductions of the surrounding countryside. Not far away is the *National Toy Train Museum,* headquarters of the Train Collector's Association. It houses a host of model trains that date back to the late 1880s.

Finally, don't miss the *Strasburg Steam Railroad.* Here you'll enjoy a 4 1/4 mile ride on America's oldest short-line railroad (dating back more than 130 years) through the heart of the Pennsylvania Dutch countryside.

NORTH TO NEW HOPE

Follow Broad Street (Route 611) north. Between Sixty-sixth and Sixty-seventh Avenues, bear to the right as 611 will become Old York Road, and at Willow Grove it will become Easton Avenue.

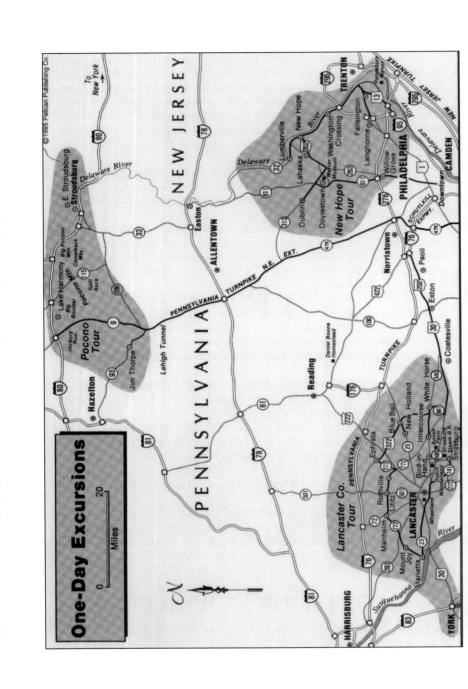

Approaching Doylestown, stay to the left as the Route 611 bypass skirts the west side of this nineteenth-century county seat of Bucks County. Exit at Route 313, turn left, and go to the town of Dublin, PA. There, turn left on Dublin Road, and go one mile to the *Pearl S. Buck House, Green Hills Farm.*

This 1835 stone farmhouse, where the famous humanitarian and winner of both the Nobel and Pulitzer prizes lived and wrote from 1935 until her death 40 years later, was declared a National Historic Landmark in 1980. She once said that the stone walls of her home symbolized, for her, strength and durability.

It's tastefully furnished in Early American and European, and because she spent so much of her life in China, where her parents were missionaries, it's accented by original Oriental touches. Among the highlights of the home is the desk upon which Miss Buck wrote her famed book, *The Good Earth.*

A guided tour of the home and the Green Hills grounds, where Miss Buck is buried, takes about two hours.

Moravian Pottery and Tile Works ————

Now take Route 313 (Swamp Rd.) back toward Doylestown. Soon, at East Court Street, on your right, you'll see the *Moravian Pottery and Tile Works*—the north part of the "Mercer Mile."

Henry Chapman Mercer (1856-1930) was an archaeologist, anthropologist, historian, and writer, as well as one of the most ambitious collectors and innovators of his time. He wasn't an architect, but he still designed and, using unskilled laborers from nearby farms and a dutiful horse named Lucy, built the Pottery and Tile Works, a home that looks more like a fortress, and the Mercer Museum.

All are worth seeing, and not just because they were the first buildings ever to be constructed solely of reinforced concrete. It was in the Pottery and Tile Works that Mercer developed the methods and formulas for manufacturing tiles that are still seen today in the casino in Monte Carlo, the Pennsylvania State Capitol, and the Bryn Mawr College Library. The factory was closed after his death and eventually turned into a museum. In 1974 it was reactivated, and now, with Mercer's original machinery, kilns, molds, and tools on display, it is once again producing tiles the way Mercer did 75 years ago.

Within walking distance is Mercer's home, *Fonthill.* Here you'll find 39 rooms in which the ceilings, walls, and floors are covered with Mercer's distinctive tiles; there are also countless engravings, prints, and artifacts that he collected on his worldwide explorations.

Now take the short drive to the *Mercer Museum,* Pine and Ashland streets, which contains 40,000 tools, implements, and utensils from pre-industrial days. The tools represent all types of manufacturing from past times, from the making of shoes, toys, hats, and candies to boats and bathtubs. There's also a fascinating collection of caskets and gallows.

Now take Route 313 southeast to Route 202, turn left, and you'll find yourself on the course that the earliest travelers took between New York City and Philadelphia. There are still areas of beautiful country-side along the way.

Peddler's Village

At Route 263, turn left for Lahaska (originally called "Lahaskeke" by the Indians, meaning "place of much writing"). Here, among the grass, streams, and waterfalls are herringboned bricked walkways that will lead you to the shops of *Peddler's Village*. They are extraordinary shops, too; so extensive is the selection of stencils, potholders, decoys, quilts, candles, brass, and other creations that if you know someone who "has everything," you'll be able to surprise them with a gift from here.

Across the street (Route 202) is *Penn's Purchase*, a group of 40 dis-count outlets. You'll also find a number of restaurants on both sides of the street.

Bucks County Vineyards & Winery

Now take Route 202 toward New Hope. Dotted with old stone houses, these few miles abound with antique shops that attract collec-tors and dealers from throughout the nation. You will then come to the *Bucks County Vineyards & Winery*.

Located on a Pennsylvania farm granted to Jacob Holcomb by William Penn in 1717, the winery now bottles about 61,000 gallons a year. You're also invited to tour the *Wine Museum* where, on the third floor, there's a *Fashion Museum* containing an astonishing collection of original costumes from the stage and screen. Arthur Gerold, the win-ery's president, once owned America's largest theatrical costume com-pany, Brooks-Van Horn. Here you'll find original costumes worn by Richard Burton and Robert Goulet in "Camelot"; Julie Andrews in "My Fair Lady"; Angela Lansbury in "Mame"; Marlon Brando in "The Godfather," and the first costume ever worn by Barry Manilow, bought for him by Bette Midler because he was short of cash.

A cheese shop has also been added, and some of what you purchase here was no doubt made by an Amish cooperative dedicated to the art.

On to New Hope

Now follow Route 202 into New Hope. Originally an art colony founded in 1900 by some internationally famous artists who had settled along the Delaware River, this is now a thriving arts center. Artists of all types live in this charming town and on nearby farms, and as you would expect, the selection of original work in New Hope's nearly 100 shops is extraordinary.

On the Corner Square is the *Parry Mansion,* a historical home that was occupied by five generations of the Parry family. Tours are available and ten of its rooms reflect the changes of lifestyle between Colonial times and the early 1900s.

On the northwest corner of Cannon Square, which commemorates the Civil War dead, is the *Logan Inn* (see LODGING). The original structure was the Ferry Tavern, built in the 1720s. It's now a splendid example of the colonials' facility for adding on to existing buildings, and long ago was named after James Logan, William Penn's secretary and another friend of the Lenni Lenape Indians.

The tavern's interior, presided over by a huge clock, is decorated with eighteenth- and nineteenth-century antiques. Townsfolk frequent the tavern and its restaurant, and 16 guest rooms are available.

Across the street is the *Bucks County Playhouse.* Once an old grist mill, it was converted into a playhouse in 1939 and is now known as the State Theater of Pennsylvania. (See PERFORMING ARTS Theater.)

An absolute must is the New Hope Station, built in 1890 and now the starting point for the *New Hope Steam Railroad.* Here, an old steam locomotive is ready to take you on a trip through the country to Lahaska and back. It takes about an hour.

On New Street are the New Hope *Mule-Drawn Barge Rides.* For an hour, you can unwind beneath the awnings of a flat-bottom barge as it's pulled by a pair of mules through the canal of the town, out into the country, and back.

Phillips Mill

If you have the time, **take the lovely country drive north on Route 32, along the Delaware River to Phillips Mill,** one of the many charming towns of Solebury Township. This is one of the most picturesque communities you'll find anywhere, and the restored grist mill from which the community got its name is still the home of the Phillips Mill Community Association, which has served area artists for decades.

Farther north on Route 32 is Lumberville, another village of stone and frame houses, pleasantly surrounded by the canal, the river, and a ridge of mountains called "the Coppernose." It has also been the home of the *Black Bass Hotel* since 1727 (see LODGING and DINING), an outstanding spot to stay, or to dine and drink in the scenery.

Washington Crossing

South of New Hope on Route 32 is *Washington Crossing,* where George Washington led his soldiers across the Delaware River on Christmas night of 1776 to defeat the Hessians in a surprise attack on Trenton. Some 500 acres of the area now comprise *Washington Crossing State Park,* including an exact replica of Emanuel Leutze's painting "Washington Crossing the Delaware," and the Old Ferry Inn, where the General ate dinner before crossing the river. Between the Inn and the Memorial Building is a boat barn containing four replicas of the boats used that historic night more than 200 years ago. (They are used every Christmas Day to re-enact the feat, beginning at 2 pm.) The northern 100 acres of the park have been devoted to an explosion of wild flowers second to none.

Farther south are three attractions—two of them historic, the other for children.

William Penn

Within five miles of each other are *Fallsington,* where William Penn worshipped, and *Pennsbury Manor,* his estate on the Delaware River. Fallsington is a lovely village along Route 13, just south of Route 1, where no less than two dozen eighteenth-century houses still stand with pride, and where the *Stagecoach Tavern,* a favorite stop for travelers between New York and Philadelphia from the 1790s to the 1920s, has been faithfully restored.

Farther south, along the Delaware River, east of Tullytown, is the Manor, which Penn began building during his first visit to his colony in the early 1680s, but which he did not occupy until his second visit in 1700. Even then, due to financial problems which prompted a return to England (and the fact that his wife and daughter really preferred city life), he lived in the Manor only two years. It is now a total recreation of what Penn so loved then (however briefly). A decade of research was invested in the Manor's reconstruction. Tours are available.

Sesame Place

Finally, there's *Sesame Place*. **Off Interstate 95 in Langhorne, PA,** next to Oxford Valley Mall, this is a twenty-first-century play park geared to children aged 3-13. Here they can meet real-life Sesame Street characters, as well as enjoy televised adventures and live science shows. Make sure they bring their bathing suits; the water games are guaranteed to get them wet.

NORTH TO
THE POCONOS

How to Get There

Take the Schuylkill Expressway west to the Pennsylvania Turnpike, travel east on the turnpike to the Northeast Extension, and follow that north to the mountains. The Poconos are served by regular bus service from Philadelphia, and major airlines land at Lehigh Valley International Airport in Allentown (610-266-6000) and Wilkes-Barre/Scranton International Airport in Avoca (570-457-3445).

A Place of Beauty

Only 85 miles northwest of Philadelphia are the majestic Pocono Mountains, a 2,400-square-mile expanse of natural beauty highlighted by a host of outdoor and indoor recreational activities. "Pocono" is an Indian name for "a stream in the mountains." This range is blessed with countless streams, creeks, lakes, and gorgeous waterfalls. With each season defined by its own breathtaking scenery and climate, the Pocono Mountains are an exhilarating experience every month of the year.

Winter Sports

In the winter, four major ski areas—Big Boulder, Camelback, Jack Frost Mountain, and Shawnee Mountain—are among the finest in the

East. Beginner, intermediate, and expert trails are available, and all facilities include fully staffed ski schools, rentals, and lodge activities. There are 12 top ski resorts in the Poconos, each offering a variety of downhill trails, cross-country trails, slopes, snowmaking equipment, and lifts. Snowmobiling, sledding, tobogganing, ice-skating, sleigh rides, and ice fishing are also extremely popular in the Poconos in the wintertime.

Summer Recreation

Warm weather means just as much fun. As "the Myrtle Beach of the North," the Poconos have more than 30 golf courses, several of championship caliber. Indoor and outdoor tennis courts abound, with many resorts offering special packages for tennis and golf. Three state parks—Delaware Water Gap Recreational Area, Big Pocono State Park, and Tobyhanna State Park—provide more than 1,000 campsites, 15 of which are open year-round. You will also find exceptional areas for fishing, boating, whitewater rafting, canoeing, swimming, hiking, horseback riding, and hunting.

Among numerous other attractions are shops where pottery, baskets, and candy are handmade before your eyes. There are various museums, a wildlife park, and the Camelback Alpine and Water Slide where, after a chair-lift ride to the top, you'll career to the bottom in a plastic sled over a 3,600-foot, toboggan-like course. For information call 570-629-1661.

The 2 1/2-mile tri-oval high-speed course of the Pocono International Raceway attracts top drivers on the NASCAR and Indy-car circuits to the mountains each summer (800-RACEWAY).

Where to Stay

Lodging in the Poconos is extensive. You can stay in a charming country inn, a modern hotel or motel, or any of the fine lodges and resorts. And then there are the honeymoon resorts. It was in the Poconos that the sunken tub, the heart-shaped pool, and the in-room swimming pool were invented; as a result, the Poconos are now the Honeymoon Capital of the world, with honeymoon resorts attracting more than 275,000 newlywed couples each year.

In view of the many types and plans of accommodations that are available in the Poconos, you may wish to order brochures in advance and study them in detail. We recommend you call or write the Pocono Mountains Vacation Bureau, 1004 Main St., Stroudsburg, PA, 18360; 570-421-5791 or 800-762-6667. Website: www.800poconos.com.

Dining Out

There are countless restaurants offering the full range of seafood and American, Continental, international, French, Italian, and Chinese cuisine. The specialty, however, is the always fresh Pocono Mountain trout.

SOUTHEAST TO ATLANTIC CITY

Leave the City via the Benjamin Franklin Bridge

Follow the signs to the Atlantic City Expressway. This will take you straight to the New Jersey shores of Atlantic City. Since the approval of casino gambling in 1976, investors have poured billions into this resort. There are 12 glittering casinos in which to enjoy table games, including blackjack, roulette, craps, baccarat, and big six wheels. There are also thousands of slot machines.

In addition, the casino hotels offer razzle-dazzle musical revues and a variety of entertainment in lounges. A boxing fan? Matches are scheduled regularly. There's also the world-famous Boardwalk, fine dining, and lots of fellow visitors. For more information, see LODGING Resorts.

THE INTERNATIONAL
VISITOR

Philadelphia continues to grow and develop as a truly international host city. Upon landing at Philadelphia International Airport, flights from foreign countries taxi to the Overseas Terminal and there international passengers are greeted by the full complement of immigrations and customs facilities and services. Consulates and ethnic societies in the Philadelphia area stand ready to help those arriving daily from around the world, to make Philadelphia a home away from home. We have listed aids and resources for international visitors and those relocating in Philadelphia, beginning with the consulates, trade offices, and ethnic societies.

International House of Philadelphia, 3701 Chestnut St., Philadelphia 19104; 215-387-5125. This residence, program, and cultural center provides a unique living experience for 450 students from 50 countries, in addition to sponsoring nationally recognized media, arts, and folklife programs and offering services for foreign students throughout the Philadelphia area.

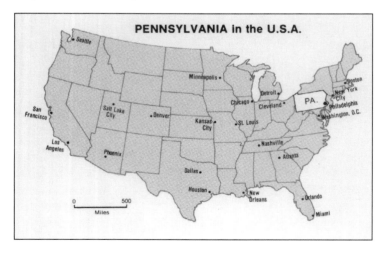

256

International Visitors Council of Philadelphia, (IVC), 1600 Arch St.; 215-686-3961. The 40-year-old IVC is the official Greater Philadelphia representative for international guests of the U.S. government and private foundations. Its goal is to create an international network of business, civic and community leaders to promote international business relationships and mutual understanding among nations. Each year, IVC arranges more than 3,000 one-on-one meetings that link international leaders with their Philadelphia-area counterparts. IVC also schedules social events, seminars and discussion groups. It has attracted members of Parliament from five continents, mayors from more than 60 cities around the globe, and heads of businesses, universities, hospitals, and government agencies to the Philadelphia area to meet their counterparts.

The World Affairs Council, 1314 Chestnut St.; 215-731-1100. This membership organization, with programs open to the public, provides lectures, seminars, debates, and conferences on international events and issues. Its International Business Forum section advances and increases the effectiveness of international companies in Pennsylvania, Delaware, and New Jersey. Call for more information.

Consulates and Trade Offices ——————

Austria, 123 S. Broad St.; 215-772-7630.

Belgium, 215-238-8729.

Chile, Public Ledger Bldg., Independence Sq.; 215-829-9520.

Costa Rica, 1411 Walnut St.; 215-564-4415.

Czech Republic, 215-646-7777

Denmark, 123 S. Broad St.; 215-772-7454.

Dominican Republic, Lafayette Building, 437 Chestnut St.; 215-923-3006.

Dubai, Eight Penn Center; 215-751-9750.

Ecuador, Sixth and Chestnut Sts.; 215-925-9060.

El Salvador, 119 Llanfair Rd., Ardmore (residence); 610-642-1354.

Finland, 112 Christian St.; 215-465-5565.

France, Honorary Consul, One Liberty Place, Suite 2500; 215-851-1474.

Germany, 1617 JFK Blvd.; 215-665-3263.

Haiti, 1600 Market St., Thirty-fourth floor; 215-751-2516.

Israel, 230 S. Fifteenth St.; 215-546-5556.

Italy, 1026 Public Ledger Bldg., Independence Sq.; 215-592-7329.

Japan, Honorary Consul, 1735 Market St.; 215-553-2170.

Liberia, 610-668-9433.

Madagascar, 610-640-7832.

Malta, 1819 JFK Blvd.; 215-563-8334.

Mexico, 21 S. Fifth St.; 215-922-4262.

Monaco, Suburban Station Building; 215-665-0152.

Netherlands, 45 Brennan Dr., Bryn
   Mawr; 610-520-9591.
Nicaragua, NE Corner Second St.
   and Girard Ave.; 215-427-2570.
Norway, 112 Christian St.;
   215-462-2502.
Panama, 124 Chestnut St.;
   215-574-2994.
Portugal, 7950 Loretto Ave.;
   215-745-2889.

Puerto Rico, Two Penn Center;
   215-851-9930.
Spain, 3410 Warden Dr.;
   215-848-6180.
Sweden, 1628 JFK Blvd.;
   215-496-7200.
Switzerland, Public Ledger Bldg.,
   Independence Sq.; 215-922-2215.
United Kingdom, 226 Walnut St.;
   215-925-0118.

Ethnic Societies

China, Cultural and Community
   Center; 215-923-6767.
France, Alliance Francaise de
   Philadelphia; 215-735-5283.
Germany, German Society of
   Pennsylvania; 215-627-2332 and
   627-4365.
Ireland, Irish Center; 215-843-8051.
Italy, Societies at Immaculata
   College and the University of
   Pennsylvania.
Jewish, Jewish Federation of Greater
   Philadelphia; 215-832-0500 and
   735-7977.

Korea, Korean American
   Association of Greater
   Philadelphia;
   215-457-8343.
Poland, Polish-American
   Association; 215-634-8191.
Spain, Council of Spanish Speaking
   Organizations; 215-627-3100.
Sweden, American-Swedish
   Historical Foundation; 215-389-
   1776.
Wales, Welsh Society of
   Philadelphia; 215-247-5790
   (president's residence).

Bank Hours

Philadelphia's banking hours vary anywhere from 9 am-3 pm, to 9 am-7 pm, Monday through Friday, and many of the branch locations have Saturday hours as well.

Currency Exchange and International Banking

Always try to exchange foreign currency at a bank or at the airport, where you will be offered the most competitive rate. However, the cashiers in some major hotels and restaurants will be able to exchange foreign currency, too.

International banking services in Philadelphia include purchase and sale of foreign currencies and foreign travelers' checks, cable transfers, foreign drafts on overseas banks, foreign collections, import/export financing, and issue of commercial letters of credit. The following banks in Philadelphia are at your service, and all have numerous branch locations.

Commerce Bank, 888-751-9000.
FirstTrust Bank, 215-722-4000.
First Union Bank, 800-ASK-FUNB (275-3862).
Keystone Financial, 800-366-9399.
Mellon Bank, 800-MELLON-24 (635-5662).
PNC Bank, 888-762-2265.

Also at your service are:
American Express, King of Prussia; 610-265-7450; 800-528-4800.
Thomas Cook Currency Services, 1800 JFK Blvd.; 215-563-7348; 800-287-7362.

For further information, call the **Federal Reserve Bank** at 215-574-6000.
Treasury Dept., Treasury Check information, 215-516-8152

Customs Allowances

You are allowed to bring into the United States from overseas the following duty free:

One liter of alcoholic beverages; fifty cigars; two hundred cigarettes. Be aware that state liquor laws supersede the national regulations.

There is a personal exemption of $200; over this amount the next $1,000 in goods is charged at a flat rate of 10%. Anything above $1,000 is charged whatever duty rates apply.

Gifts that are mailed to the United States under the value of $100 are duty free; over that amount the recipient will be charged duty. For further information, call the **U.S. Customs House,** Second and Chestnut Sts.; 215-597-4605. Website: www.customs.treas.gov.

Driving

Driving in the United States is in the right lane. An international driver's license should be secured through your local automobile association before you leave home. United States gallons of gasoline are one-fifth smaller than the United Kingdom's imperial gallon. Gasoline stations along the highways are generally open on weekends or in the evenings, and some remain open 24 hours; watch for signs.

The 55 mph (miles per hour) speed limit is observed and strictly enforced by the use of police radar observation. Some highway speeds are higher where posted. In Pennsylvania, you are allowed to turn right at a red traffic light except where posted, and the law dictates you must call the police immediately when you have an accident.

Electricity

110 volts, 60 cycles A.C. Bring an adapter for your razor and/or hair dryer.

Medical Insurance

Medical insurance should be secured prior to arrival. There is no national health service in the United States.

Money

The United States dollar ($) is divided into 100 cents (¢). The coins are: penny worth 1 ¢ (copper-colored); nickel 5 ¢; dime 10 ¢; quarter 25 ¢; half-dollar 50 ¢ (all of which are silver-colored), and the silver dollar and the new gold dollar $1. The bills or notes are all one color, green, and are in denominations of one dollar, five dollars, ten dollars, twenty dollars, fifty dollars, one hundred dollars, and one thousand dollars.

Postage

Mail service is generally good and letters cross the country in one to three days. Zip codes must be used for guaranteed delivery. Express mail, which guarantees next-day delivery, is available. Check with the nearest post office for information on rates. 800-275-8777.

Public Holidays

The following holidays are considered legal holidays in most businesses, including government offices. Banks and businesses will not operate on these days. Some holidays are celebrated on the closest

Monday to the holiday in order to give working people a long weekend. This is indicated in the listing.

January 1, New Year's Day.

January 15, Martin Luther King's Birthday.

February 22, George Washington's Birthday, celebrated on closest Monday.

May 31, Memorial Day, celebrated on closest Monday.

July 4, Independence Day.

September, Labor Day, first Monday after first Tuesday.

October 12, Christopher Columbus Day, celebrated on closest Monday.

November 11, Veterans Day.

November, Thanksgiving Day, fourth Thursday.

December 25, Christmas Day.

Telephone and Telegrams

Most public pay phones require a 35 ¢ coin deposit, but read the instructions before inserting your coin. When calling long distance, dial 1, the area code, and the number. Telephone numbers preceded by an (800) number are toll-free in the United States; you dial 1-800 and number.

To send a mailgram (guaranteed next-day delivery by mail and less expensive than a telegram), telegram, international message, or charge-card money order, call Western Union, 800-325-6000.

Tipping and Taxes

Tipping is your way of rating and rewarding service. These several guidelines will help you adjust the size of the tip you wish to give. A 15% tip is customarily considered for restaurant service, hotel laundry and valet service, room service, bar bills, and taxi fares. Bellhops and porters generally receive $1.50 per bag. Pennsylvania levies a 6-7% sales tax on some merchandise and food; there is no tax on clothes, except for bathing suits (and umbrellas). There is a 13% tax on hotel and motel rooms in Philadelphia.

Translators

Berlitz Translation Services, 800-523-7548, provides translations by international language experts, and language classes.

Inlingua Intercultural Communications Organization, 215-735-7646, and 800-361-6444, offers translation service in any language, language school, interpreting, video film narration, typesetting, and more.

Nationalities Service Center, 215-893-8400, provides interpreting and translation of documents.

Radio and Television Stations
Broadcasting in Foreign Languages ———

WPHE 690 (AM) Spanish.
WEMG 900 (AM) Spanish/English dance/contemporary.
WSSJ 1310 (AM) Spanish oldies.
WNWR 1540 (AM) Ethnic/multilingual.
TV Channel 28 (UHF) Spanish language.
TV Channel 35 (UHF) International/multilingual.

Visa Requirements ————————————

Be sure to obtain your visa from the United States Embassy in your country several weeks prior to departure.

For passport information, call the U.S. Passport Agency; 215-597-7480. The message is in English and Spanish.

METRIC CONVERSIONS

Length

1 millimeter	=	.039 inch (in.)	1 inch	=	2.54 cm.
1 centimeter	=	.39 in.	1 foot	=	0.30 m.
1 meter	=	3.28 feet (ft.)	1 yard	=	.91 m.
1 kilometer	=	.62 mile (mi.)	1 mile	=	1.61 km.

To convert miles to kilometers, multiply the number of miles by 8 and divide by 5.

Weight

1 gram	=	.04 ounce (oz.)	1 oz.	=	28.35 g.
1 kilogram	=	2.2 pounds (lb.)	1 lb.	=	.45 kg.
			1 ton	=	.91 metric ton

Liquid

		2.11 pints (pt.)	1 pt.	=	.47 liter
1 liter	=	1.06 quarts (qt.)	1 qt.	=	.95 liter
		.26 gallon (gal.)	1 gal.	=	3.79 liters

Temperature

To convert Fahrenheit temperatures to Centigrade (Celsius): Take the Fahrenheit temperature, minus 32, and divide by 1.8. This equals the Centigrade temperature.

CONVERSION CHARTS FOR CLOTHING

Dresses, coats, suits and blouses (Women)

British	10	12	14	16	18	20
American	8	18	12	14	16	18
Continental	40	42	44	46	48	50

Suits and overcoats (Men)

American/British	34	36	38	40	42	44
Continental	44	46	48	50	52	54

Shirts (Men)

American/British	14	$14^1/_2$	15	$15^1/_2$	16	$16^1/_2$	17	$17^1/_2$
Continental	36	37	38	39	40	41	42	43

Shoes (Men) for $^1/_2$ sizes add $^1/_2$ to preceding number

British	6	7	8	9	10	11
American	7	8	9	10	11	12
Continental	$39^1/_2$	$40^1/_2$	$41^1/_2$	$42^1/_2$	$43^1/_2$	$44^1/_2$

Shoes (Women) for $^1/_2$ sizes add $^1/_2$ to preceding number

British	3	4	5	6	7	8	9
American	$4^1/_2$	$5^1/_2$	$6^1/_2$	$7^1/_2$	$8^1/_2$	$9^1/_2$	10
Continental	35	36	37	38	39	40	41

The L.O.V.E. Sculpture in Center City

Bob Krist for the Greater Philadelphia Tourism Marketing Corporation

SPECIAL PEOPLE

SENIOR CITIZENS

The older traveler is recognized as an integral part of the large traveling population in the United States and abroad. Travel agencies nationwide focus many of their travel promotions and group trips on the interests of the mature traveler—interests that range from fixed-income capabilities to comfortable transportation and accommodations; from available medical facilities to theme tours and social life. These are the same concerns of the older person who is visiting Philadelphia.

Most major airlines in Philadelphia offer special rates for senior citizens, but be sure to check with your respective airline for its discounts and when they apply. **AMTRAK** (800-USA-RAIL) offers a 15% reduction on all trips for persons 65 years and over, and **Greyhound** bus company (800-231-2222) offers up to 15% off "walk-up" fares, as opposed to advance purchase fare, for people over 55.

Public transportation on **SEPTA** (215-580-7800; TDD: 215-580-7853) discounts its fares for senior citizens as follows: Off-peak hours free (9 am-3:30 pm, 6:30 pm-6 am, all day Saturdays, Sundays, and holidays). Peak hours, the regular fare of $1.50, transfers 40 ¢ (6 am-9 am, 3:30 pm-6:30 pm). **SEPTA Red Arrow and Frontier** divisions: off-peak hours free (9 am-3 pm, 6:30 pm-6 am, all day Saturdays, Sundays, and holidays). Peak hours full fare.

Note: SEPTA's free and reduced rates apply only to persons 65 years and over. Proof of age must be presented to operator when boarding transit vehicle, such as Medicare card or special SEPTA I.D. card. Card can be obtained at SEPTA Building, 200 W. Wyoming Ave., Philadelphia 19140; 215-580-7800; or SEPTA General Office, 841 Chestnut St., Ground Floor, Philadelphia 19107; 215-580-7852; or at the Sixty-ninth St. Terminal. Be sure to bring proof of age.

SEPTA's Regional Commuter Rail Program offers free transportation during off-peak hours. Trip must terminate prior to the start of peak hours. Full fare during peak hours. The senior commuter must present

265

I.D. when on board. This I.D. can be a Medicare card, a PACE (prescription) card, a Public Assistance card, or an Access card. Without these cards, the senior must pay $1. For further information call the Mayor's Commission on Services to the Aging, Room 906, 1401 Arch St., Philadelphia 19102; 215-686-3587. The Commission can also assist the senior citizen with rent or property tax rebates.

Many hotels and motels in the Philadelphia area discount rooms for senior citizens. It is recommended to inquire when making your reservations or checking in. (Also check Bed-and-Breakfast under LODGING.)

Two organizations stand ready to assist senior citizens visiting or traveling through Philadelphia. They are excellent places to obtain referrals for specific needs.

The **American Association of Retired Persons** is a non-governmental, non-partisan, non-profit national organization for men and women 55 and older, whether employed or unemployed. Among the benefits of the $8 annual membership are 10-25% discounts at major hotel and motel chains. Members should always call in advance to confirm the discounts available. AARP members are entitled to discounts of up to 30% on car rentals from Hertz, Avis, Thrift, and National; but once again, call in advance for reservations and information. For further information regarding the AARP, write or call the AARP, Attention Membership Communications, 601 East St. NW, Washington D.C. 20077-1214; 800-424-3410.

Also available is the **Traveler's Aid Society,** which provides emergency service to travelers of all ages and background. This organization is headquartered at 121 N. Broad St., Suite 1001, Philadelphia 19107; 215-523-7580 and 546-0571; branch offices are located at the Greyhound Bus Terminal (215-238-0999), and Thirtieth St. Station (215-386-0845).

HANDICAPPED PERSONS

Thousands of handicapped persons pursue active, fruitful lives, and Philadelphia has made admirable strides in making itself accessible to the disabled in all aspects of urban living. The Mayor's Commission on People with Disabilities provides information or referral concerning transportation, employment, parking, housing, education, recreation, accessibility, attendant care, legislation, city compliance with the Americans With Disabilities Act, and more. The **Mayor's Commission on People with Disabilities** is in City Hall; 215-686-2798.

The expansion and remodeling of **Philadelphia International Airport** has made it much more accessible and convenient for the handicapped person. Specially designed areas in the parking garage provide direct and level access to the terminals, and wheelchairs are available with prior notification. Specially equipped restrooms are located throughout the airport. Most terminals are equipped with jetways, enabling direct and level access to planes. Elevators operate between the departure/arrival and baggage areas. For information or assistance, call the Public Transportation Director at 215-686-1776.

Regarding rental cars, **Hertz** and **Avis** are among the companies that provide automobiles with hand controls. It is advisable to make reservations 48 hours in advance. For information call 800-654-3131 (Hertz) or 800-831-2847 (Avis).

At **Thirtieth Street Station,** a level entrance provides access from the sidewalk. If previously arranged by telephone, a porter will meet the disabled traveler and assist him or her to the track level via elevator. For AMTRAK service, the person in a wheelchair usually transfers to a regular seat, unless traveling in a special car. For information call: 215-824-1600.

For information about access, elevators, and escalators at various SEPTA stations, call SEPTA Paratransit at 215-580-7145.

Some SEPTA routes offer lift-equipped buses. For a listing and schedule, call 215-580-7800.

In the suburbs, lift-equipped buses can be arranged with one-day advance reservation by contacting "Suburban On Call" at 215-580-7700. Hearing-impaired persons can call the TTY number: 215-580-7712.

SEPTA also offers Paratransit service. Visitors and residents should register by calling 215-580-7145.

SEPTA enables handicapped persons to ride half-fare during off-peak hours, provided they have obtained the required card through SEPTA. For information about the card, call 215-580-7145.

For information regarding the **PATCO** high-speed line, call 215-922-4600.

Many hotels and motels in the Philadelphia area provide rooms and facilities tailored to the needs of the handicapped person. For specific information call your hotel in advance.

When planning to attend a theater, concert, or sporting event, the handicapped person should telephone in advance for information and any special arrangements where available.

Easter Seal Society, 3975 Conshohocken Ave.; 215-879-1000. The Society offers a wide variety of services to all handicapped people.

Library for the Blind & Physically Handicapped, Free Library of Philadelphia, 919 Walnut St.; 215-683-3213. Books and magazines are available for adults and children in Braille, large print, and recorded form, including *The New York Times*.

Radio Information Center for the Blind, 919 Walnut St.; 215-627-0600, ext. 208. Special radio programs are provided that include the reading of local newspapers, books, and popular magazines. Special receivers are necessary, but are available for a $50 donation the first year and $25 per year thereafter. Daily 8:30 am-3:30 pm.

Travel Information Service for the Handicapped, provided by MossRehab Hospital, 215-456-9900. Telephone information is available regarding the needs of travelers with disabilities in Philadelphia, as well as those traveling in the United States and abroad.

STUDENTS

Students visiting Philadelphia will find camaraderie at the many colleges and universities in the area. Your most important document is your student identification card, which certifies your student status and helps stretch the travel budget. Always ask if a student discount is applicable for accommodations or travel systems, at restaurants, theaters, cultural programs, museums, and at places of entertainment.

Lodging

Bank Street Youth Hostel, 32 S. Bank St.; 215-922-0222 and 800-392-HOST. An old nightclub completely transformed into an attractive, dormitory-style hostel. It can accommodate more than 50 people at $14-16 per night.

Chamounix Mansion, located on Chamounix Drive in West Fairmount Park, is a dormitory-style hostel that can accommodate 44-88 people. It charges $11 per night for members, as well as for those with International Youth Hostel membership. Fee is $14 per night for non-members. Kitchen facilities and common rooms are available. Closed from December 15-January 15. Open 8 am-11 am and 4:30 pm-midnight.

Hostelling International, Chamounix Mansion, Fairmount Park; 215-878-3676 or 800-379-0017. This organization offers 12 youth hostels in Pennsylvania. A membership card allows you to use these hostels and all others internationally. The card costs $25 per year for ages 18-54 and $10 for those under 17 and over 60. Website: www.libertynet.org/chmounix.

International House, 3701 Chestnut St.; 215-387-5125. This is a high-rise dormitory on the University of Pennsylvania campus with housing for foreign students and nightly guests.

Philadelphia Colleges and Universities

Philadelphia and its surrounding counties are graced by almost 90 colleges and universities, which offer degrees and advanced degrees in every conceivable course of study. Among them are:

Art Institute of Philadelphia, 1622 Chestnut St.; 215-567-7080.

Community College of Philadelphia, 1700 Spring Garden St.; 215-751-8000.

The Curtis Institute of Music, 1726 Locust St.; 215-893-7902.

Drexel University, Thirty-second and Chestnut Sts.; 215-895-2400.

LaSalle University, Twentieth and Olney Sts.; 215-951-1500.

The Medical College of Pennsylvania and Hahnemann University, Broad and Vine Sts.; 215-762-7000.

Moore College of Art, Twentieth and Benjamin Franklin Pkwy.; 215-568-4515.

Pennsylvania College of Optometry, 1200 W. Godfrey Ave.; 215-276-6000.

The Philadelphia College of Textiles and Science, School House Lane and Henry Ave.; 215-951-2700.

St. Joseph's University, 5600 City Ave.; 610-660-1000.

Temple University, Broad St. and Montgomery Ave.; 215-204-7000.

Temple University College of Podiatric Medicine, Eighth and Race Sts.; 215-625-5243.

Thomas Jefferson University, Eleventh and Walnut Sts.; 215-955-6000.

University of the Arts, Broad and Pine Sts.; 215-875-4800.

University of Pennsylvania, Thirty-fourth and Walnut Sts.; 215-898-5000.

University of the Sciences in Philadelphia, Forty-third St. and Kingsessing Mall; 215-596-8800.

Colleges and Universities in Suburban Philadelphia

Bryn Mawr College, Bryn Mawr; 610-526-5000.
Haverford College, Haverford; 610-896-1000.
Rosemont College, Rosemont; 610-527-0200.
Swarthmore College, Swarthmore; 610-328-8000.
Villanova University, Villanova; 610-519-4500.

Popular Student Hangouts

Casa Mexicana, 4002 Chestnut St.; 215-387-4477. A casual Cantina restaurant that has good Mexican food available at good prices.

Cavanaugh's Restaurant, 119 S. Thirty-ninth St.; 215-662-5000. A dinner theater that is lots of fun.

Khyber Pass Pub, 56 S. Second St.; 215-238-5888. This funky, earthy pub features local music every night of the week.

O'Hara's Fish House, Thirty-ninth and Chestnut Sts.; 215-349-9000. It's not just fish, but steaks and a salad bar, too. You can drink and eat on a shoestring here. Live jazz, pop, karaoke, and blues, Wed-Sat.

Smart Alex, Thirty-sixth and Chestnut Sts.; 215-386-5556. This multilevel bar and restaurant in the Sheraton University City is especially fun when the six-foot TV screen comes alive with a major sporting event. There's dancing nightly, too. Steaks, hamburgers, and omelets highlight the menu.

Smokey Joe's, Fortieth and Walnut Sts.; 215-222-0770. The carved booths in the rathskeller of this super-popular watering hole date back to the Prohibition years. Food from hamburgers to ribs, and live entertainment.

CHILDREN

Children will enjoy many of the sights listed in this book. Try to accent their visits with some of the fascinating places to eat in Philadelphia, among them, **The Bourse** and **The Gallery,** both of which feature international fast-food and dining. The **Reading Terminal** is another interesting spot to catch a bite to eat; here you will find authentic Pennsylvania Dutch cooking, as well as many more over-the-counter delights.

Remember that Philadelphia is the ice cream capital of the nation, and Reading Terminal offers **Bassett's** ice cream, one of Philly's favorites. Other spots to try the city's ice cream delights are **More Than Just Ice Cream** on Locust Street, and throughout Center City and suburban counties, **Hillary's** and **Baskin-Robbins.**

Undoubtedly, at the top of any child's list of places to visit will be the **Philadelphia Zoo** (including the Daniel W. Dietrich Memorial Children's Zoo, the enchanting Tree House and the exciting monorail), and the **Elmwood Park Zoo,** where children can pet animals in their natural habitat. Then there's the **Academy of Natural Science's** hands-on mini-museum, **Outside-In.** The **Please Touch Museum,** designed for children seven years or younger, is most unusual, and the only one of its kind. The **Franklin Institute's** many exhibits always fascinate children, especially the **Fels Planetarium's** special programs, and the sensational films in the four-stories-high IMAX Theater. Of course, children will love touring the real submarine and historic battleship at the Independence Seaport Museum. Then they can take the RiverLink ferry across the Delaware to the New Jersey State Aquarium and Camden Children's Garden. The Garden is so wonderful for younger

Polar Bears at the Philadelphia Zoo   *Bob Krist for the Greater Philadelphia Tourism*
Marketing Corporation

children, they might postpone actually going into the aquarium for another day! Meanwhile, further into New Jersey is the Garden State Discovery Museum, (856-424-1233) another bonanza for the young.

In Broomall, **Kehler's Kids Fun Factory** is a climbing, sliding, crawling, jumping treat (610-359-9999), while in Bucks County, there's Big Bird, Bert, and Ernie at the marvelous **Sesame Place** amusement park. In Lancaster County, in addition to the rollercoasters and shows at Hershey Park and the delicious tour at Hershey's Chocolate World, the younger set never misses **Dutch Wonderland.** After enjoying the spectacular train display at the **Choo Choo Barn** nearby, they must take a ride on the **Strasburg Railroad** (see ONE-DAY EXCURSIONS). Or they can travel toward Allentown to make a splash at **Dorney Park Wild Wildwater Kingdom,** or north on the New Jersey Turnpike and have a blast at **Great Adventure** and its wild animal park.

Two other fascinating experiences for children and families are within an hour's drive of the city. The **Crayola Factory** at Two Rivers Landing (30 Centre Square, Easton; 610-515-8000) offers crayon and marker manufacturing demonstrations and hands-on activities for all ages. And **Herr Foods** (Rt. 272 and Herr Dr., Nottingham; 800-63-SNACK) presents free tours of its potato chip, pretzel, and other goodies factory, and usually sends people off with samples.

If the kids want a hayride, they can climb aboard at **Linvilla Orchards,** 137 W. Knowlton Rd., Media; 610-876-7116. The wagon will cart them to orchards of peaches, blueberries, or whatever fruit is in season and they can fill baskets to take home. Be careful, though—it's easy to pick more than you can use and more than you want to pay for. There are hayrides in the fall, too, to see pumpkin patches and sample apple cider.

Another type of experience awaits at Ridley Creek State Park in Delaware County (610-892-3900), where children can visit the **Colonial Plantation** and see history being lived by re-enactors. Or in the fall they can watch a battle re-enactment at **Brandywine Battlefield**, and in December see Washington crossing the Delaware at **Washington Crossing State Park.**

Throughout the year, many of Philadelphia's theaters and museums offer special programs for children. The **Philadelphia Orchestra** even holds special concerts (see PERFORMING ARTS and SIGHTS). The **Free Library of Philadelphia** presents popular book concerts, free of charge, for families (215-686-5322). And then there's the **Keswick Theatre** in Glenside, 215-572-7650, with its summer and winter series of plays tailored for the young and the youthful.

Finally, don't forget that this is Philadelphia, where U.S. history began, and let the kids enjoy the **Independence Mall** area where most attractions are free (see SELF-GUIDED CITY TOURS).

The **Liberty Bell** and **Independence Hall** always fascinate, as does the very special **Franklin Court**—and the **U.S. Mint** is an eye-opener. When everyone can't walk another step, treat the family to a narrated historic carriage ride from which you'll see Old City at a clip-clop colonial pace. And for an experience the children and the whole family will never forget, walk the area after dark with the sensational **Lights of Liberty** interactive tour. (See SIGHTS for information.)

FOR RESIDENTS

Philadelphia is your new home. Welcome to the City of Brotherly Love. This is both an exciting time, and, sometimes, a confusing one: locating housing, opening bank accounts, relocating your family, moving furniture, and the adjustment of living in a new area. Here we offer some important facts to help ease this transition period. You will find that Philadelphia and its surrounding counties have a lot to offer. It is a wonderfully exciting place in which to live.

Welcome Services

Welcome Wagon, regional office: 215-677-0113. This is a nationally recognized organization that offers friendly assistance, introducing you to local merchants and offering coupons to be used in local stores.

AN INTRODUCTION TO PHILADELPHIA LIVING

Philadelphia is the birthplace of the United States. Both the Declaration of Independence and the Constitution were adopted in Philadelphia's Independence Hall. Very few other cities can match the many historic attractions here.

In addition to the historical attributes, this city takes pride in its world-famous orchestra; the excellent schools of higher education; its many scenic parks, and museums of art, history, and science. Philadelphians also have an enormous pride in their championship sports teams—the football Eagles, hockey Flyers, baseball Phillies, and basketball 76ers.

This city swells with opportunities. It ranks as one of the greatest industrial and commercial centers of the United States.

What often makes a city interesting are the people who reside there.

Philadelphia is populated with many ethnic groups. Virtually every national and racial group in the U.S. lives within this city. Many of these nationalities enjoy sharing their customs through organized programs such as street parties, parades, and information centers. William Penn very appropriately named this city Philadelphia, Greek for "brotherly love."

GEOGRAPHICAL PROFILE

Philadelphia is, by population, the fifth largest city in the United States, with its 45,330 square miles surrounded generously by bounties of nature that include many lakes and rivers, parks, lush woodlands, and the rolling green hills of countryside. This rich combination provides us with a vast diversification of industrial endeavors and human pleasures. You may enjoy a visit with a farming family in the Pennsylvania Dutch country or a day rafting down the Delaware River; camping in one of the many state parks or skiing the challenging slopes of the Pocono Mountains. Wherever you go, you will find adventure and warm, hospitable people.

PHILADELPHIA INSIGHT

Automobiles

Auto Insurance

As a new resident, Pennsylvania law requires every driver to carry financial responsibility; you are required to have a Pennsylvania Insurance Identification card in your possession at all times. These cards are issued at the time of the purchase of insurance. Check with your local insurance agency.

Driver's Licenses

A new resident must obtain a Pennsylvania driver's license within 30 days of establishing residency. The driver's license is good for four years, and the fee is $29. For information call: 215-698-8100; 800-932-4600.

A junior license can be obtained at age 16, and a regular one at 18. If you have a driver's license from another state or an international one, you are expected to visit a State Police Examination Point to apply for a Pennsylvania license. Take with you:

1. A valid out-of-state license
2. Your vehicle registration
3. Proof of insurance
4. Proof of birth date
5. Your Social Security card or W2 form
6. Your passport and I-94 card

To obtain a license, you must have a medical form filled out, pass an eye test, demonstrate your knowledge of the traffic laws and signs, and pass a driving test. This is done at a State Police Examination point nearest you (refer to the telephone book, under "Government, State").

If you are a new driver, you must obtain a learner's permit before you may drive. The combined fee for the permit and license is $29. To drive with a permit, you must be accompanied by a person who is 18 or older and has a valid Pennsylvania license. This person is expected to occupy the seat next to you while you are driving.

Before applying for a learner's permit, you need to pass an eye test, a traffic law test, and a physical examination. Consent from a parent or guardian is necessary if you are between 16 and 18 years old. To apply, you also must present proof of your age (state birth certificate or passport), and Social Security card.

Car inspections are due on a yearly basis. Check your local phone book for the inspection center (usually a gas station or repair shop) nearest you.

Emission Control Inspection

State law requires that all owners of passenger cars and/or small trucks in the five-county Philadelphia area are annually required to have their vehicles inspected for emission control.

Inspection stations are located throughout the five-county region. For more information, call 800-932-4600.

Reporting of Auto Accidents

If you are involved in an accident, stop your car at or near the scene of the accident. When possible, move your car off the road so that you don't block traffic.

Notify police if the accident involves death or injury, or if the car requires towing. Obtain names and addresses of all people involved in the accident, as well as those of witnesses and of any injured persons.

If the accident involves a parked car and you are unable to locate the owner, leave a note on the car and notify the police. The note should contain your name and address, driver's license number, date and time of accident, and your insurance company's name and policy number.

If the police do not investigate the accident and if it involves death, injury, or a vehicle which requires towing, then forward a written report within five days to the Bureau of Highway Safety and Traffic Engineering, Department of Transportation, P.O. Box 2047, Rm. 212, Harrisburg, PA 17175.

Banking

The first United States financial institution was established in Philadelphia, where today there are close to 40 major commercial banks, trust companies, and savings and loan companies. There are many others, however, mostly branches in the surrounding counties.

Philadelphia banks continue to move forward with the changing times. There has been development of interstate banking with neighboring states. Electronic banking is prevalent throughout the area, and some people bank from home through computerized communication.

Banks vary with the services they provide, so shop around and choose the one which serves your needs best. For information, call the Pennsylvania Department of Financial Institutions at 717-787-2665, or the Federal Reserve Bank of Philadelphia at 215-574-6000, or 800-PA BANKS.

Chambers of Commerce

Chambers of Commerce are ideal sources of general information for newcomers and prospective home buyers. They are vital to the development of business, and most companies subscribe to their many services to the community.

Available through the Philadelphia Chamber of Commerce is a newcomer's kit that includes maps, transportation information, a guide to city services, and brochures on activities and historical sights. The fee for this kit is nominal.

Below is a list of chambers in principal areas of metropolitan Philadelphia and the outlying regions:

Bucks County: **Chamber of Commerce of Central Bucks;** 215-348-3913.

Chester County: **Chamber of Commerce of West Chester;** 610-696-4046.

Delaware County: **Chamber of Commerce of Delaware County**; 610-565-3677.

King of Prussia: **Chamber of Commerce of King of Prussia**; 610-265-1776.

Main Line: **Main Line Chamber of Commerce**; 610-687-6232.

Montgomery County: **Greater Montgomery County Chamber of Commerce**; 610-277-9500.

Philadelphia: **Greater Philadelphia Chamber of Commerce**; 215-790-3685. Website: www.libertynet.org/phila-visitor.

Churches, Synagogues, and Temples ————

Sometimes Philadelphia is referred to as the "Quaker City" because it was the Quakers—the first settlers of Pennsylvania—who laid the foundation of religious thought and custom here. Today, there is the widest possible variety of religious and ethnic groups in the area. The largest denomination is Roman Catholicism. Other denominations include Baptist, Episcopalian, Lutheran, Methodist, Jewish, Quaker, and many others. The principle established 300 years ago still prevails today: "Religious freedom to all."

Churches in Philadelphia are actively involved with the community. They offer assistance in many areas of social service, including daycare, health care, food programs, and activities for senior citizens and teenagers.

For more information regarding your religious organizations, call one of the major denominational and ecumenical organizations listed below:

Archdiocese of Philadelphia, 222 N. Seventeenth St.; 215-587-3600.

Episcopal Diocese of Pennsylvania, 240 S. Fourth St.; 215-627-6434.

Jewish Federation of Greater Philadelphia, 2100 Arch St.; 215-832-0500; 215-893-5821.

Lutheran Synod of S.E. PA, 4700 Wissahickon Ave.; 610-278-9400.

Philadelphia Baptist Association, 100 N. Seventeenth St.; 215-563-7393.

Philadelphia Board of Rabbis, 1616 Walnut St.; 215-832-0675.

Quaker Information Center, 1501 Cherry St.; 215-241-7024.

Reformed Church in America, 1380 Bristol Rd., Churchville; 215-357-5636.

Talmudical Yeshiva of Philadelphia (Orthodox Jewish), 6063 Drexel Rd., Wynnefield; 215-477-1000.

United Church of Christ, 505 S. Second Ave., Collegeville; 610-489-2056.

United Methodist Church, P.O. Box 820, Valley Forge; 610-666-9090.

United Presbyterian Church in the U.S.A., 2200 Locust St.; 215-732-1842.

Education

Public Schools, Primary and Secondary

Public education is free in Pennsylvania for children from kindergarten through the twelfth grade. There are more than 200 public schools in Philadelphia alone.

As a newcomer, you are certainly concerned with your child's education. It is often a major consideration in choosing where you will live. For information regarding the elementary schools, you should contact the Board of Education at 215-299-7000, or the superintendent of parochial schools in the district you have in mind. Set an appointment with the school principal to inspect the school and discuss the curriculum and special courses for the gifted and handicapped.

The Philadelphia school district works to meet the needs of the handicapped and exceptional students. If there is no appropriate program within your district, it will place your children within state-approved private schools, free of charge.

The Philadelphia school system also offers Magnet schools, which offer studies not available in the regular schools. Students need to apply for admission. Career education, including vocational-technical training and courses, is found within the regular schools or at the independent vocational high schools. Alternative education programs are offered primarily to juniors and seniors and are designed to increase learning experiences and other diverse career opportunities. Adult education programs are available throughout the city and are free of charge to anyone 18 and older who wishes to earn a high school diploma.

Public school kindergarten is available to five-year-olds. Children entering the first grade must be at least six years old before September 1 of the entering year. Enrollment requires your child's birth certificate and immunization documents, and for a transfer student, the latest report card.

For phone numbers of the local school board in your district, refer to the yellow or blue pages of your telephone book under "Schools."

In the suburbs, the elementary schools are broken down by county into school districts. Many of these schools are rated among the finest in the United States.

Each school district has its own school board. Once you have determined the county where you may be living, call the school administrative office within your district and make an appointment with the superinten-dent. He or she will be able to answer any questions you may have.

Private Schools

Philadelphia has a wealth of excellent private schools, many of which are located in the suburbs. In all, there are at least 62 private schools in the area.

For more information on accredited private schools, a booklet may be obtained from the **Middle States Association of Colleges and Schools,** 3624 Market St., Philadelphia 19104, or call 215-662-5600. Also, your local library has an invaluable reference book, **The Handbook of Private Schools,** which provides pertinent information as well as the general characteristics of each school.

For Catholic parochial schools, call the **Catholic Archdiocese of Philadelphia** at 215-587-3600. For other parochial schools, refer to the "Churches, Synagogues, and Temples" listing.

Colleges and Universities

Philadelphia boasts of its major impact on higher education and with good reason. There are almost 90 colleges and universities in the area, many of them offering degrees in medicine, law, music, art, reli-gion, business, and science.

Major Philadelphia and suburban colleges and universities are listed in the SPECIAL PEOPLE chapter.

Government

City Government

Philadelphia's is a mayor-council form of government. The mayor is the chief executive officer of the city and is responsible for the admin-istrative functions of the city. The elected mayor appoints a managing director who, with the mayor's approval, appoints the commissioners heading each department. The legislative branch of the city's govern-ment is composed of 17 members of the City Council. Ten council members represent the city districts, and seven of them are elected at large. Elections for mayor and councilmen are held every four years; city representatives are elected every three years.

County Government

The surrounding counties of Philadelphia are, by and large, gov-erned by a Board of Commissioners. Refer to the information below for a synopsis by county.

Bucks County, Court House, Doylestown, PA 18901; 215-348-6000. Its Board of County Commissioners consists of three members.

Chester County, County Court House, West Chester, PA 19380; 610-344-6000. Its Board of County Commissioners is comprised of three members.

Delaware County, County Court House, Media, PA 19063; 610-891-4000. Operates under a Home Rule Charter. Five county council members are elected.

Montgomery County, Court House, Norristown, PA 19401; 610-278-3000. A board of county commissioners.

Congressional Districts

Philadelphia has three representatives; Montgomery County, four; Chester County, two; Delaware County, four; and Bucks County, one.

U.S. Senators from Philadelphia

Senator Rick Santorum, Republican, Widener Building, One S. Penn Square, Suite 960, Philadelphia 19107; 215-864-6900.

Senator Arlen Specter, Republican, William Green Federal Building, Suite 9400, 600 Arch St., Philadelphia 19106; 215-597-7200.

Senatorial elections are held every six years.

For legislative and voter information, call the League of Women Voters. For Philadelphia: 215-829-9495. For Pennsylvania: 717-234-1576 and 800-692-7281.

Health Care/Philadelphia ─────────

Philadelphia is one of the leading medical centers of the world. The city as well as the suburbs has all types of general and specialized hospitals. Wherever you reside, you will find an excellent full-service hospital nearby.

Medical schools, health institutions, and physicians work together to provide the best possible medical care. Good quality and comprehensive services are available at reasonable prices. At most clinics, both specialized and general, you will find services on a par with those found in private practices. Information and listings are available from the Delaware Valley Health Care Council, 1315 Walnut St., Philadelphia 19107; 215-735-9695.

Hospitals

Of the 52 hospitals in Philadelphia, we have listed some below:

Albert Einstein Medical Center, York and Tabor Rds.; 215-456-7890.
Chestnut Hill Hospital, 8835 Germantown Ave.; 215-248-8200.

Children's Hospital of Philadelphia, Thirty-fourth St. and Civic Center Blvd.; 215-590-1000.

Fox Chase Cancer Center, 7701 Burholme Ave.; 215-728-6900; 888-369-2427.

The Graduate Hospital, 1800 Lombard St.; 215-893-2000.

Hospital of the University of Pennsylvania, 3400 Spruce St.; 215-662-4000.

Hahnemann University Hospital, 230 N. Broad St.; 215-762-7000.

Philadelphia Child Guidance Center, Thirty-fourth and Civic Center Blvd.; 215-243-2700.

Scheie Eye Institute, 51 N. Thirty-ninth St.; 215-662-8100.

St. Christopher's Hospital for Children, Erie Ave. at Front St.; 215-427-5000.

St. Joseph's Hospital, Sixteenth and Girard; 215-787-9000.

Temple University Hospital, Broad and Ontario Sts.; 215-707-2000.

Thomas Jefferson University Hospital, Eleventh and Walnut Sts.; 215-955-6000.

Wills Eye Hospital, Ninth and Walnut Sts.; 215-928-3000.

Medical Facilities for Specialized Treatment and Aid

Addiction Hotline, 610-645-3610.

Children's Hospital, 215-590-1000.

Poison Control, 215-386-2100.

Renfrew Center, 475 Spring Lane; 215-482-5353. Specializes in eating disorders such as bulimia and anorexia nervosa.

Suicide and Crisis Intervention Service, 215-686-4420.

Women Organized Against Rape, 215-985-3333.

Referral Associations

American Dental Association, 215-925-6050.

Department of Public Health, 215-686-5000.

Pennsylvania Department of Health, 800-692-7254.

Philadelphia County Medical Society, 215-563-5343.

Planned Parenthood, 215-351-5560.

Health Care/Montgomery County ————

Hospitals

Abington Memorial Hospital, 1200 Old York Rd., Abington; 215-576-2000.

Bryn Mawr Hospital, 130 S. Bryn Mawr Ave., Bryn Mawr; 610-526-3000.

Lankenau Hospital, 100 Lancaster Ave. (near City Ave.), Wynnewood; 610-645-2000.

Montgomery Hospital, 1300 Powell St., Norristown; 610-270-2000.

Pottstown Memorial Medical Center, High St. and Firestone Blvd., Pottstown; 610-327-7000.

Suburban General Hospital, 2701 DeKalb Pike, Norristown; 610-278-2000.

Medical Facilities for Specialized Treatment and Aid

Addiction Hotline, 610-853-7010.

Montgomery County Emergency Psychiatric Service, 610-279-6100.

Poison Control, 215-386-2100.

Women Against Rape, 610-566-4342.

Referral Associations

Dental Society, 215-925-6050.

Pennsylvania Department of Health, 800-692-7254.

Planned Parenthood, 215-351-5560.

Health Care/Delaware County ———

Hospitals

Crozer-Chester Medical Center, One Medical Center Blvd., Upland; 610-447-2000.

Delaware County Memorial Hospital, Lansdowne and Keystone Aves., Drexel Hill; 610-284-8100.

Mercy Community Hospital, 2000 West Chester Pike, Haverford; 610-853-7000.

Riddle Memorial Hospital, Baltimore Pike, Media; 610-566-9400.

Springfield Hospital, Sproul and Thompson Rds., Springfield; 610-328-8700.

Medical Facilities for Specialized Treatment and Aid

Alcoholism and Addictions Council of Delaware County, 610-352-8943.

Contact-Crisis Intervention, 215-879-4402.

Delaware County Medical Society, 610-892-7750.

Dental Society of Chester and Delaware Counties, 610-876-5680.

Planned Parenthood Association of Southeastern Pennsylvania, 215-351-5560.

Poison Control Center, 215-386-2100.

Health Care/Chester County —————

Hospitals

Brandywine Hospital, 201 Reeceville Rd., Coatesville; 610-383-8000.
Chester County Hospital, 701 E. Marshall St., West Chester; 610-431-5000.
Paoli Memorial Hospital, 255 W. Lancaster Ave., Paoli; 610-648-1000.
Phoenixville Hospital, 140 Nutt Rd., Phoenixville; 610-983-1000.
Veteran's Administration Medical Center, Coatesville; 610-384-7711.

Medical Facilities for Specialized Treatment and Aid

Chester County Department of Drug and Alcohol Services, 610-344-6620.
Crisis Intervention Service, 610-918-2100.
Poison Control, 215-386-2100.
Rape Crisis Council, 610-692-7273.

Referral Associations

Center for Addictive Diseases, 610-648-1130.
Chester County Cares (useful information for residents), 610-436-4040.
Chester County Health Department, 610-344-6225.
Chester/Delaware Dental Society, 610-876-5680.
Planned Parenthood of Chester County, 610-692-1770.

Health Care/Bucks County —————

Hospitals

Frankford Hospital, Pond and Wilson Sts., Bristol; 215-949-5000.
Doylestown Hospital, 595 W. State St., Doylestown; 215-345-2200.
Quakertown Community Hospital, 1021 Park Ave., Quakertown; 215-538-6400.
Warminster General Hospital, 225 Newtown Rd., Warminster; 215-441-6600.

Medical Facilities for Specialized Treatment and Aid

Alcoholics Anonymous, 215-788-9920.
Bucks County Department of Health, 215-345-3318.
Bucks County Rescue, 215-348-5803.
Planned Parenthood Association of Bucks County, 215-785-4591.

Referral Associations

Bucks County Commissioner's Office of Public Information and

Referral, 215-348-6415.

Home Decorating

Decorating a new home is a creative challenge which is a pleasure for some, but a confusing chore for others. For everyone the home is meant to be a tranquil place, a place of comfort, a reflection of the individual and his or her family.

Bloomingdale's, Strawbridge & Clothier, and Macy's are just a few of several department stores which offer a staff of decorators whose services may be complementary to your style.

One exciting concept, a wholesale showroom complex for interior design, is the **Market Place** at 2400 Market Street; 215-561-5000. The main function of The Market Place is to display, in 53 showrooms, everything for the home: furniture, carpets, fabrics, wallcoverings, lamps, and accessories. Designers often shop here for their clients. Generally the showrooms are not open to the public, except when specially arranged, usually through a designer.

As a consumer seeking the services of a designer, information may be obtained through the Eastern Pennsylvania chapter, The American Society of Interior Designers, 215-568-3884.

Jury Duty

For the state and county courts, jurors are called from the registered voter lists of persons 18 and older. The Petit Jury and the Grand Jury are the two levels of court service in the state federal court. Jurors are called from the ten districts. Exceptions include: convicted felons who have not had their rights restored; elected officials; those with a physical handicap; and primary caretakers of children ten years and under.

There are 1-5 days of duty at $9 a day, rising to $25 after the third day.

The above information does not necessarily apply to the county courts. Contact your county courthouse for details. Jury Commission: 215-686-1776. Website: http:\\courts.phila.gov\gijrydty.htm.

Legal Services

For references call the Lawyer Referral and Information Service of the Philadelphia Bar Association: 215-238-6333.

County referrals are:

Montgomery County—**Bar Association,** 610-279-9660.
Delaware County—**Legal Assistance Association, Inc.,** 610-874-8421.
Chester County—**Legal Aid of Chester County,** 610-436-9150.
Bucks County—**Legal Aid of Bucks County,** 215-781-1111.
Refer to the phone book in the blue pages for the list of numbers to call for various legal questions.

Libraries

The Free Library of Philadelphia (215-686-5322) has a central library at Logan Square, Nineteenth and Vine streets. In addition to the main library, there are 49 neighborhood branches and three regional libraries; refer to the white pages of the phone book under "Free Library of Philadelphia" for locations and phone numbers. A free Library Borrowers Card may be obtained at any of the libraries.

Major county libraries are:

Abington Free Library, 215-885-5180.
Bucks County Main Library Center, 215-348-0332.
Chester County Library, 610-280-2600.
Free Library of Springfield Township, 610-543-2113.
Lower Merion Library Association, 610-525-1776.
Pottstown Public Library, 610-970-6551.
West Chester Public Library, 610-696-1721.

For the **Library for the Blind and Physically Handicapped,** 919 Walnut St., Philadelphia, call 215-683-3213.

Local Laws

Liquor Laws

State Law requires that you must be 21 to buy and to be served liquor. Possession of a photo driver's license or a non-driver's I.D. card is acceptable identification for service and purchases.

In Pennsylvania, all alcoholic beverages except beer are sold in State Liquor Stores. Beverage distributors sell beer.

An establishment selling liquor on Sunday must have a Sunday Sales Permit; by law they may serve liquor from 1 pm-2 am.

Property Laws

Philadelphia has established firm zoning laws that require certain procedures for changes in residential districts from one use to another. Variances or minor changes of a structure within the same zoning classification require obtaining a work permit from the Licenses and Inspection Department at City Hall.

In the surrounding counties, the laws differ from one county to the other, or from each borough. Contact your township building for clarification.

Medical

See Health Care in previous section.

Newspapers and Publications

The two major newspapers are *The Philadelphia Inquirer* (morning paper), 215-854-2000, and *The Philadelphia Daily News* (evening paper), 215-854-2000.

Popular Philadelphia neighborhood papers include 41 weeklies from the Associated Neighborhood Newspapers, 610-941-3555.

Other small newspapers from the surrounding counties include:

Bucks County Courier Times (Levittown), 215-338-0499.
Chestnut Hill Local (Chestnut Hill), 215-248-8800.
Daily Local News (West Chester), 610-696-1775.
King of Prussia Post (King of Prussia), 610-630-6200.
Main Line Times (Ardmore), 610-642-4300.
News of Delaware County (Havertown), 610-446-8700.
Suburban and Wayne Times (Wayne), 610-688-3000.

The most recognized Philadelphia magazine is the *Philadelphia Magazine* (215-564-7700), which is published monthly.

Pets

Laws require rabies vaccinations for pets by a licensed veterinarian. Pets must be confined to the owner's property except when on a leash. Dogs running at large will be picked up by the Animal Control Unit, and the owner will be fined.

Laws require every dog owner to buy an annual license.

In 1981, the City Council enacted the "Pooper-Scooper" law, which places the responsibility on the owners for cleaning up their pet's litter. Violators will be fined.

For additional information, call the Humane Society of PA (215-426-6300) or the Women's Humane Society (215-750-3100). There are local SPCA's in the suburban areas.

Public Services

Philadelphia

City of Philadelphia Services are supplied by the following:

Electric: **PECO Energy**; 800-494-4000. Emergency: 800-841-4141.

Natural Gas: **PGW (Philadelphia Gas Works)**; 215-236-0500. Emergency: 215-235-1212.

Garbage collections: Household pickup for trash, garbage (foodstuffs), and recyclables is free for Philadelphia residents. Each is collected separately, but it is optional to separate garbage from trash. If you choose to do so, garbage must be placed in tightly fastened metal containers; trash into covered containers, or sturdy bags securely tied. You must separate recyclables into their own designated containers, and newspapers must be tied or bagged. For information regarding pick-up days for your area, and to arrange for a separate garbage pick-up, call 215-686-5560 (trash) and 215-686-5564 (garbage). For inquiries about recyclables, call 215-686-5504.

Water/Sewage: **Philadelphia Water Dept.**; 215-686-6880. Emergency: 215-685-6300.

The suburban counties are supplied by the following:

Montgomery County

Electric and Natural Gas: **PECO Gas and Electric**; 800-494-4000. Emergency: 800-841-4141.

Sewage: There are many authorities in the county. Call the Montgomery County Sewer Authority. Fee for services.

Water: **Philadelphia Suburban Water Co.**; 800-711-4779. Emergency, evenings, and weekends: 610-525-1402.

Delaware County

Electric and Natural Gas: **Philadelphia Electric Co.**; 800-494-4000. Emergency: 800-841-4141.

Water: **Philadelphia Suburban Water Co.**; 800-711-4779. Other water services are privately and municipally operated. Refer to the Pennsylvania Department of Environmental Resources, 610-832-6000.

Sewage: There are various sewer authorities in Delaware County. Fee for services.

Chester County

Electric and Natural Gas: **Philadelphia Electric Co.**; 800-494-4000.
Water: Water services are privately and municipally operated. See above for phone number of PA Dept. of Environmental Resources.
Sewage: Refer to the Municipal Authorities. Fee for services.

Bucks County

Electric and Natural Gas: **Philadelphia Electric Co.**; 800-494-4000.
Water: Water services are privately and municipally operated. See above for phone number.
Sewage: **Bucks County Water and Sewage Authority**; 215-536-2391. Fee for services.

Taxes

Individual Income Tax

Philadelphia requires a tax on all sources of income unless they are exempt by statute. Employers are required to withhold state income tax for both the resident and non-resident employees.

Property Tax

Property taxes are levied by counties, municipalities, schools, and special districts. Philadelphia homeowners should refer to the Property Tax Assessment Committee for questions regarding property taxes.

In Philadelphia, a state sales and use tax of seven percent is added to all retail purchases, rentals, uses, and consumption of tangible goods, personal property, and special services (take-home food and clothing are exempt). For clarification of what is and is not taxable, contact the Revenue District Office in Philadelphia, State Office Building, Rm. 201, 1400 Spring Garden St., Philadelphia, PA 19130-4088; 215-560-2056.

City Wage Tax

The city of Philadelphia has a wage tax of 4.56 percent of the gross wages for those who work and reside within the boundaries of Philadelphia. For those who work in Philadelphia but do not reside there, the tax is 3.97 percent. For more information, contact the Philadelphia Revenue Department of Customer Service, 215-686-6600.

TV and Radio

Television

There are many television stations available to you. The VHF TV stations include Channels 3 (CBS), 6 (ABC), 10 (NBC), and 12 (PBS). On UHF, there are channels 17, 28, 29, 35, 48, 57, and 61.

Cable television has made an impact on the Philadelphia area. Most areas are fully serviced by one or more companies. To inquire about the availability of cable television in your area, contact your local Township Office.

Radio

The Philadelphia area offers many excellent radio stations. There are more than 30 radio stations in the eight-county area (see MATTERS OF FACT).

Volunteering

For those people who wish to volunteer their time and talents, call United Way First Call for Help Volunteer Centers, 215-665-2474; in the suburbs, 610-558-5639. Their primary function is to screen you for your interests, and they will then place you accordingly.

Voting

1. Eighteen years old by the day after election.
2. A resident 30 days prior to election.

It is required that you register to vote at any courthouse. Take with you proof of age (driver's license, birth certificate, etc.) and proof of residency (rental agreement or home sale agreement). To register by mail, obtain a mail-in registration form from the following places—borough or city office, township office, U.S. Post Office, Pennsylvania State Liquor Store, or free library.

For further information, contact your County Board of Elections, Voter Registration Division:

Bucks County: 215-348-6163.
Chester County: 610-344-6410.
Delaware County: 610-891-4659.
Montgomery County: 610-278-3280.
Philadelphia: 215-686-3469 or 215-686-1505.

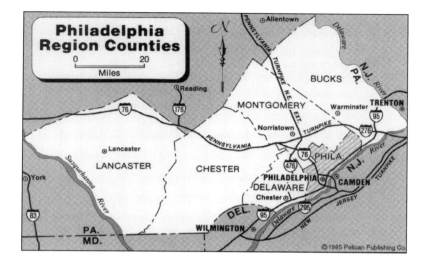

The local League of Women Voters (215-829-9495) is a non-partisan, informed source that may be able to assist you with registration requirements and provide information on elected state and community representatives.

PHILADELPHIA REAL ESTATE

An Overview

Philadelphia is often referred to as the "city of homes." As an incoming resident, you will find that this city has many diverse neighborhoods, with a variety of styles and concepts.

Each Sunday, *The Philadelphia Inquirer* has a comprehensive Real Estate section. The Chamber of Commerce offers an in-depth briefing on the region in the Relocation Center, as well as Real Estate brochures.

Information and Referral

The Board of Realtors has information on residential property and a list of realtors. Contact the Board of Realtors in the area in which you are interested. Listed below are Boards of Realtors:

Bucks County 215-956-9176.
Chester County 610-363-2056.
Delaware Valley 610-356-6505.
Montgomery County 610-260-9931.
Philadelphia 215-925-2607.

Other sources include the **Apartment Referral Service**, 215-638-9898, servicing Northeast Philadelphia and Bucks and Montgomery counties; and the **Real Estate Commission of Harrisburg**, 717-783-3658.

Buying and Renting

Consider the many variables that confront you when you are seeking to buy or rent a home. The proximity of your residence to your place of employment is important. For those who are employed in city government jobs, there is the requirement which states that they must reside within the city limits. Be clear on the geographical territory according to the rule before you begin looking. Spend time checking out the neighborhood of your choice. Consider less space, for a better location. Be certain of how much you can afford. Inquire about school systems. Many apartment complexes have exquisite landscaping, pools, social centers, racquet sports, and health clubs.

The season from April through October is regarded as the key time when renters select their accommodations for the coming year.

Regional and Neighborhood Profiles

As in many other big cities, Philadelphia's close-in residential areas are experiencing a resurgence of popularity. If you want old-world charm at a reasonable price, consider Old City, University City, Wynnefield, or Overbrook Farms.

The following is an analysis in brief of some of Greater Philadelphia's most recognized neighborhoods to facilitate your choice and introduce you to the many possibilities for settling in. Most civic associations have newsletters; ask your real estate agent to make these available to you. You can sense the spirit of a neighborhood from these publications, along with your inspection of houses, condominiums, and apartments.

Public transportation, SEPTA, is available to all parts of the city within the perimeter and beyond to the suburbs. SEPTA also operates a network of subway-elevated systems, trolley lines, and bus services. Street and transit maps that show the scheduled routes are available for

$6.95 each at main stations, or write to SEPTA Sales, P.O. Box 7780-1834, Philadelphia, PA 19182-1939; Telephone: 215-580-7440 or 580-7800. By mail, there is an additional fee of $1.50 per map.

Intown Neighborhoods

Center City's ability to attract a growing number of homebuyers has been linked to the ever-increasing employment market. Developers are concentrating on developing new vacant properties, upgrading existing housing, and converting industrial buildings to residential use. Federal tax incentives have encouraged restoration of old historical properties.

The in-town neighborhoods in brief profile are:

Abbott Square is a condominium complex within Society Hill. These lovely units were completed in 1985.

Bella Vista is one of the oldest areas in South Philadelphia. Here you'll find the Italian Market, which is widely known as a mecca for food shoppers. The neighborhood is characterized by two- and three-story rowhouses and is one of the more affordable areas. Significant residential investment activity began in the latter part of the 1970s. This is primarily a blue-collar neighborhood with rentals from inexpensive to expensive.

Chestnut Hill is a posh suburb within Philadelphia County. For the most part, "The Hill" is a town of stately homes, fine shops, and superb restaurants. Many of the residents have passed their homes down from one generation to the next. Some of the best private schools in the country were founded here. Commuter train services into the city are excellent. Expect rentals to be expensive.

Chinatown is located in the north central part of the city. It is best known for its streetscape, restaurants, and the magnificent Chinese Friendship Gate at Tenth and Arch Sts. An exceptionally large part of this area is rental. Housing values continue to rise quickly each year, and much attention has been placed on new subsidized housing construction. The residents are predominately foreign born.

Fairmount Park. The *neighborhood* called Fairmount Park lies just outside of the city in the upper Roxborough area. It is surrounded on three sides by the *actual* Fairmount Park, and is a semirural residential enclave of single homes. There are trees and open spaces, a wish come true for the city dweller, especially for those who are required to live in the city limits.

Manayunk nestles along the banks of the Schuylkill River canal just west of Center City. It is one of the newest hot spots in the area. Named a National Historic District in 1983, "Philadelphia's Main Street" boasts more than 65 chic boutiques and galleries and dozens of restaurants. The residential streets are narrow and steep and contain affordable row homes.

Chestnut Hill   *Greater Philadelphia Tourism Marketing Corporation*

Northern Liberties is something of a continuation of Old City in that it has become the latest habitation of local artists who are often in search of cheap, well-lighted homes and studios. Commercial properties are being converted into airy and expensive spaces. This area is a mixed bag, sociologically and structurally. Rentals are moderate to expensive.

Old City is located in the northeast corner of Center City. It was the original commercial center of the city. Today, the area is characterized by obsolete industrial loft buildings. These once old, decaying warehouses have been converted into spacious, charming, and architecturally creative spaces. The area contains the most exciting collection of art galleries on the East Coast. It attracts mostly young, single professionals and childless married couples. Rentals are moderate to expensive.

Parkway/Museum District. Stretching from City Hall to the Philadelphia Museum of Art, the Benjamin Franklin Parkway is flanked by some of the city's most acclaimed institutions. The Parkway is also the location of numerous festivals and events throughout the year, including Fourth of July fireworks. The area contains high-rises and row homes and attracts singles, young families, and those who love the culture and excitement of the city.

Penn's Landing is located on Philadelphia's waterfront. It has had exciting real estate development. Residential towers and low-rise condominiums have been incorporated with shops, restaurants, museums, and attractive landscaping. The biggest appeal is having a home with a waterfront view within the city.

Rittenhouse Square. This area was developed between 1850 and 1880 as a residential neighborhood. Many of these large nineteenth-century homes are still maintained as private homes; others have been converted into apartments or condominiums. This affluent area is comprised primarily of single-person and non-family households, and most are rentals. In the warm weather months, this square is a popular site for flower shows, art exhibits, concerts, and a general gathering place.

Society Hill. South of Center City lies Society Hill, one of Philadelphia's chief historical neighborhoods. Restoration of this area began in the 1950s. Once a wholesale food center, it is now characterized by restored eighteenth-century rowhouses and some contemporary structures as well. It is considered to be among the more exclusive residential neighborhoods in the city.

Spring Garden/Franklin Town is another neighborhood in the Art Museum area. These large nineteenth-century rowhouses have seen substantial reinvestment activity through private funding. The neighborhood was designated as a historic district by the Commonwealth of Pennsylvania. The location is popular with young folks and couples with children. There is a wide range of rental prices.

Suburban Neighborhoods ─────────────

Philadelphia's Main Line is a series of communities located along the "main line" of the old Pennsylvania Railroad from Philadelphia to Paoli. As an area, the Main Line is considered symbolic of wealthy society and gracious suburban living. Here you will find turn-of-the-century estates with glorious gardens and great tall trees. The area boasts some of the best schools in the country. There are some of the country's most challenging golf courses, as well as some of the best known country clubs, swim clubs, and equestrian centers. The Main Line offers a variety of housing styles. In recent years there has been a surge in townhouse and condominium construction. Many units offer affordable prices, a variety of architectural styles, and recreational facilities. Many of the smaller private homes are affordable too. Contact the Delaware Valley Association of Realtors for assistance in getting you acquainted with the area, 610-356-6505.

Montgomery County ─────────────

Montgomery County has a diverse mix of religious, social, and income groups. Generally, it is a community comprised of middle to upper middle class families. There are many small, older communities with garden complexes, new townhouses or condominiums, a few high-rises, and single homes. Rentals and homes run from moderate to very expensive.

Delaware County─────────────

In Delaware County, as a rule, the farther north and west you go, the more expensive the housing becomes. Springfield, Media, Wallingford, and Swarthmore are lovely and expensive; Upper Darby, Drexel Hill, Lansdowne, Havertown, Pilgrim Gardens, and Alden are more reasonably priced. For rent, there are mostly older converted houses, garden apartments, mid-rise buildings, and single family homes. Prices range from moderate to high.

Chester County ─────────────

Chester County is tucked into rolling hills and meadows. An afternoon drive may take you through historic Valley Forge, over wooden bridges, passing a foxhunt, or stopping at an inn for brunch. There are acres and acres of preserved open spaces wonderful for picnics, walking, bicycling, riding, or for living. You'll find many old stone farmhouses, Cape Cods, and contemporaries with solar details. In recent years, developers have put an emphasis on townhouses and condominiums with recreational facilities and beautiful landscapes. Rental prices vary from moderate to expensive.

Bucks County

Bucks County is a rustic artist community. The area abounds with rolling farmlands, charming country inns, elegant dining, or simple country fare. A home may be a converted barn or mill. Many of the village shops have maintained their original style of yesteryear. There is much growth in new housing construction. It is a young family area. Prices are moderate.

HOME AND GARDEN SHOPPING NEEDS

Air Conditioning Repairs— Matthew Borden; 610-449-6720.

Appraisals—Freeman Fine Arts; 215-563-9275.

Auto Repairs—Claude Baldino Auto Repair; 610-853-4737.

Beauty Salon—JonLauri Salon; 610-446-8242.

Blinds and Shades—Bed Bath and Beyond; 610-642-9296.

Building Materials—Rock Hill Supply Co.; 610-664-0820.

Carpet and Rug Cleaners—A. Talone; 610-642-9000.

Cleaners—Golden Touch; 610-649-0106; also A. Talone; 610-642-9000.

Doors—Doors Unlimited; 215-455-2100.

Electrical Repairs—Peter Yeremian; 610-353-1844.

Furniture Rentals—IFR Furniture Rentals; 800-223-3600.

Furniture Repairs—V.R. Bernabeo & Sons; 610-789-1110.

Glass (Auto and Home Mirrors)— Jem Auto Glass; 215-739-2624.

Home Accessories—Home Depot; 610-394-9600.

Lamp Repairs—Lectric Light House; 610-446-5656.

Landscaping—Waterloo Gardens; 610-363-0800.

Leather Cleaning—A. Talone, Cleaners; 610-642-9000.

Locks—Yearsley's; 610-642-2262.

Painting, Residential—Michael Gorman; 610-626-2299.

Paintings Restored—Newman Galleries; 215-563-1779.

Pest Control—Jones Pest Control; 610-328-9980.

Picture Frames—Merion Art & Repro Center; 610-896-6161.

Plaster Moldings and Character Items—Wells Vissar; 215-763-1663.

Photography—Edward Moskow Studio; 215-877-1823

Plumbing—Anthony Doherty; 610-853-0514.

Pool Services—Nichols; 800-343-3760.

Printing—Print Quick; 610-667-8234.

Realtor—Rachel Levin; 610-896-7400 or 610-649-5228.

Remodeling—Reber McLean Builders.; 610-356-3300.

Rentals (tools, machines, cleaning equipment)—U Haul; 610-789-0316.

Silver Repair—Chelsea Silver Plating; 215-925-1132.

Stained Glass—Cathedral Stained Glass; 215-379-5360.

Wrought Iron—DeVito Bros.; 610-896-2869.

LET'S HAVE A PARTY

It's time to try something different for that special occasion. Let us make a few wild and wonderful suggestions. If you can't afford the time to research sites and services for your wedding, birthday party, or whatever the occasion, the following people are excellent for handling all the details from A to Z: **Party Productions,** Bala Cynwyd, 610-667-9070. And if your party is in need of live music, call **Stone Groove Productions** at 215-698-9679 and ask for the **Fooling April** band. They play all the popular hits from the 50s to the present. Website: www.foolingapril.com.

Buy the Bus

Climb aboard a motorized replica of the original trolleys that clanged through Fairmount Park. Ask your friends to come along for a celebration (maximum of 40 adults). You can have food, drink, live music, and have the trolley decorated. The minimum is $300 for two hours. Call **Philadelphia Trolley Works**; 215-923-8522.

Get Me to the Church on Time

If you are looking for the unusual with a touch of Colonial and a romantic flair, then how about a horsedrawn carriage to get you to the church? Call **Philadelphia Carriage Co.**; 215-922-6840; or **'76 Carriage Co.**; 215-923-8516.

Rolling Down the River

Landlubbers will enjoy that special birthday, graduation, or retirement party aboard the cruiseship, *The Spirit of Philadelphia,* with cocktail lounges and dance floors. This boat glides out of Penn's Landing down the Delaware River, rain or shine, from around noon and into the moonlight hours. Call **Spirit Cruises**; 215-923-1419.

Up, Up, and Away in a Balloon ────────

It's your anniversary, and you're looking for something really out of the ordinary. Have you experienced soaring in the sky at sunrise or sunset in a hot-air balloon? Glide for an hour enjoying a moment you'll never forget. After the flight, if you choose, champagne will be served to celebrate, and a picnic lunch may be included. Call **Air Ventures** in Paoli; 610-889-9386; or **The U.S. Hot Air Balloon Team**; 800-763-5987.

A Barge Party ───────────────────

Hans and Spooky could be the names of the mules that draw your barge down the Delaware Canal in New Hope. The **New Hope Mule Barge** offers a private barge party for rent. Call 215-862-2842. Party packages include flowers, music, food, and a stop at a secluded picnic grove an hour and a half out of town. Sit back and enjoy the view of Bucks County countryside.

A Rafting Adventure ──────────────

For those who thrive on adventure, a rafting trip is a must. Laugh, scream, get soaked, and enjoy the raw beauties of Mother Nature's own health spa. Bring your party to the Lehigh River in the Poconos. All equipment is provided and trained guides will lead your group. Or raft more serenely on a river closer to home. (See SPORTS TO DO Rafting.)

Christmas Cheer ───────────────

Have a family party or bring together your favorite families to spend a day celebrating in the Christmas spirit. Begin by driving out to Chester Springs in Chester County to **Wind Ridge** Christmas tree farm; 610-469-9299. Once you've cut down the perfect tree, take it back to the shed and they will tie it up while you sip a hot drink and warm your hands.

Continue on over to Chadds Ford to the **Brandywine River Museum** for a show of Christmas decorating and interesting art; 610-388-2700. For the children and the children-at-heart there are displays of antique dolls and model trains.

Just down the road is **Longwood Gardens,** a holiday wonderland during the Christmas month. Stroll through the Christmas Tree Lane of illuminated trees to the indoor gardens which are transformed into a splendor of poinsettias, decorated wreaths and trees, and many other plantings. Organ concerts are featured daily. Call 610-388-1000. And now . . . to all a good night.

Let's Party With the Ponies

To get that child's party hopping, or trotting, invite some ponies to the bash. **Chelsea Hill Farm** in Aston will bring gentle, well-groomed equines for the children to ride. Don't forget to put some hay in the party bags. Call 610-494-9884.

Kids' Time Out

Please Touch Museum is really the name of the place. It is a delightful spot to charm a child's friends at birthday time. Everything here is scaled for the children's enjoyment and nothing is off-limits, as the name implies. The Museum is in Philadelphia; call 215-9630666.

High-Flying Dinner Date

What can be more romantic than a champagne and roses helicopter flight to a five-star restaurant or hotel? **Philadelphia Helicopter** flies you in style to locations in this area, Atlantic City, New York, or elsewhere. Call for details: 215-969-3100; 888-506-0560. Website: www.philadelphiahelicopter.baweb.com.

BITS AND PIECES

For a city as old and historic as Philadelphia, traditions and interesting facts inevitably arise through the years. Here we offer by no means a history lesson, but rather a collection of intriguing information that may enhance your position in some future trivia contest.

Did you know that:

—Since 1871, when William Penn's statue was mounted on the tower of City Hall, it was traditional that no other building tower above this monument (548 feet from the top to bottom). Not until the 1980s, with the building of Liberty Place, did the skyline grow taller.

—Philadelphians buy more tickets to professional sporting events than residents of any other city in the nation, including New York and Los Angeles.

—Two people can fit inside one of the pipes of the huge organ at Longwood Gardens.

—Philadelphia has the smallest and most concentrated center of any major city in America. It doesn't extend much beyond the city of William Penn's original plan of more than 300 years ago.

—It is still against the law to sleep in a barbershop and to take a cow to Logan Circle.

—The Benjamin Franklin Parkway is one of the widest streets (250 feet) in the world.

—In 1816, property developers came close to convincing the city fathers that Independence Hall should be torn down and Independence Square divided into housing lots. The Liberty Bell was to be sold for scrap metal.

—The vending tradition, which is so popular in Philadelphia, dates back to 1723, when Benjamin Franklin bought a loaf of bread from a street peddler.

—The only statue of Charles Dickens in the world is located in Clark Park at Forty-third and Baltimore.

—The intersection of Frankford and Cheltenham avenues is the only one in the world with a cemetery on each of its four corners.

—Giant strawberries are painted on telephone poles and light standards on Ridge Avenue in the Strawberry Mansion area.

301

—The width of the stage at the Academy of Music is half the length of a football field.

—Market Street is the oldest business district in the world.

—Philadelphia Brand Cream Cheese, which has been on the market for 106 years, has always been manufactured in upstate New York.

—In Philadelphia, there are 32 bridges spanning the Schuylkill River.

—A manuscript collection of more than 14 million documents fills seven miles of shelves in the Historical Society of Pennsylvania at Thirteenth and Locust streets.

—William Penn originally planned to call Pennsylvania "Cambria," the ancient name of Wales.

—According to legend, William Penn unwittingly named Fairmount Park, too. As the story goes, he was standing on the hill where the Art Museum is now, gazing across the expanse of green toward the Schuylkill River, when he remarked what a "Faire mount" it was. In any event, the park was included as "Faire Mount" on Thomas Holmes' plan for Philadelphia that was drawn up in 1862.

—John Wilkes Booth played a one-week engagement at the old Arch Street Theater a few months before he assassinated President Abraham Lincoln. (His acting performances were panned by the reviewers.)

—Thomas U. Walter, who designed the dome of the Capitol building in Washington, also designed the four cantilevered stairways in the corners of City Hall.

—The first steel-bladed ice skates were made in 1850 and were known as "Philadelphia skates."

—Both the telephone and television were introduced to the world in Philadelphia—the phone at the Centennial Exhibition in Fairmount Park in 1876, and the television at a demonstration in the Franklin Institute in 1934.

—Philadelphia was the first capital of the United States—from 1790 to 1800—since it was the wealthiest city in the Union at that time and the most centrally located.